I0795763

IMAGES
of America

AFRICAN-AMERICAN LIFE IN LOUISVILLE

IMAGES
of America

AFRICAN-AMERICAN LIFE IN LOUISVILLE

Bruce M. Tyler

ARCADIA
PUBLISHING

ISBN 978-0-7385-5375-7

Published by Arcadia Publishing
Charleston, South Carolina

Printed in the United States of America

Library of Congress Catalog Card Number: 98-86341

For all general information contact Arcadia Publishing at:
Telephone 843-853-2070
Fax 843-853-0044
E-mail sales@arcadiapublishing.com
For customer service and orders:
Toll-Free 1-888-313-2665

Visit us on the Internet at www.arcadiapublishing.com

I dedicate this book to my deceased parents
Corine Tyler-Walker and Robert Tyler, and my step-father, Henry N. Walker.
They did the best they could under the apartheid system and society in America.

Contents

BIBLIOGRAPHY

Hall, Wade. *Passing for Black: The Life and Careers of Mae Street Kidd*. Lexington: The University Press of Kentucky, 1977.

Hall, Wade. *The Rest of the Dream: The Black Odyssey of Lyman Johnson*. Lexington: The University Press of Kentucky, 1988.

Horton, Colonel John Benjamin. *Not Without Struggle*. New York: Vantage Press, 1979.

Wright, George C. *Life Behind a Veil: Blacks in Louisville, Kentucky, 1865–1930*. Baton Rouge: Louisiana State University Press, 1985.

INTRODUCTION

These images of African Americans in Louisville reveal the rich, varied, and complex life of a people engaged in a struggle for progress, prosperity, peace, and patriotism despite living in the American system of racial apartheid. Their lives were prosperous despite anti-democracy restrictions. African-Americans, in their lives, times, and culture, were a pro-democracy force that fought on two fronts. They fought for democracy within the larger society and for cultural and social democracy and self-help within African-American society. They did so by developing institutions that would assist them in their struggle from the late 1800s to the 1960s and beyond. African Americans made progress despite anti-democratic opposition forces arrayed against them. These photographs are a vital part of African Americans' collective visual memory of their life and times.

African Americans supported and attended public schools that were under-funded and neglected. They developed Lincoln Institute with the support of sympathetic white citizens. They built and operated important religious institutions such as Quinn Chapel A.M.E. Church and Broadway Temple A.M.E. Zion, both of which hosted community, state-wide, and national conventions of African-American professional groups and fraternities and sororities. The African-American community of faith undergirded a large part of the social and communal life of its community.

Louisville's African Americans attended local churches, schools, and colleges and lived in neighborhoods or in public housing areas that were, apparently, designed for them in order to maintain racial separatism. On the other hand, these institutions and their African-American leaders and workers nurtured a hunger for democracy and institutional freedom and opportunity. Their faith allowed them to gradually develop and mature as individuals and as a society. They fought in both world wars for freedom that they did not fully enjoy in the

United States. Yet, they joined the military and trained at Fort Knox, Kentucky, and they struggled for democracy in the armed forces.

Louisville's African Americans developed the night life on Walnut and Chestnut Streets and in other sections of the city. They had a highly developed musical and dance culture, which they and many other citizens enjoyed and participated in with enthusiasm. Most African Americans were blue-collar, working class people, but they took great pride in their formal dress. They often made their own clothing, especially the women's apparel that was worn to nightclubs and social events. Their formal dress reflected the African-American genteel culture, and, mixed with jazz, jive, and jitterbug dancing, two great social and cultural traditions were brought together. African Americans of this generation proved that they could progress, live in new public housing, dress in formal garb, and live well and elegantly despite the national doctrine and practice of racial caste that rejected their human rights and personal dignity and safety.

ACKNOWLEDGMENTS

This pictorial publication of African-American life in Louisville, Kentucky, is my effort to capture some of the major institutions and people that formed the core of life and times of a people in the Greater Louisville area. The personal and family photos of many people made this project worth the time and effort to reveal their lives and the institutions that fostered a rich and deep history worth preserving.

I started out researching African-American life and culture in Los Angeles while attending graduate school at California State University, Long Beach, and at the University of California, Los Angeles. In 1985, I moved to Louisville to teach at the University of Louisville. I received funding from Jefferson County Commissioner Darryl Owens in 1990 to begin research on Louisville's African-American history. Mr. Owens's support was soon followed by grants from Louisville's city Alderman Arthur Smith and Mayor Jerry Abramson. Their support has been greatly appreciated.

This book is part of my ongoing research to preserve and publish my findings for the benefit of the Louisville community so that it may understand its culture and the outstanding contributions African Americans have made to enrich the community, despite a national and local legal system of apartheid that rejected democracy for all citizens.

Commissioner Darryl Owens gave me a list of people to interview in researching Louisville's African-American history. That list included retired photographer James Sydnor. I spent many hours—over a period of several years—interviewing Sydnor and cataloguing the few remaining pictures made during his long photographic career. Some of his pictures appear in this book. Meeting with him led me to broaden my project by collecting and copying many more pictures and building historical information around them.

I received photos from Dr. Alice Hasim of the Mammoth Life and Accidental Insurance Company where her father, E.A. Bettis Jr., worked. Des Moines Beard provided pictures of Louisville's public housing, and I spent many hours (and years) interviewing him on his work and local history. Edward Churchill provided me with pictures of old Walnut Street and Edward Sumpter shared with me his pictures of the Brock Building and its splendid night life. Ken Clay provided pictures of Helen Humes and stories about Louisville people and society. The University of Louisville's Archives allowed me to copy pictures from Earle Pruitt's materials.

Hughlyn Wilson literally handed over to me the entire archives of Quinn Chapel A.M.E. Church to research and use. I was assisted by Rev. Larry Crossland of Broadway Temple A.M.E. Zion Church, and he allowed me to use his church's photos and materials. Frederick L. Stith provided me with photos of himself and of his father's cleaners and lodge. Charles Thomas's photos were provided by his wife. Although both Thomas and Sydnor died a few years ago, their work and materials have been very helpful in the creation of this project.

Rev. Joseph Graffis of St. Augustine Catholic Church gave me permission to use the church's materials and photos.

Dr. Eleanor Young-Love, my colleague, and Dr. Samuel Robinson of the Lincoln Foundation provided their records and photos of the Lincoln Institute. Ms. Young-Love, who is now retired from the University of Louisville, is the sister of Whitney M. Young Jr.

Louisville's Division of Fire provided a few photos, and the other fire department photos were given to me by family members of deceased firefighters.

The photographs of Central Colored High School are from school books and other materials from that grand public institution.

The photos of the U.S. Army are courtesy of Patton Museum, Fort Knox, Kentucky.

Throughout the book, dates in parentheses following the captions refer to the date the photograph was taken.

One

Family Photos

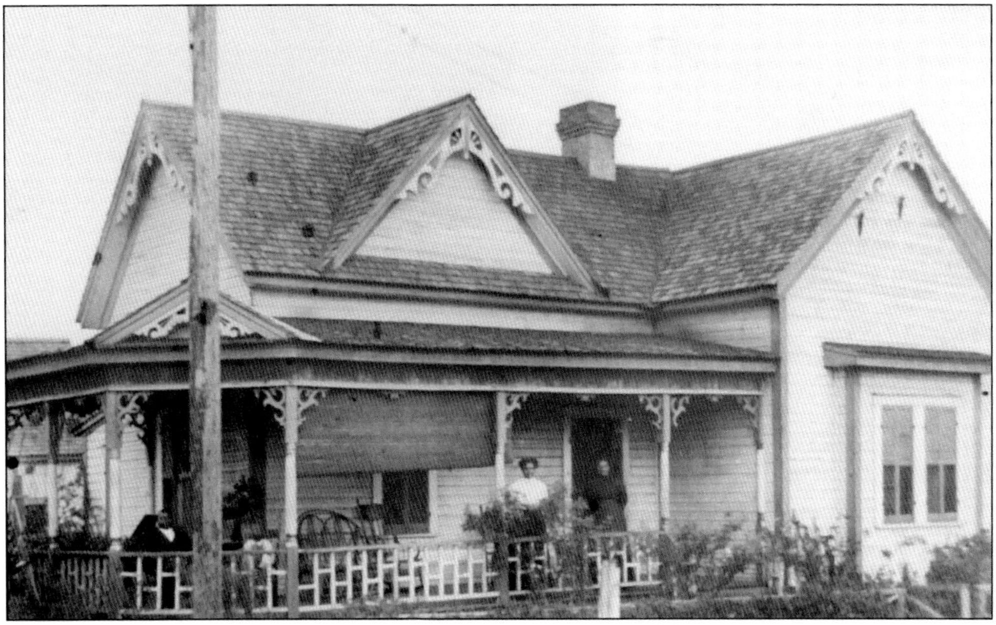

This postcard view of a Louisville family's home was donated by a member of the Louisville Quinn Chapel A.M.E. Church. (*1904*.)

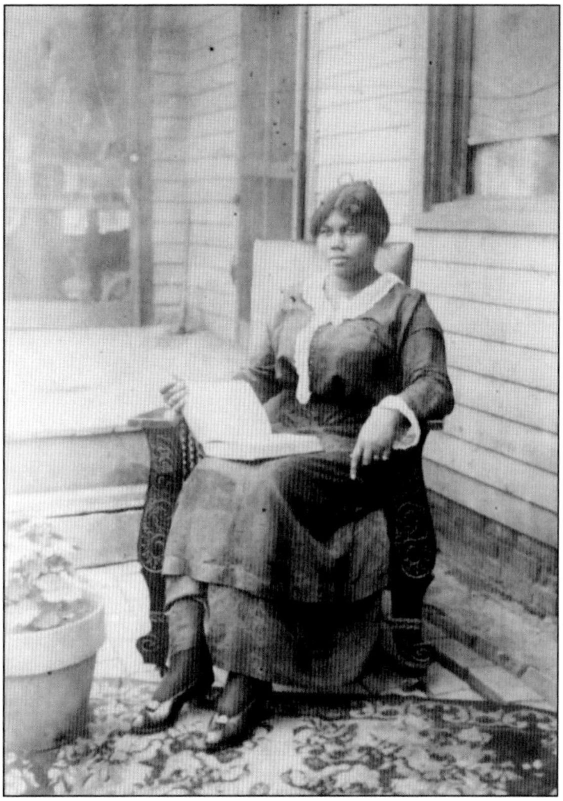

Pictured is Mrs. James E. Sydnor at her home in Louisville. (*c.* early 1900s.)

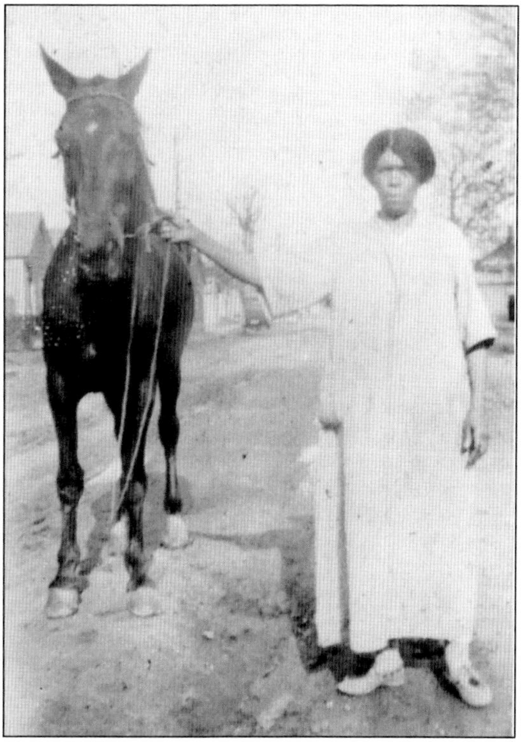

In this view, Mrs. James E. Sydnor is pictured with her horse. (*c.* early 1900s.)

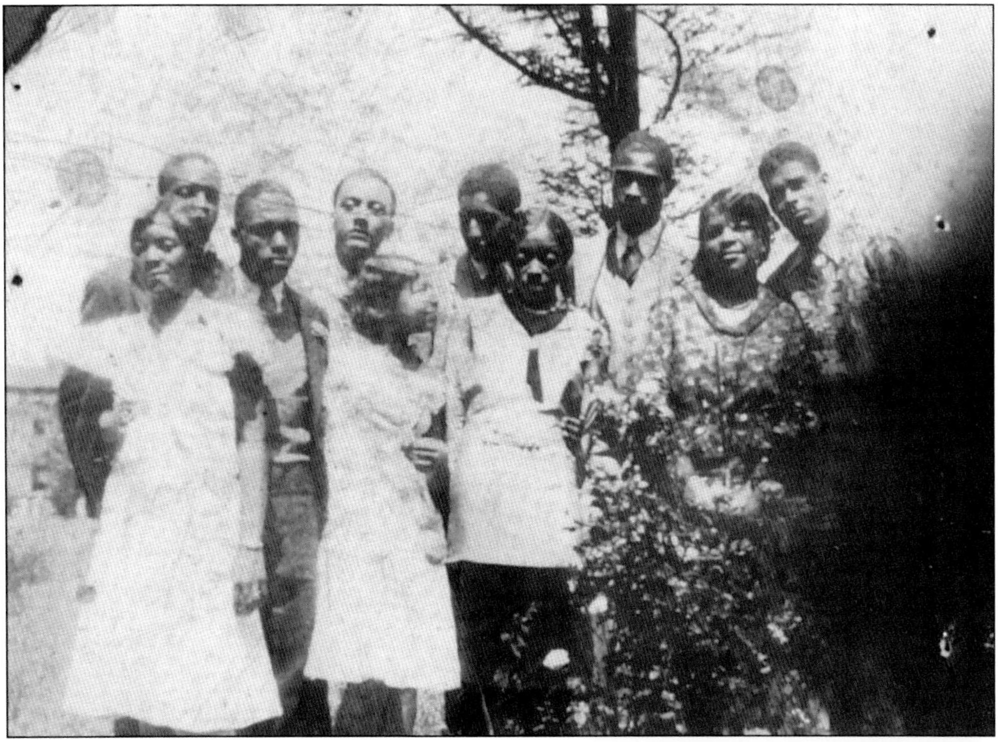

James Sydnor Jr. is the third man from the left seen in the background of this photograph. He was a member of the graduating class of 1928 at Simmons University in Louisville.

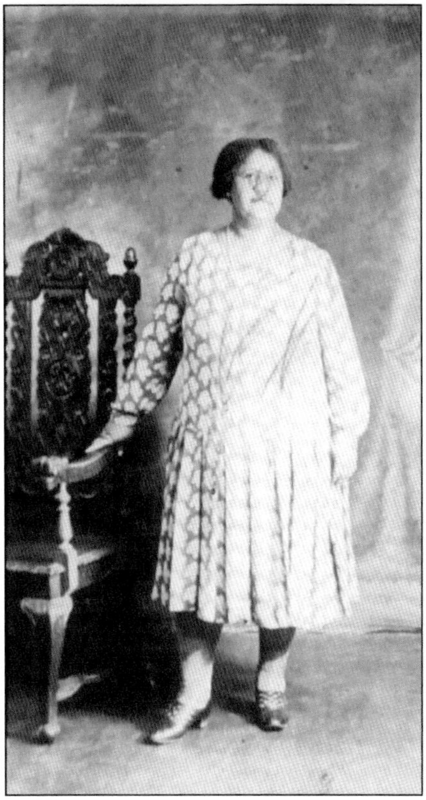

Pictured is a friend or relative of the Sydnor family. (c. 1920s.)

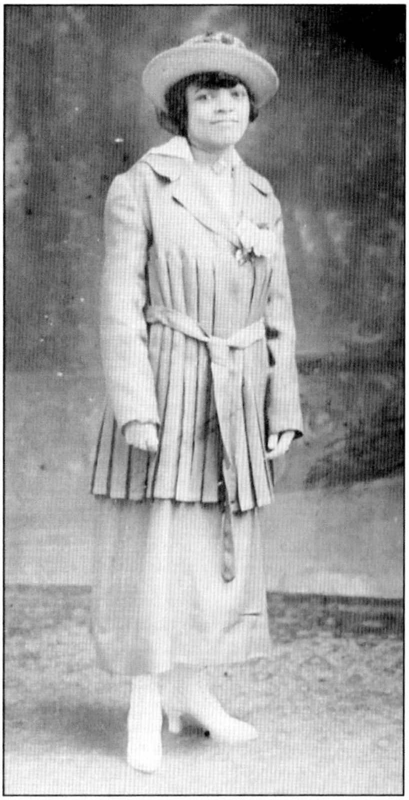

This c. 1920s photograph shows another friend or relative of the Sydnor family.

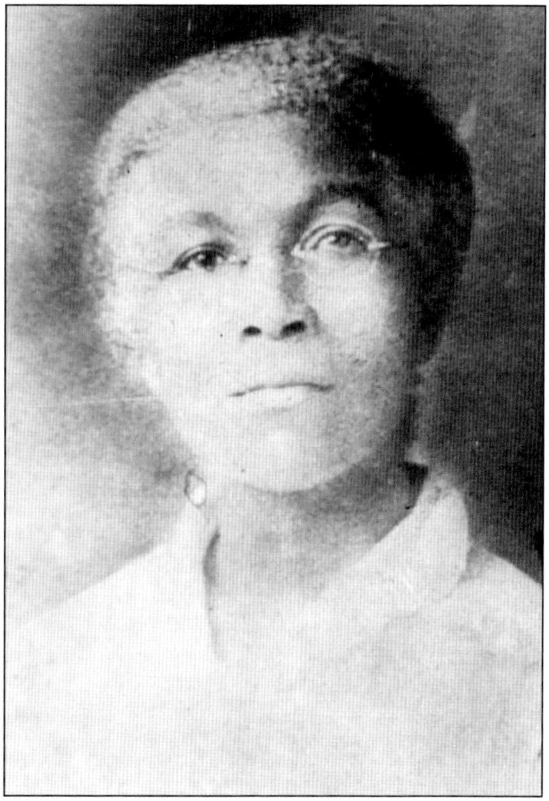

Elizabeth Battle Withers of Louisville was a Baptist missionary for Calvary Baptist Church and the grandmother of Mrs. Ann Spann. (c. early 1900s.)

Pictured is Jenny Clay Alsop, who was born in Lexington, Kentucky. She was also a grandmother of Mrs. Ann Spann. (c. late 1800s.)

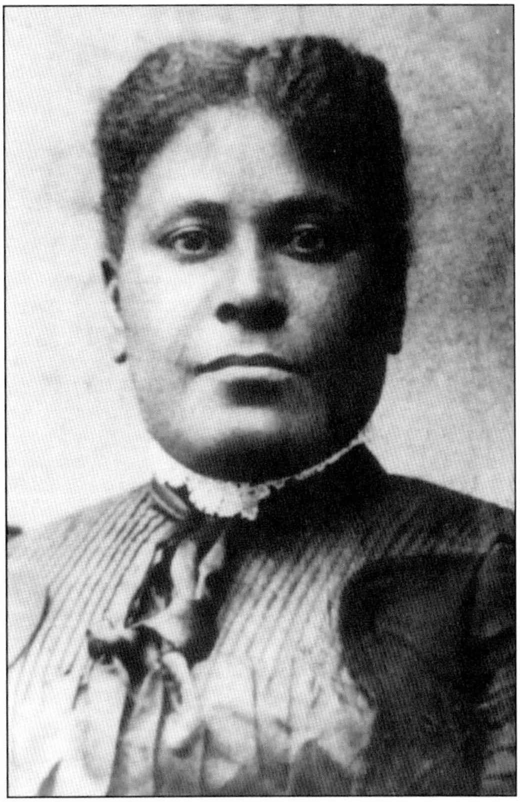

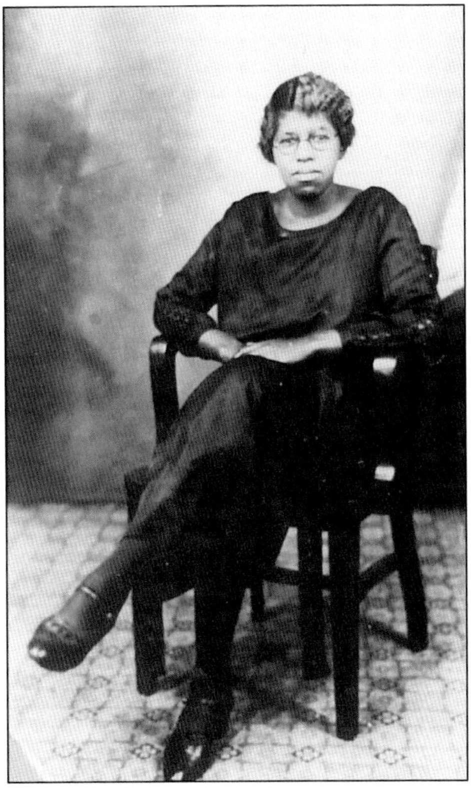

The lady seated here was a member of Quinn Chapel A.M.E. Church. (c. 1920s.)

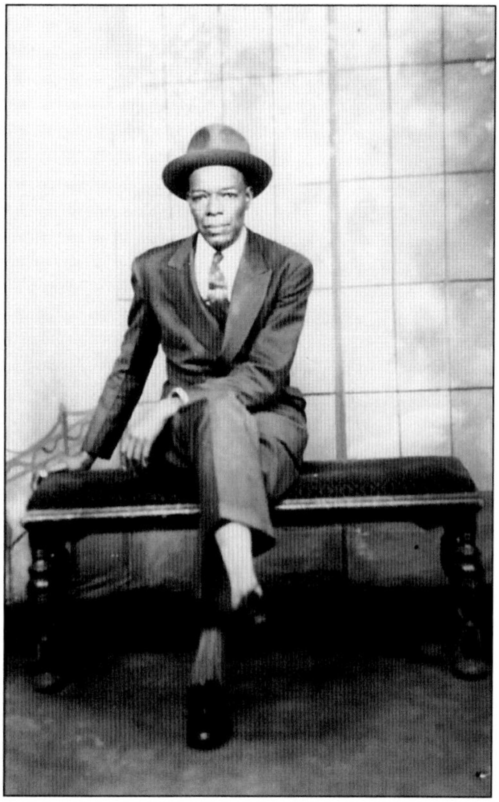

Pictured is a member of the Crosley family. The family attended Quinn Chapel A.M.E. Church.

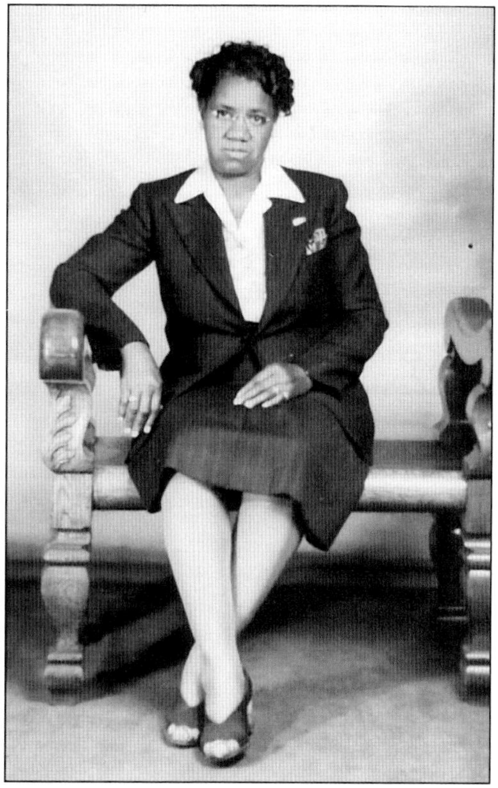

This photograph shows another member of the Crosley family.

Two

LINCOLN INSTITUTE

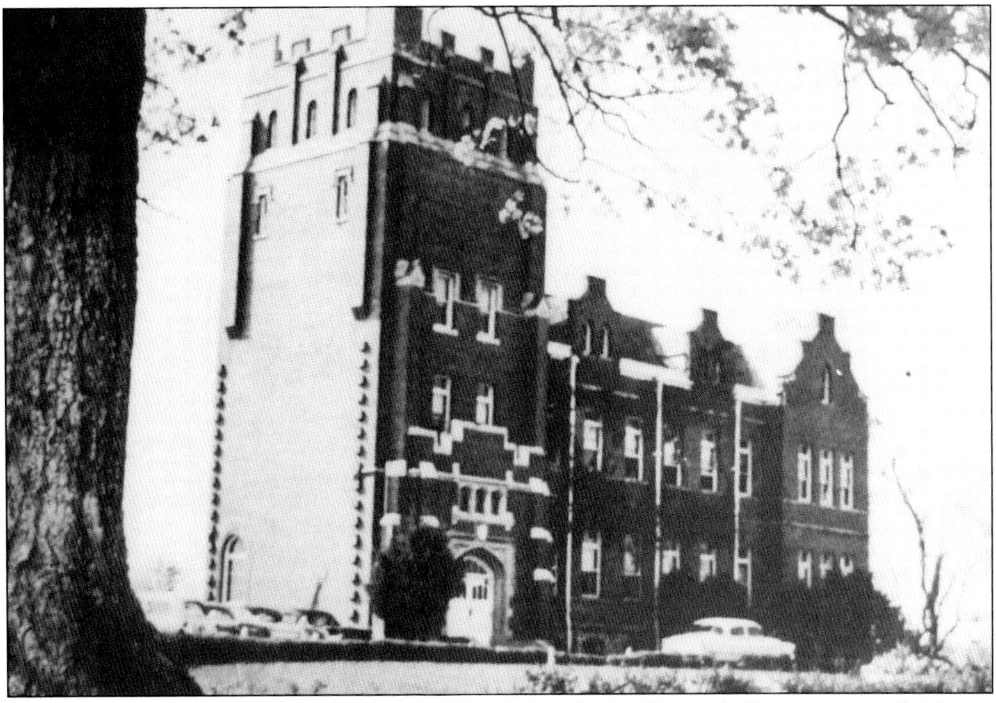

Berea Hall, the campus administration building named after Berea College, permitted African Americans and white students to jointly attend classes until Kentucky's legislature, supported by the United States Supreme Court in 1908, segregated all schools in the state.

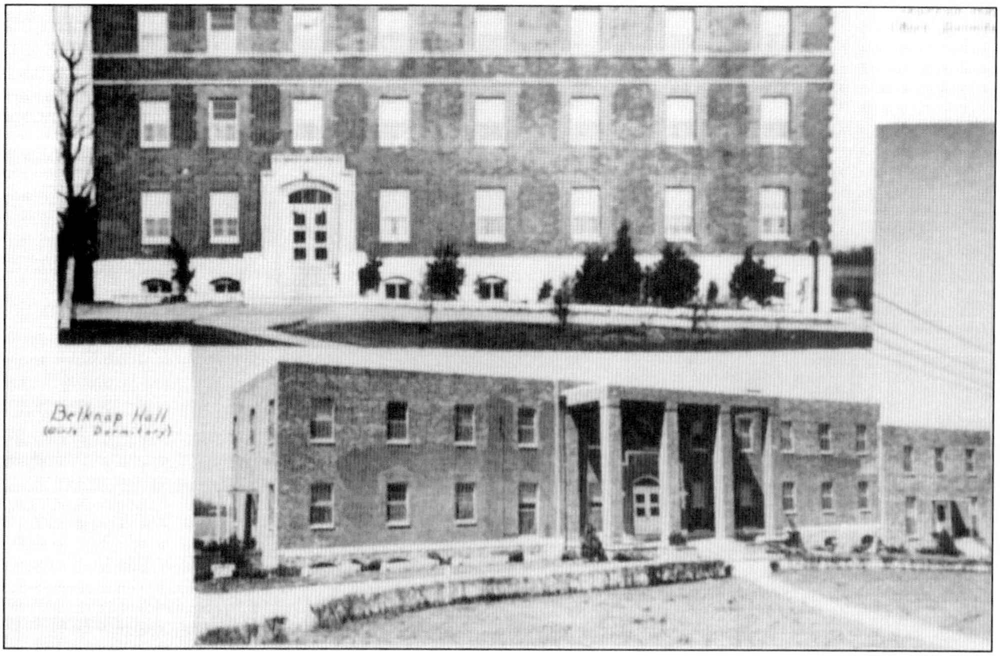

Lincoln Institute opened in 1911 to educate neglected African-American students in Kentucky. Eckstein Norton Hall housed about 180 male students, and Belknap Hall housed 172 female students and practice teachers from Kentucky State College. The building had a music room, beauty parlor, large recreation rooms, and a clinic managed by a trained nurse. (c. 1954.)

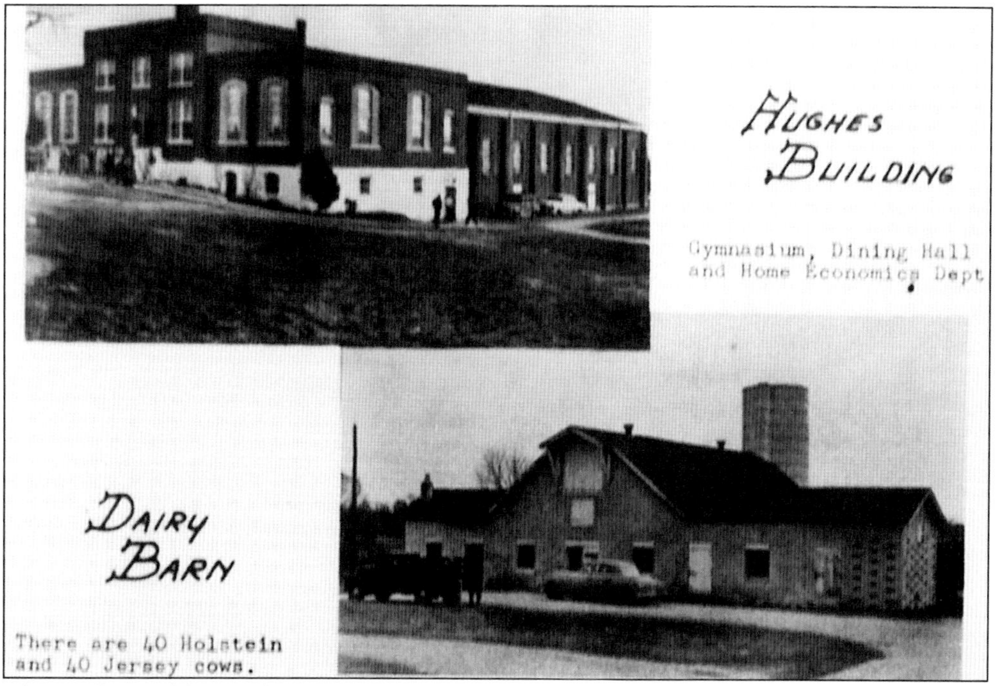

The Hughes Building included a gymnasium, dining hall, and home economics department. In 1935, to keep Lincoln Institute out of bankruptcy, Hughes of Lexington gave Lincoln Institute $10,000 under President Whitney M. Young Sr.'s Faith Plan.

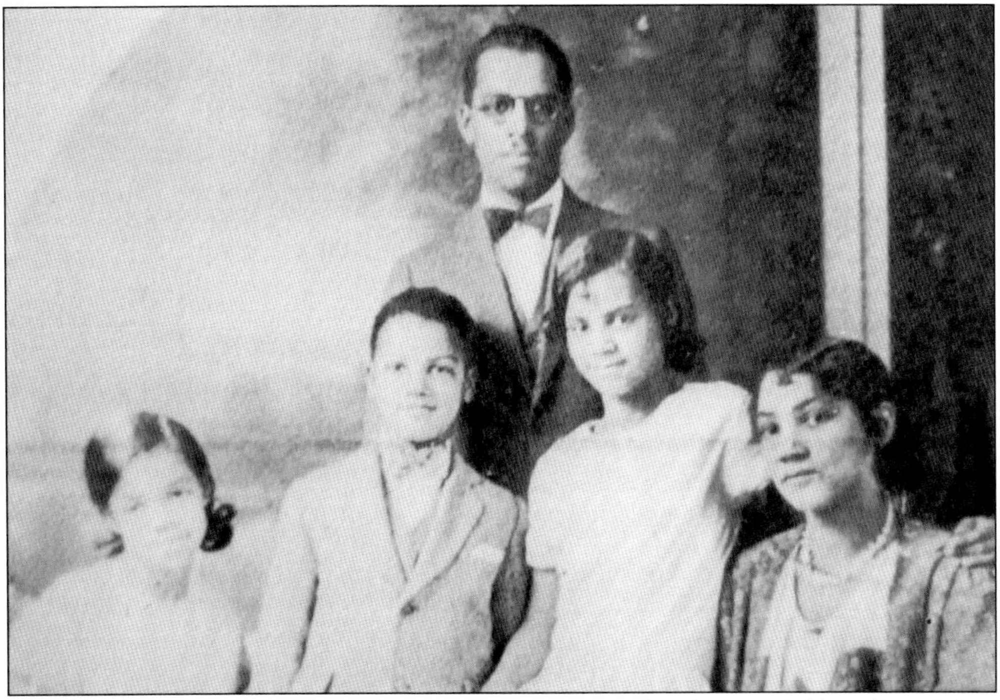

Whitney M. Young Sr., and his wife, Laura Rae, are pictured with their children (from left to right), Eleanor, Whitney Jr., and Arnita. The Lincoln Institute's service motto was "education of the head, heart, and hand."

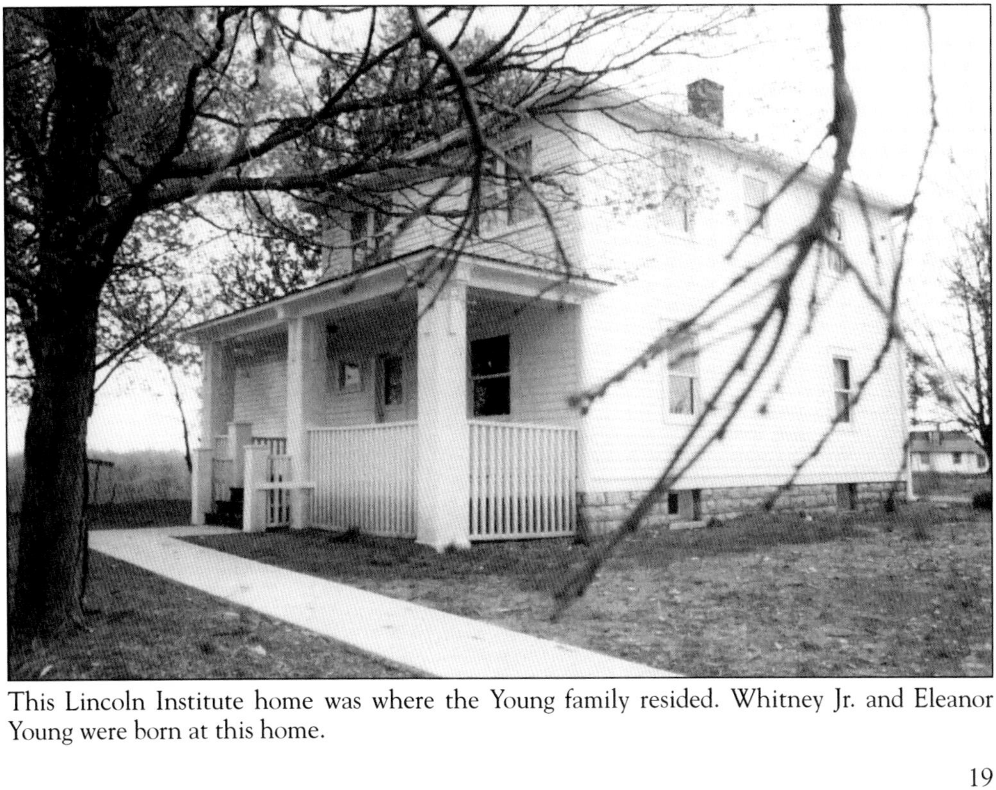

This Lincoln Institute home was where the Young family resided. Whitney Jr. and Eleanor Young were born at this home.

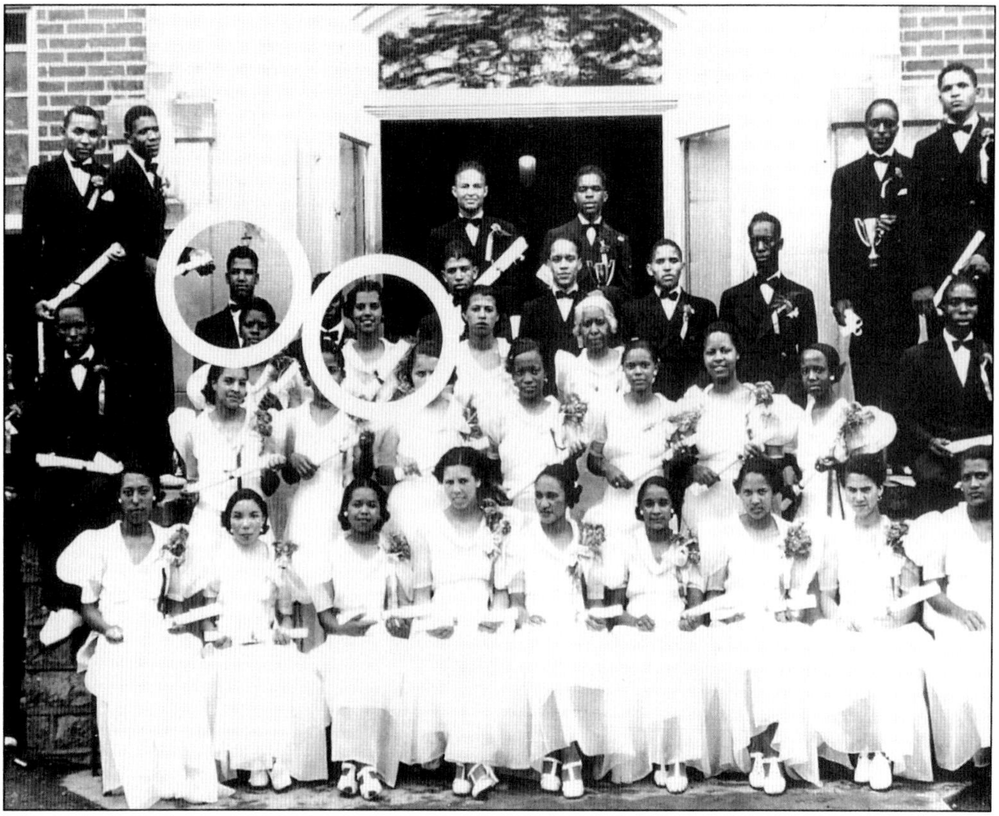

This view of Whitney Jr. and Arnita Young standing on the steps of Berea Hall was made at their graduation from Lincoln Institute High School in 1936.

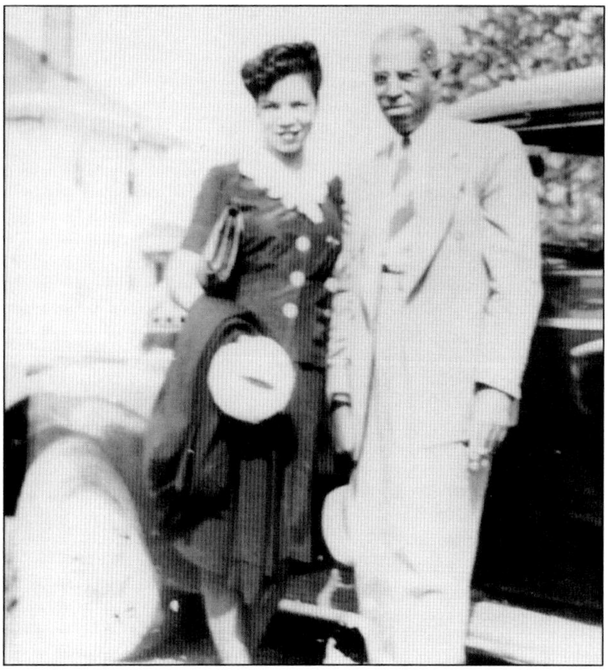

Pictured in this view of Lincoln Institute are Dr. Young Sr. and his daughter, Eleanor.

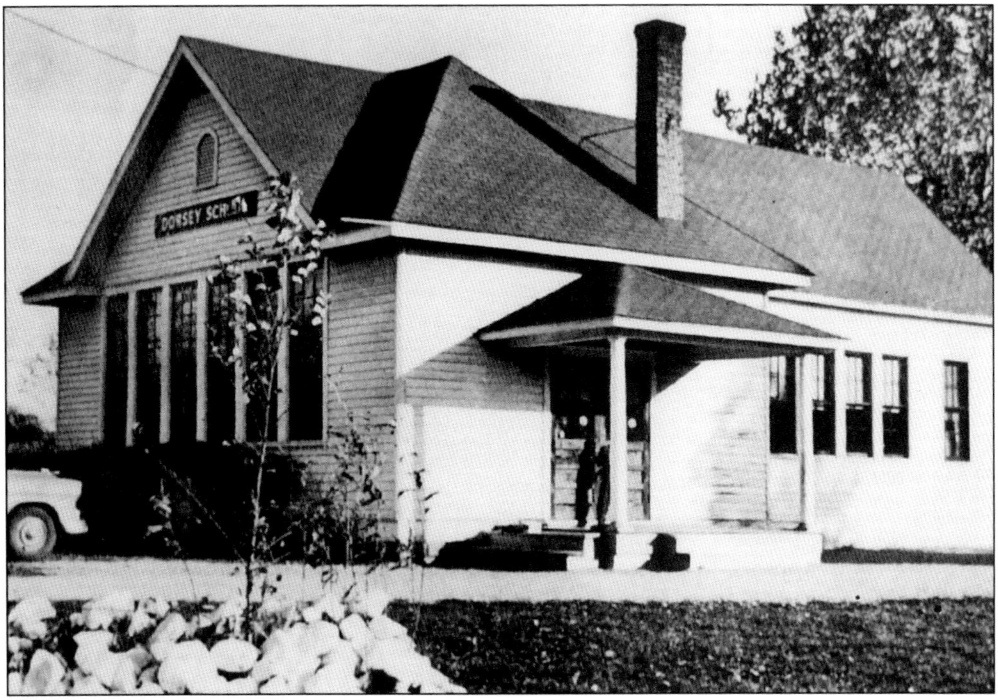

Dorsey School was one of many schools in seven counties that Lincoln Institute served with programs designed to improve education and health. It assisted with beautification projects and designed a program to bring books to the school from the state library. Dorsey School won the first beautification award. (c. 1954.)

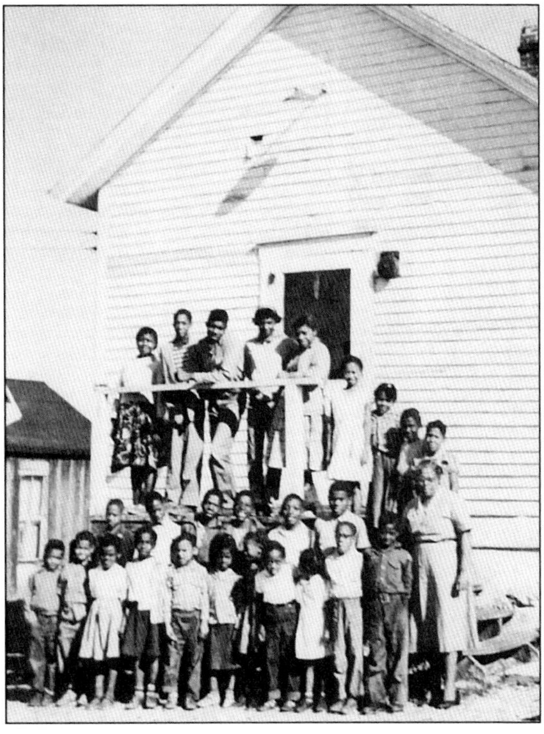

This is another school that was assisted by Lincoln Institute. Its program was designed to improve teachers' and students' health and education, and it recruited students to attend Lincoln Institute to further their education.

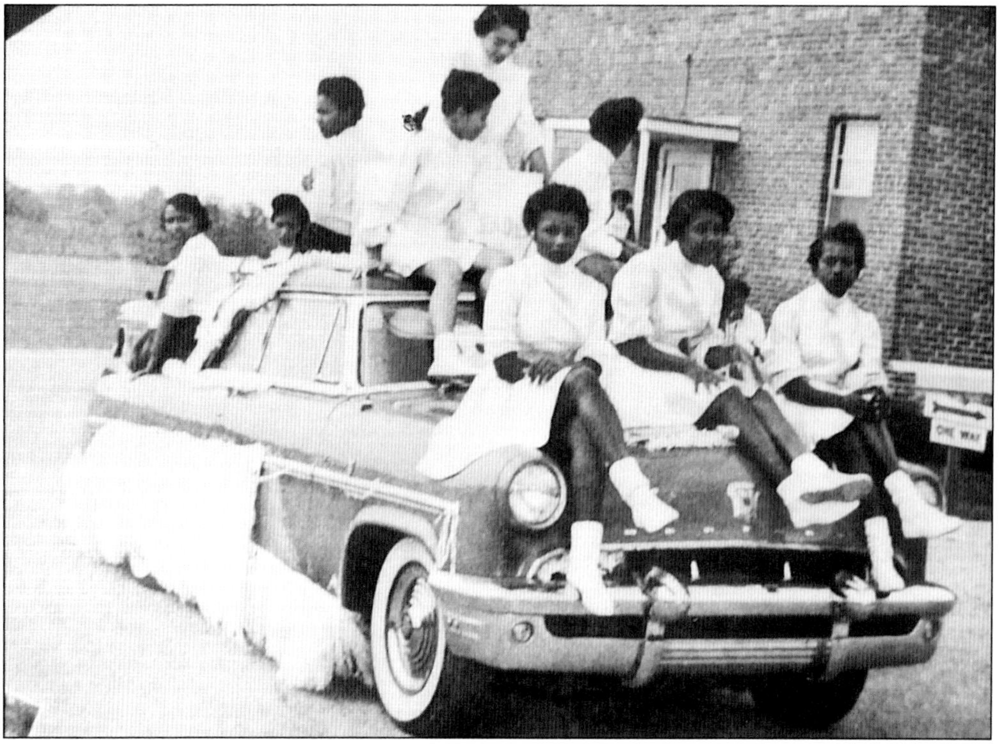

In this view, students celebrate homecoming at Lincoln Institute. (*c*. 1954.)

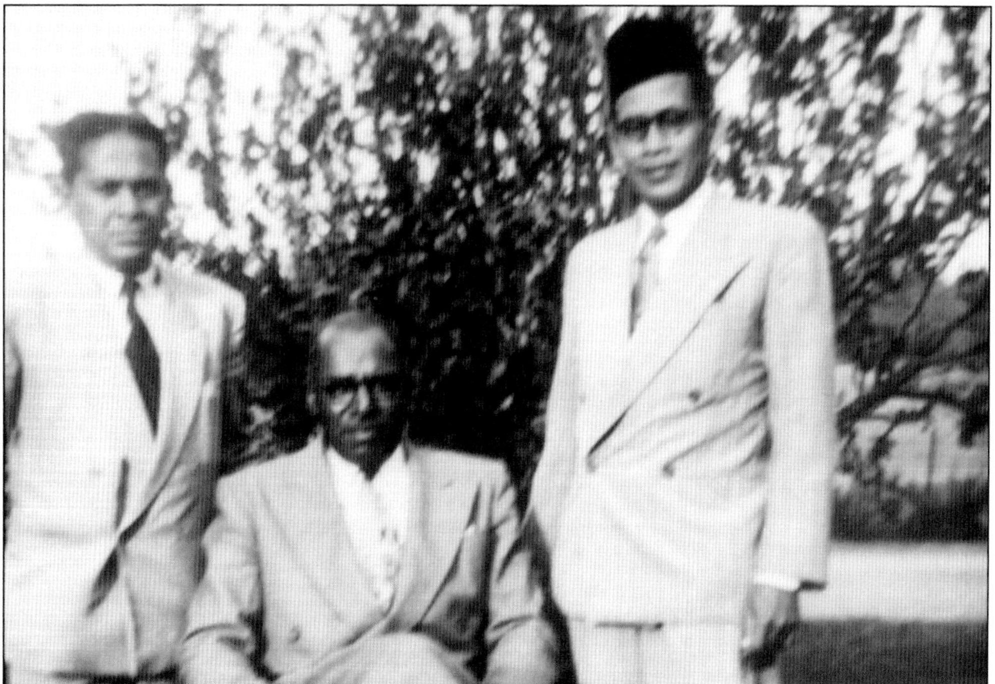

President Young is pictured with international visitors who came to investigate Lincoln Institute's methods of education.

President Young and Kentucky Gov. Bert T. Combs (second from left) attend a graduation ceremony. (c. 1960 view.)

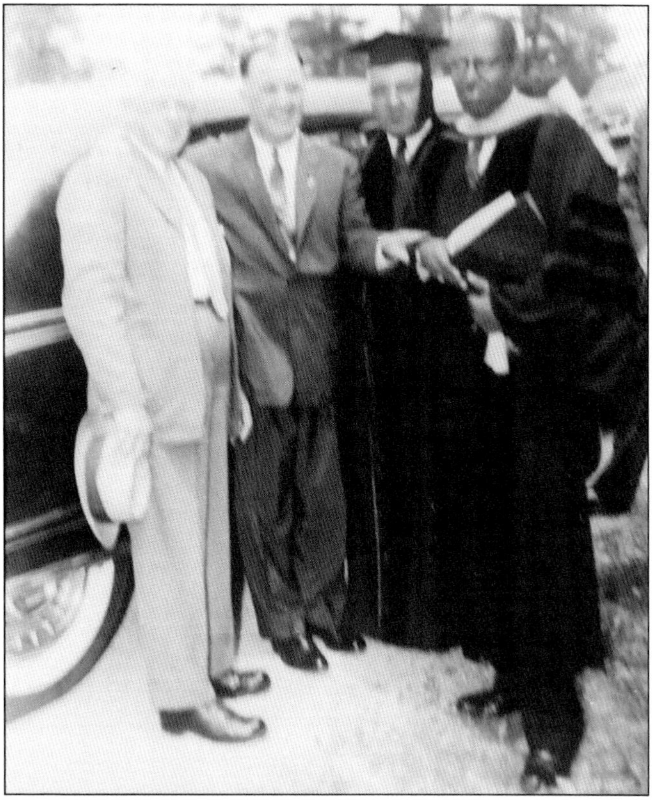

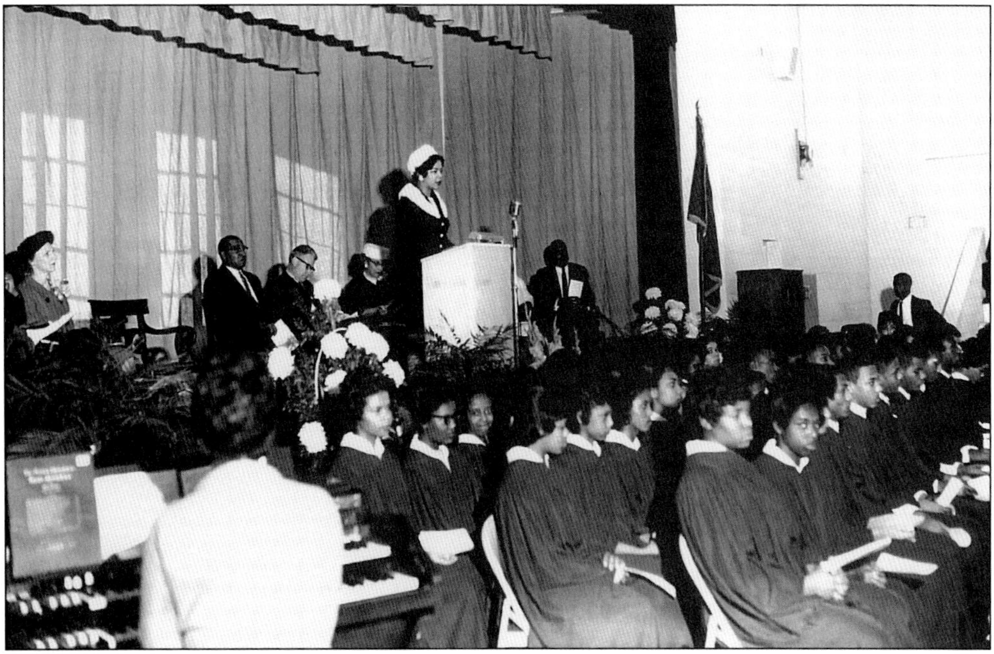

Pictured on-stage in this view of commencement are, from left to right, as follows: Eleanor, Laura Young, Dr. Young, and Gov. Bert T. Combs. Eleanor and her mother are wearing similar hats. This was Eleanor's graduating class when she was principal.

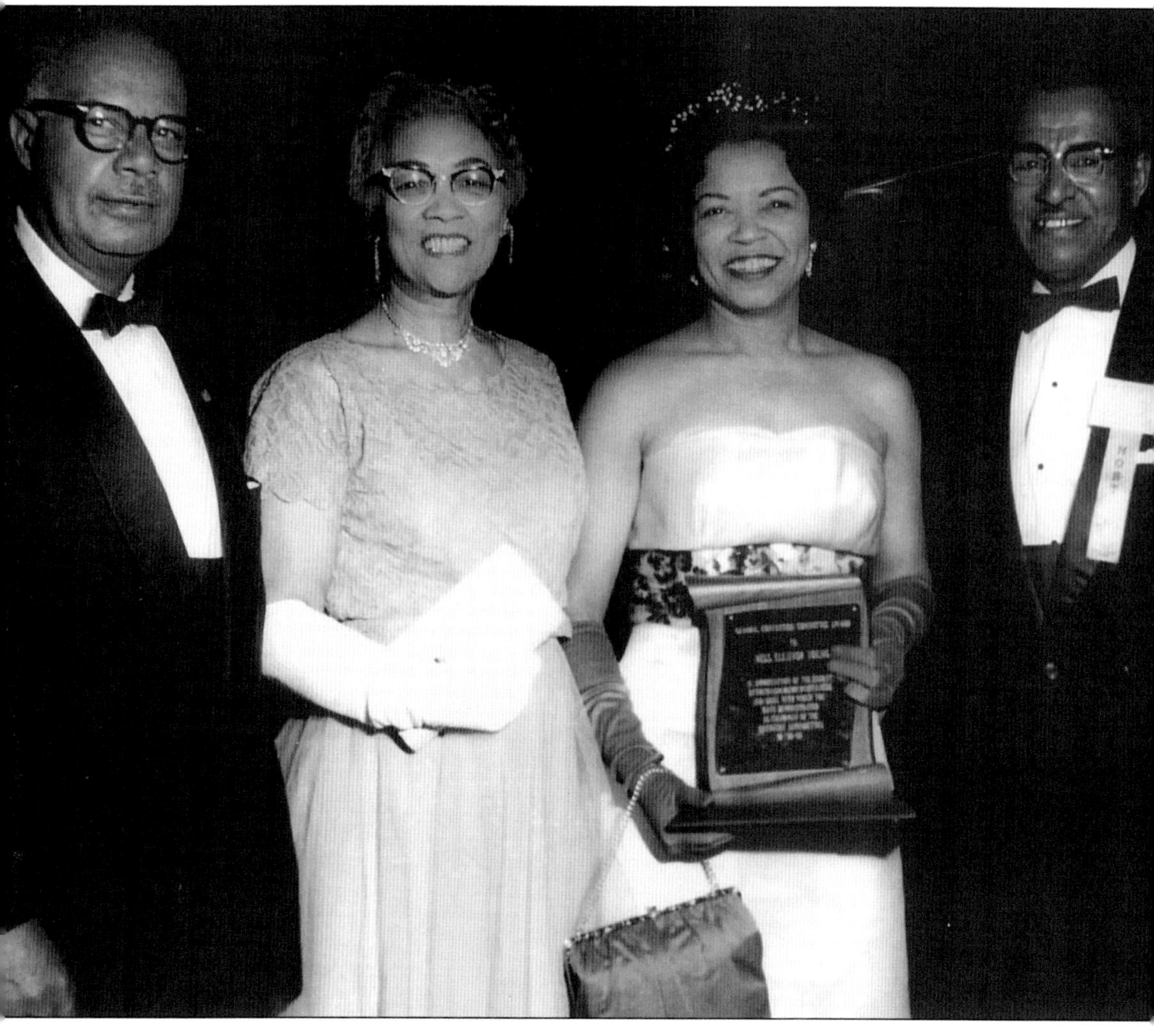

Pictured in this 1961 view of the Alpha Phi Alpha national convention (held in Louisville) are, from left to right, as follows: Lester Granger (National Urban League), Laura Young, Eleanor Young, and Dr. Whitney M. Young Sr. Eleanor received an award for her service as president of the Alphabettes, the group that hosted the convention. Dr. Young was an Alpha.

Three

Central Colored High School

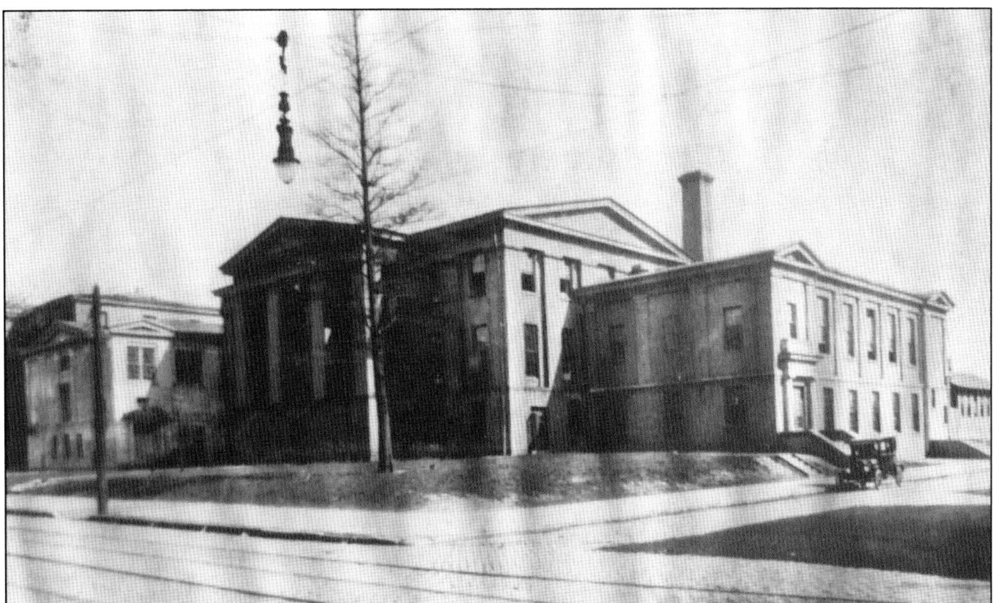

Central Colored High School was once a Civil War hospital. Central became a public institution that permeated nearly every family who had students in Central or were the friends or parents of students. It was a mutual bond that tied the community together.

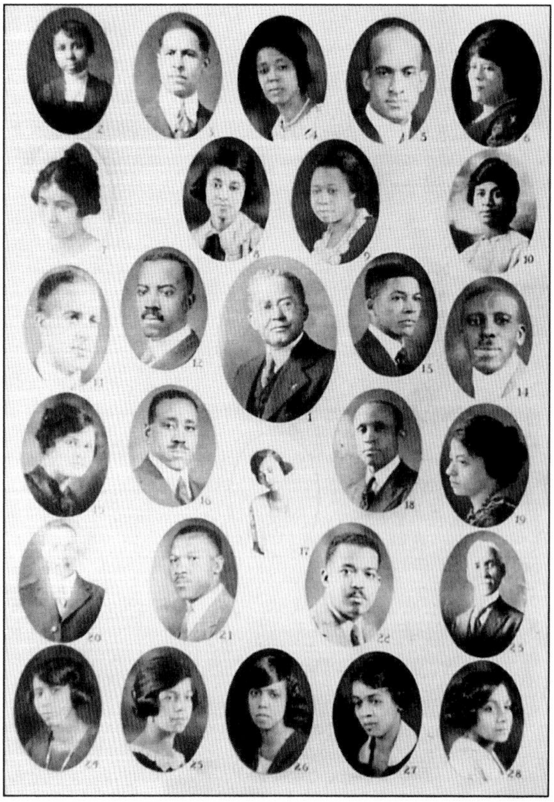

Pictured is Central Colored High School's African-American faculty in the era of racial segregation and anti-democracy practices. For many years, Central was the only high school available for African Americans. African-American teachers held an honored status in the community. (*c*. 1921.)

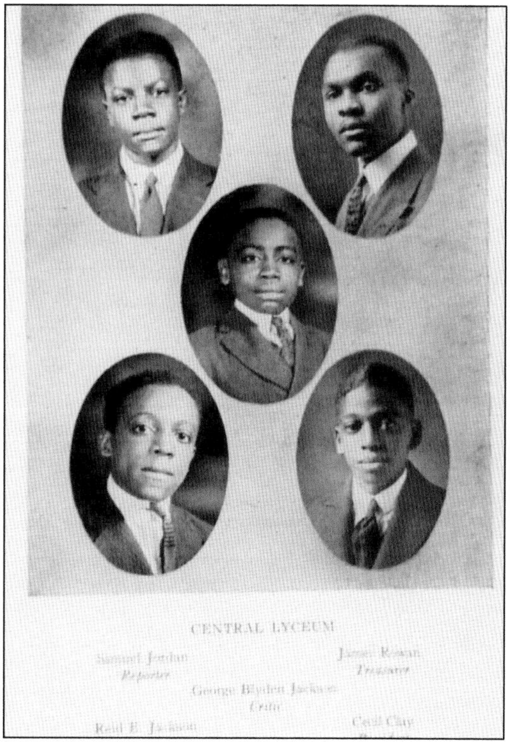

Central's Lyceum student group excelled in their studies. (*c*. 1921.)

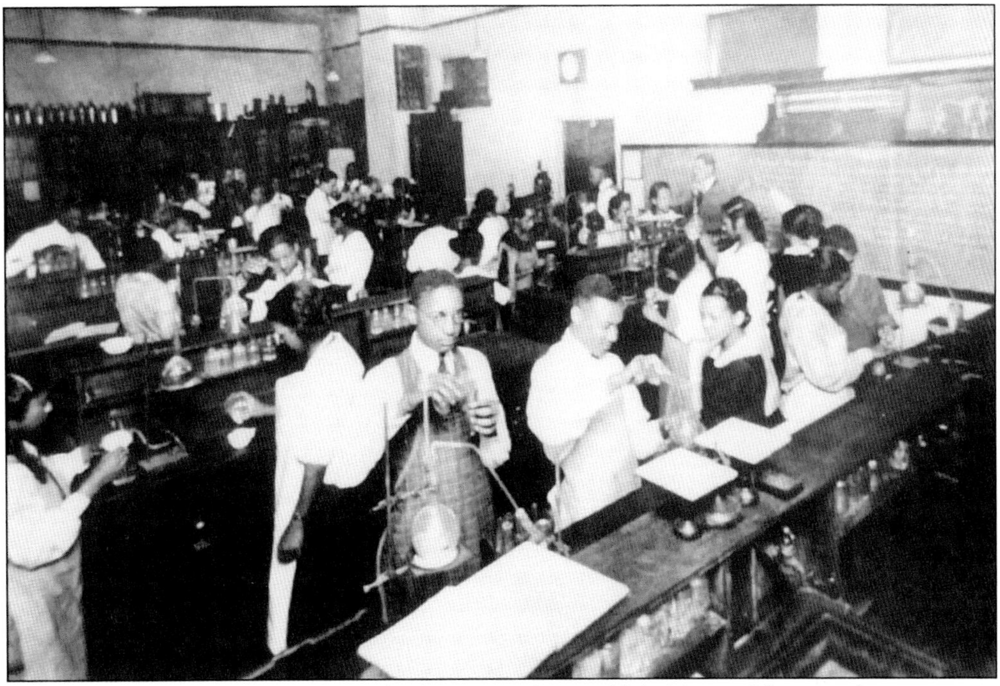

This photograph is a view of Central's chemistry class and lab. Many of these students went on to become doctors, dentists, and science teachers. (c. 1921.)

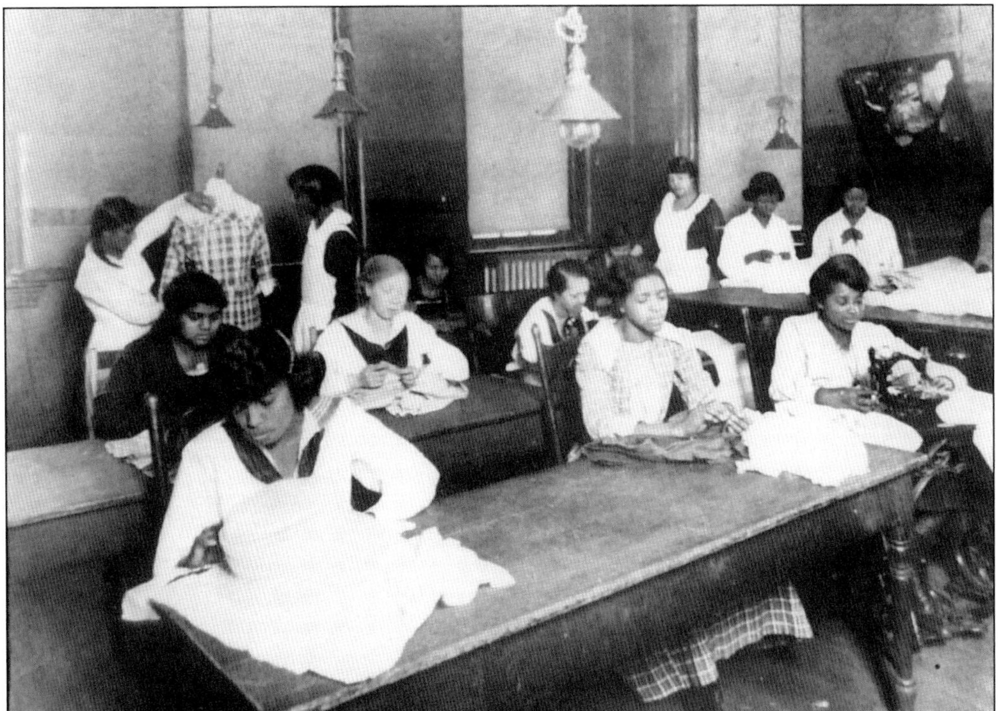

Central's sewing class produced innovative students who utilized their skills for family and employment purposes. (c. 1921.)

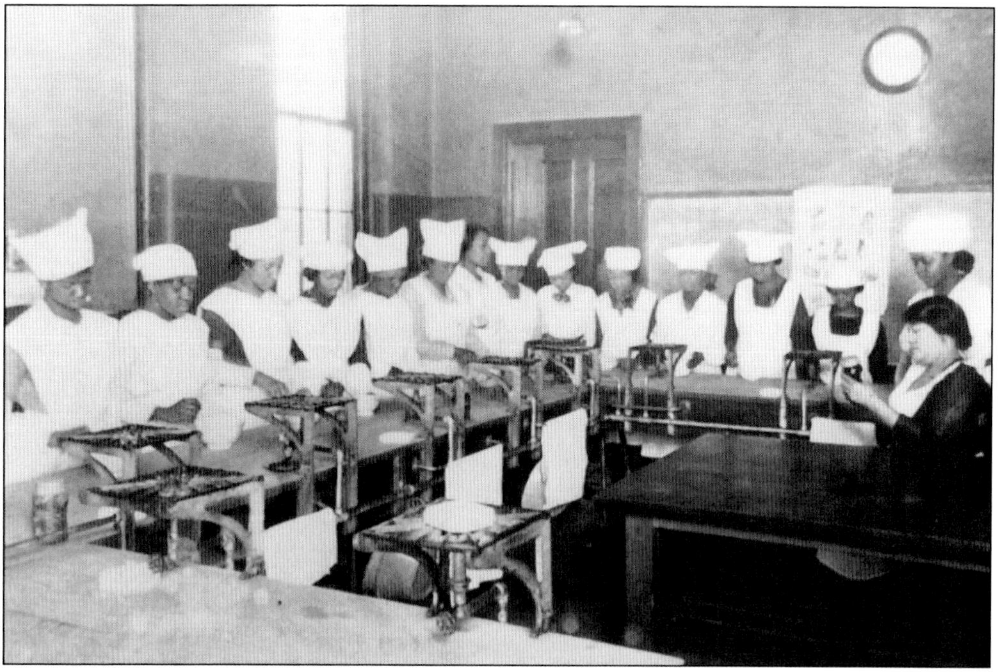

Seen in this view is a freshman class in domestic science at Central. Since many women found employment as domestic servants, these classes prepared them for work, family, and homemaking skills. (c. 1921.)

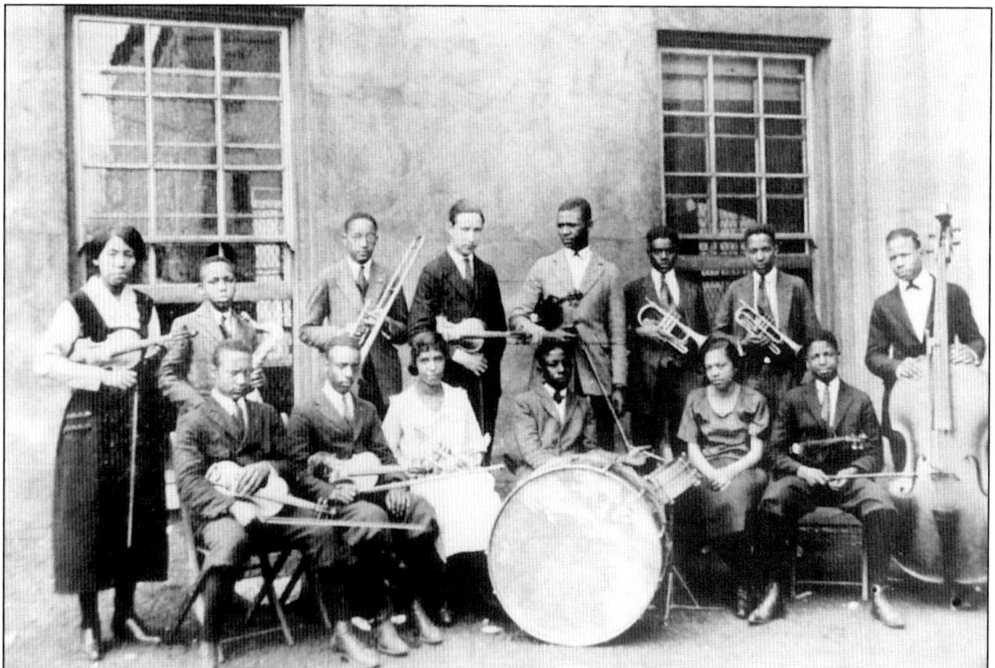

Pictured is Central Colored High School's orchestra. Musical training was a vital part of the curriculum and provided church, community, and professional music groups with trained musicians. (c. 1921.)

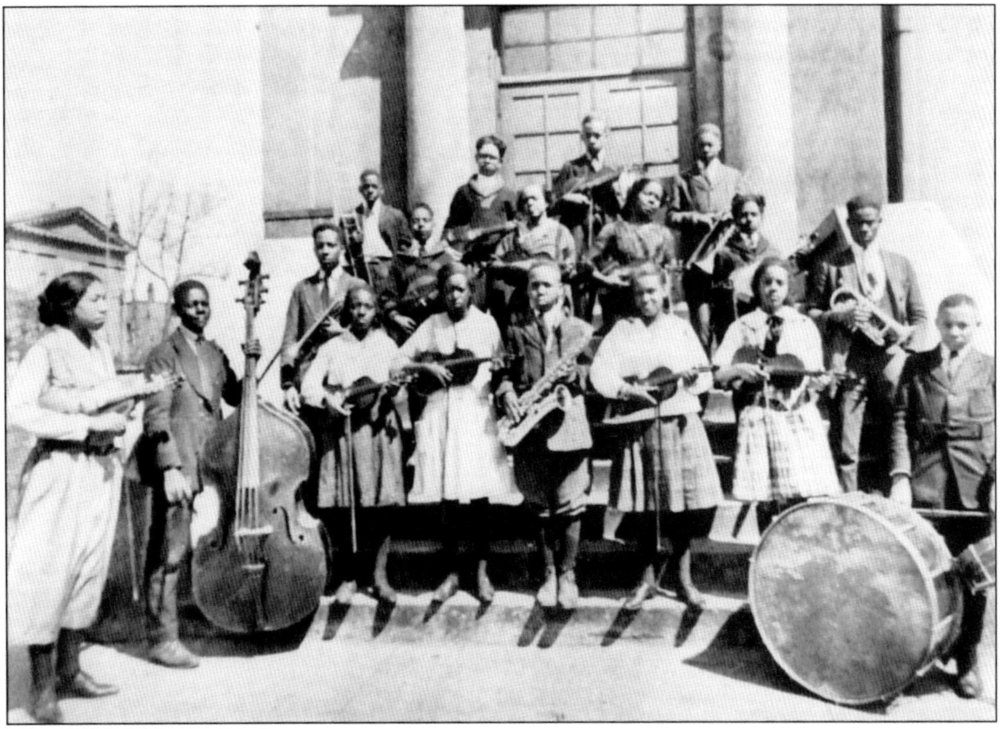

This is a view of Central Colored High School's junior orchestra. (*c.* 1921.)

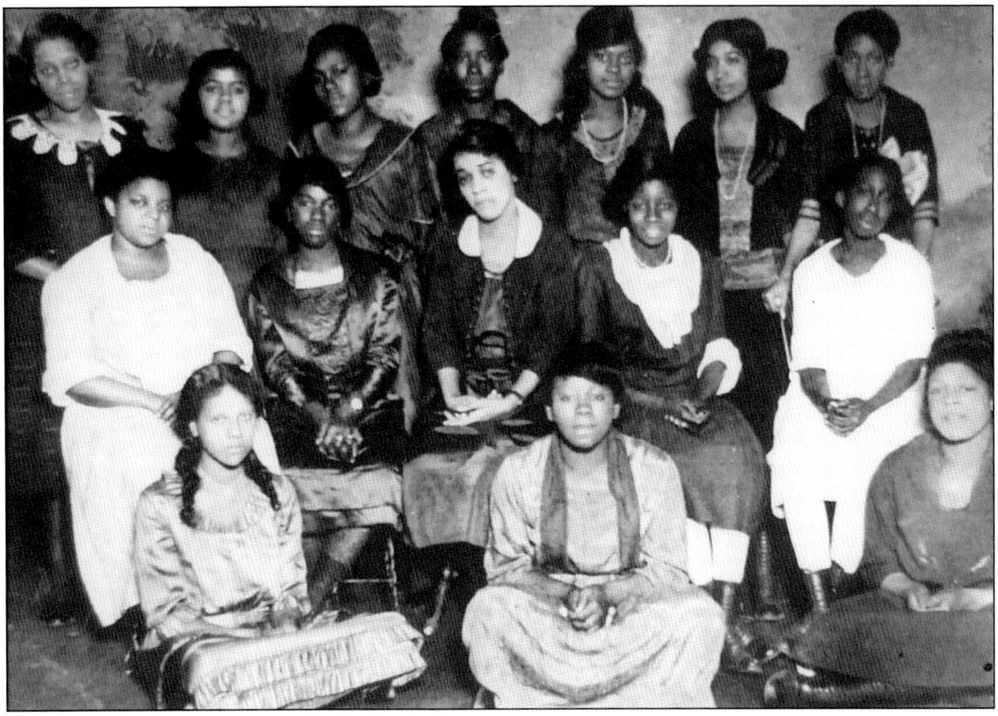

Pictured is the Central Colored High School girls' glee club. Central and community churches produced well-trained singers. (1922.)

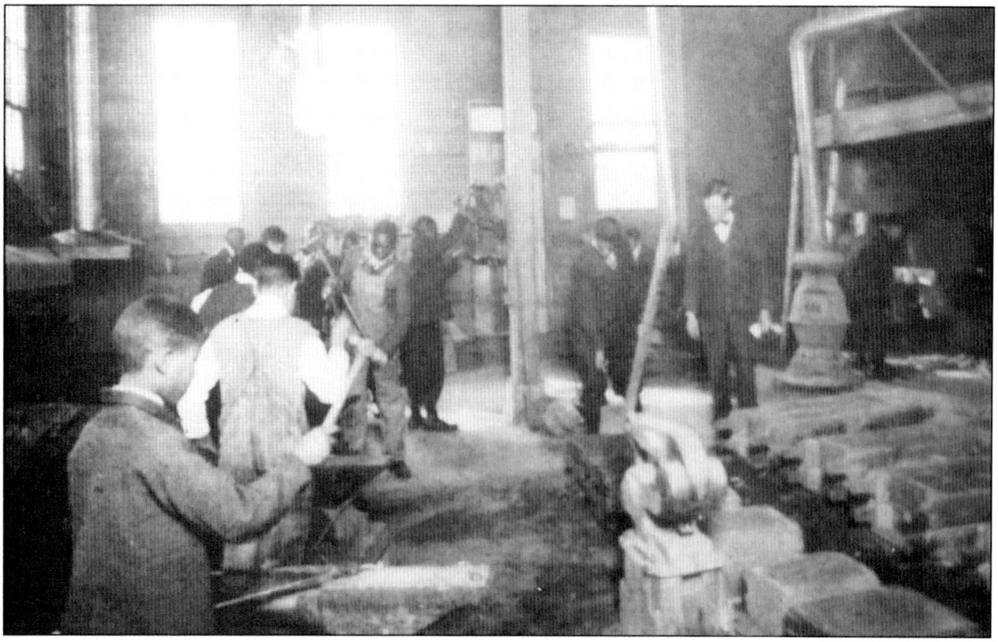

Central Colored High School offered a blacksmith shop class to male students. They prepared for industrial jobs by learning techniques in class. (1922.)

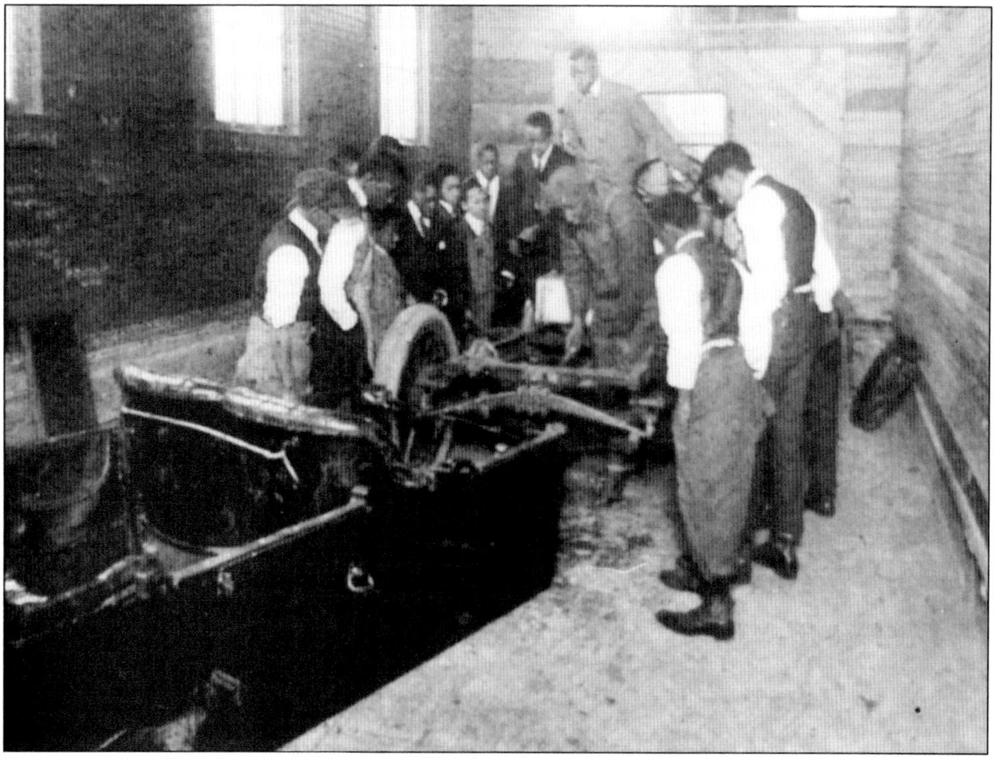

Central Colored High School also offered a class in automobile repair. Central quickly adapted its curriculum to teach students to repair cars since transportation by car was becoming vital to modern society. (1922.)

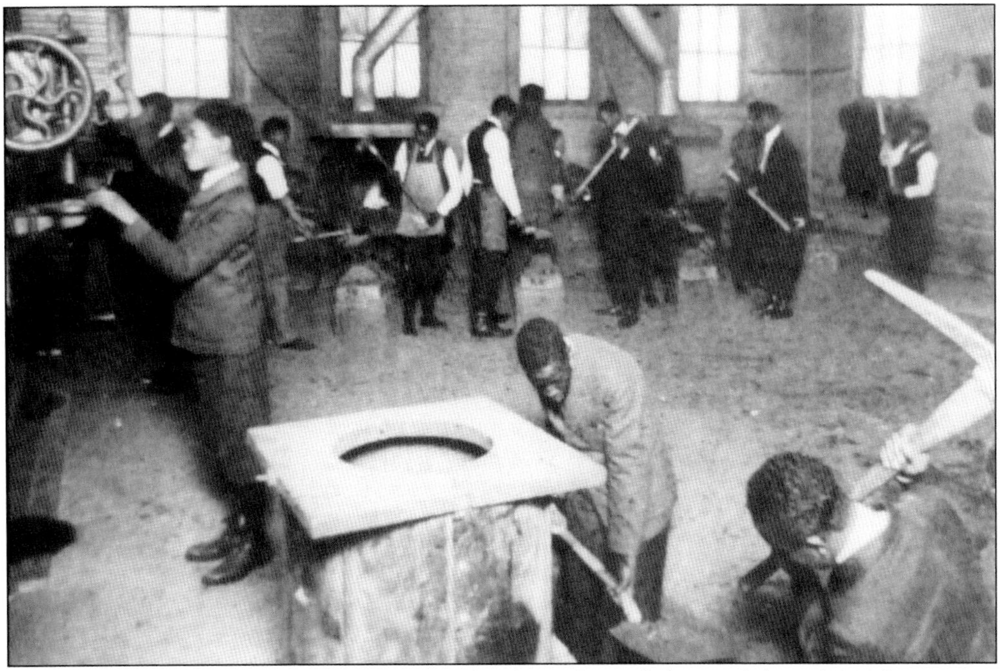

Pictured is the Central Colored High School industrial metal class and shop. (1922.)

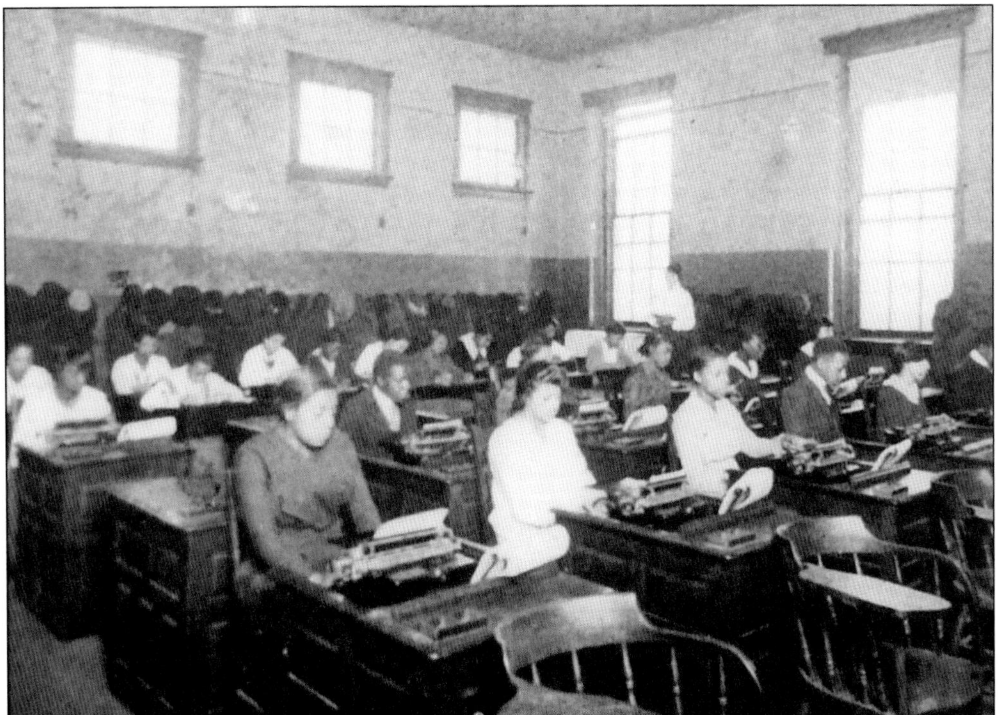

Central Colored High School offered classes in business and secretarial work. Many of these students became white-collar clerical workers. (1922.)

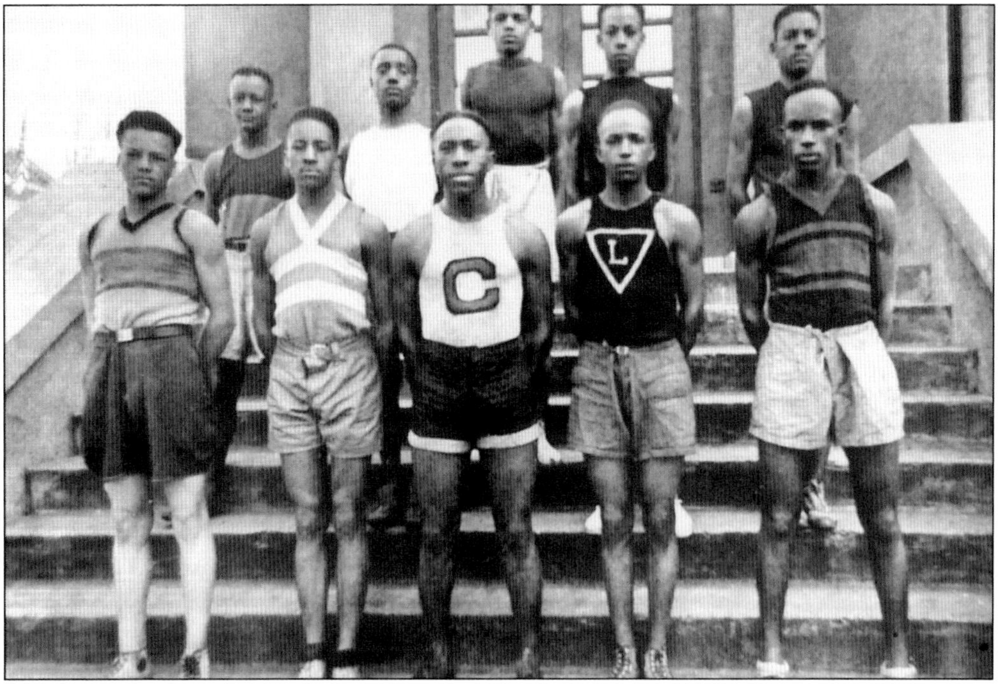

Pictured in this 1922 photograph is the Central Colored High School track team.

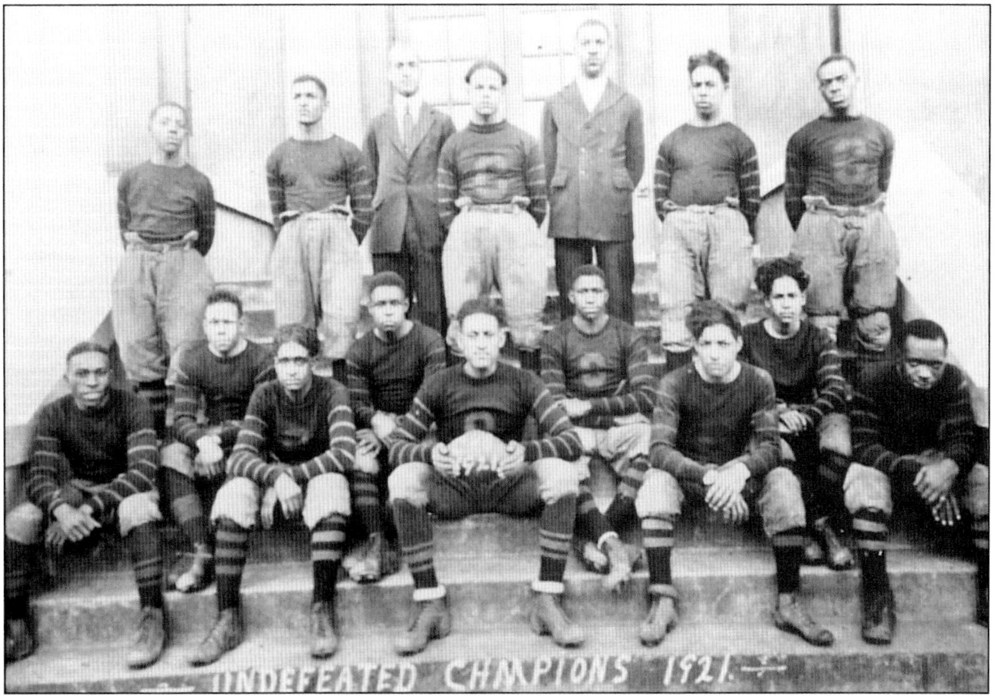

This is the Central Colored High School's undefeated Varsity Football Squad as photographed in 1921.

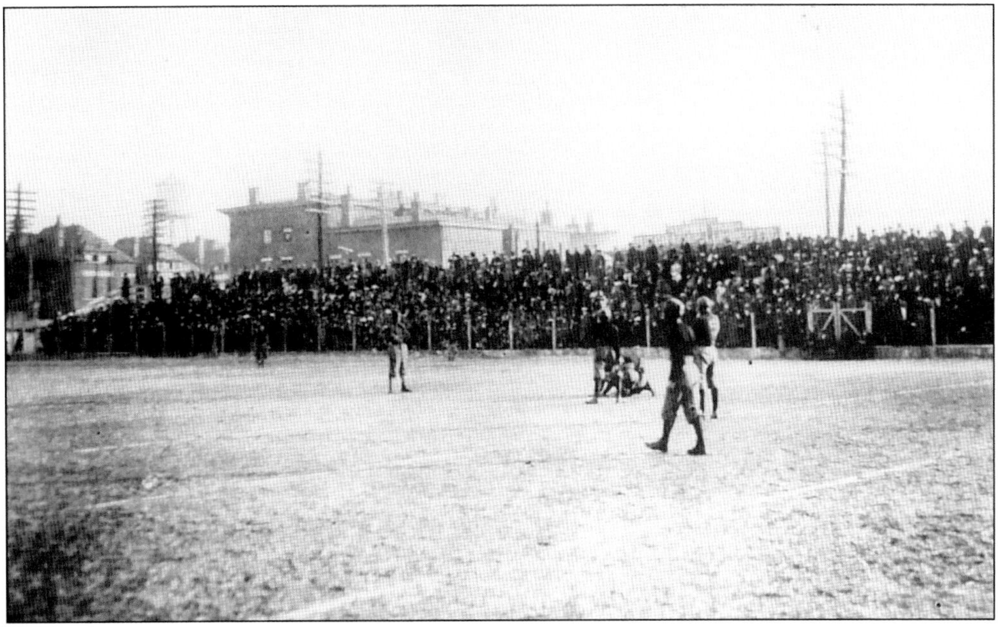

Pictured is the football team on the playing field at Central. (1922.)

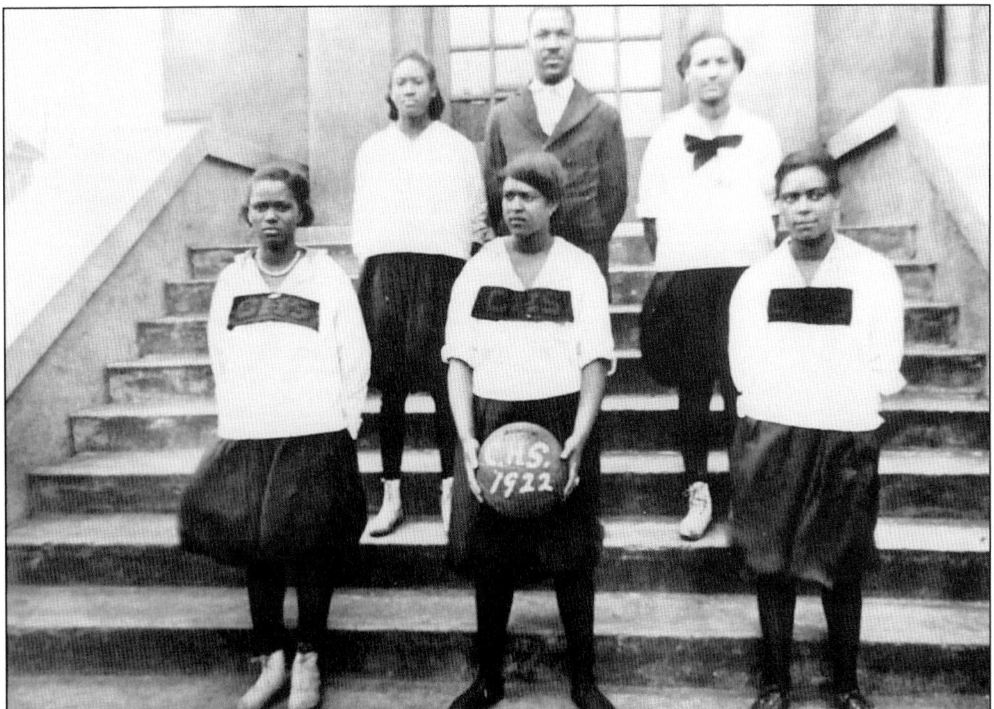

Seen in this 1922 view is the Central Colored High School Girls' Varsity Basketball team with their coach.

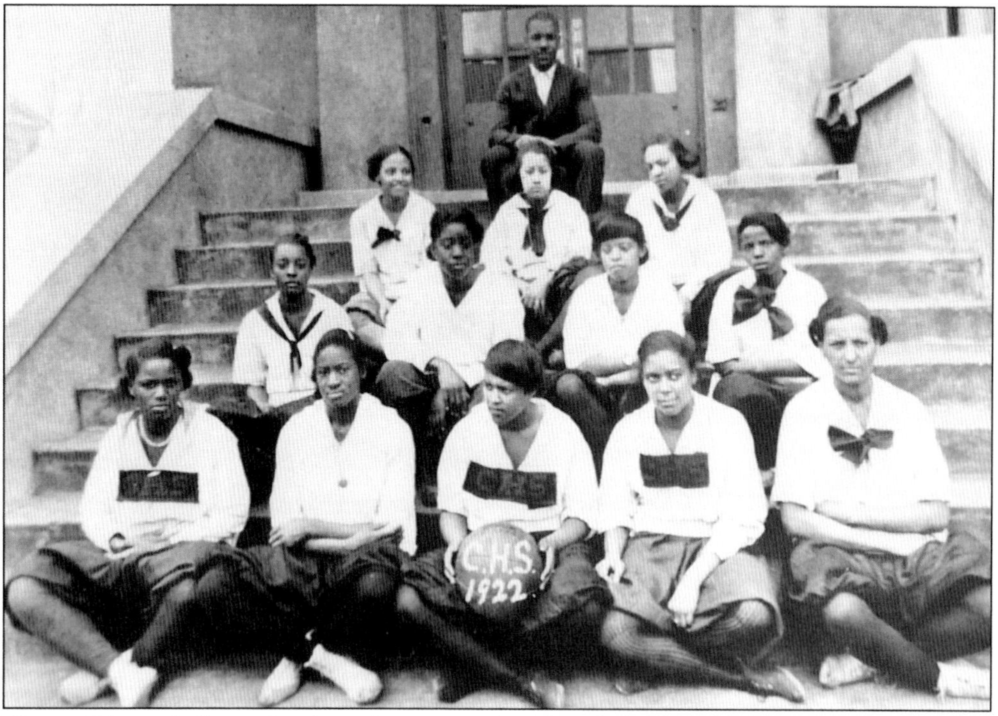

The girls' basketball squad and coach is pictured in this 1922 photograph.

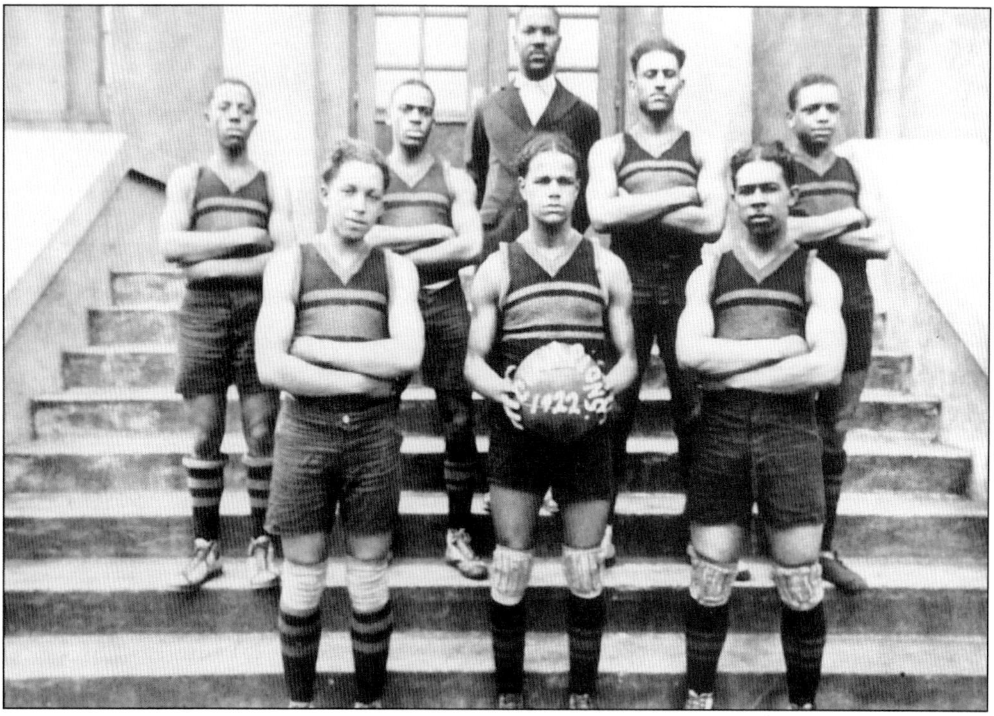

Pictured is the 1922 boys' basketball squad and coach.

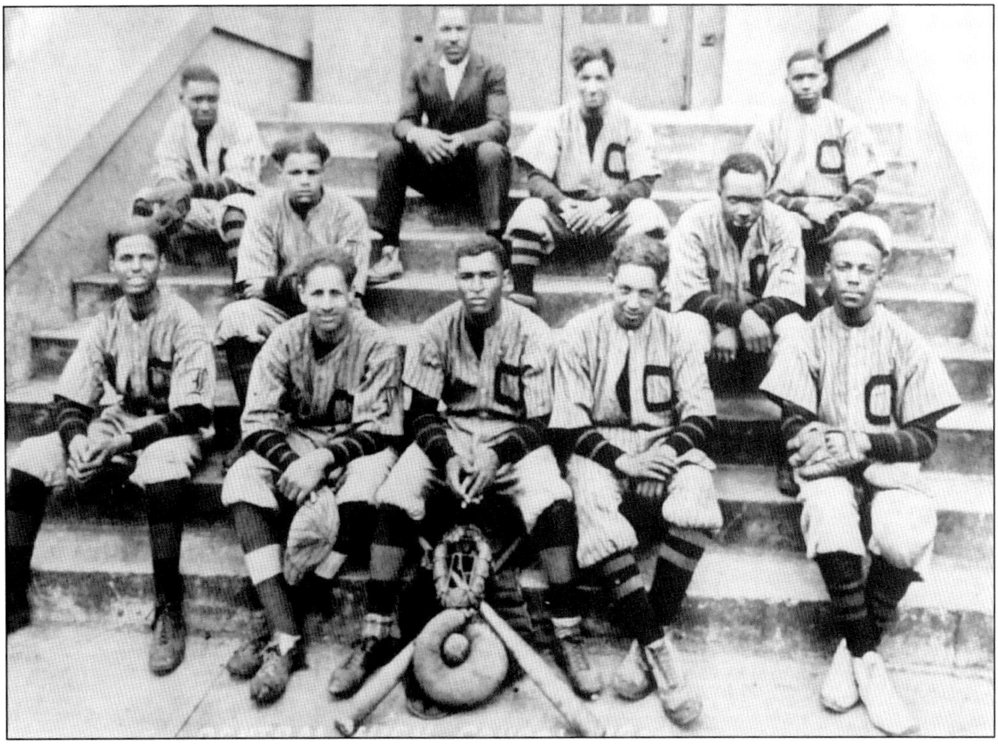

Pictured in this 1922 view is the boys' baseball team and coach.

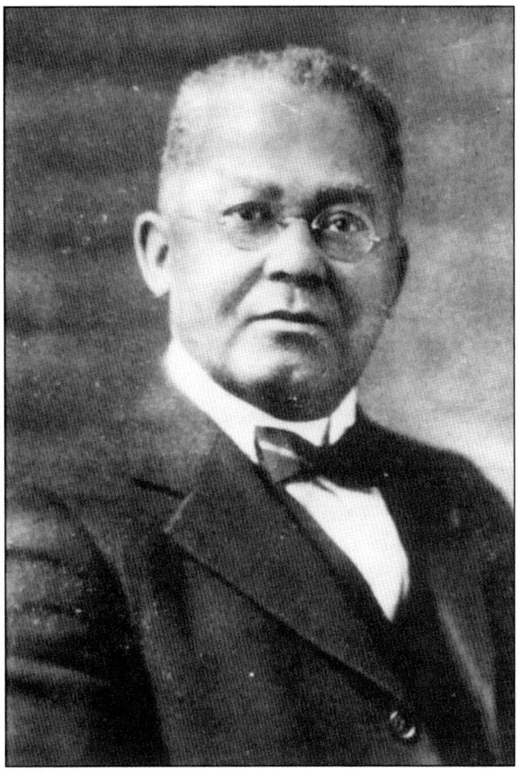

William B. Matthews was the principal of Central Colored High School at the time this photograph was made in 1933.

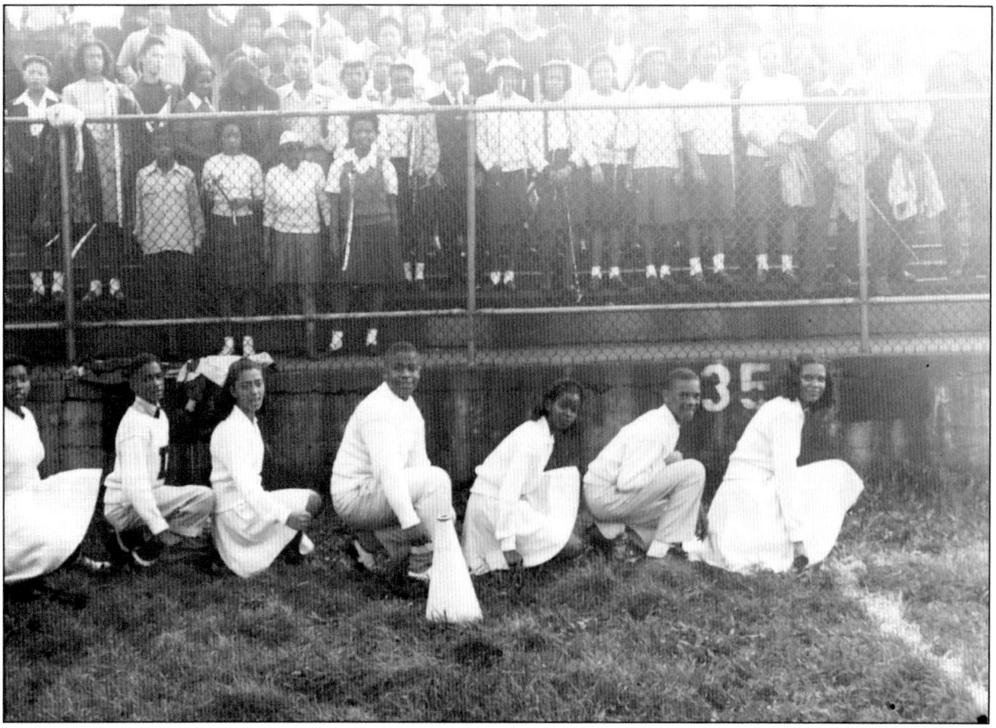

Pictured are the cheerleaders at Central Colored High School stadium. (*c.* 1939.)

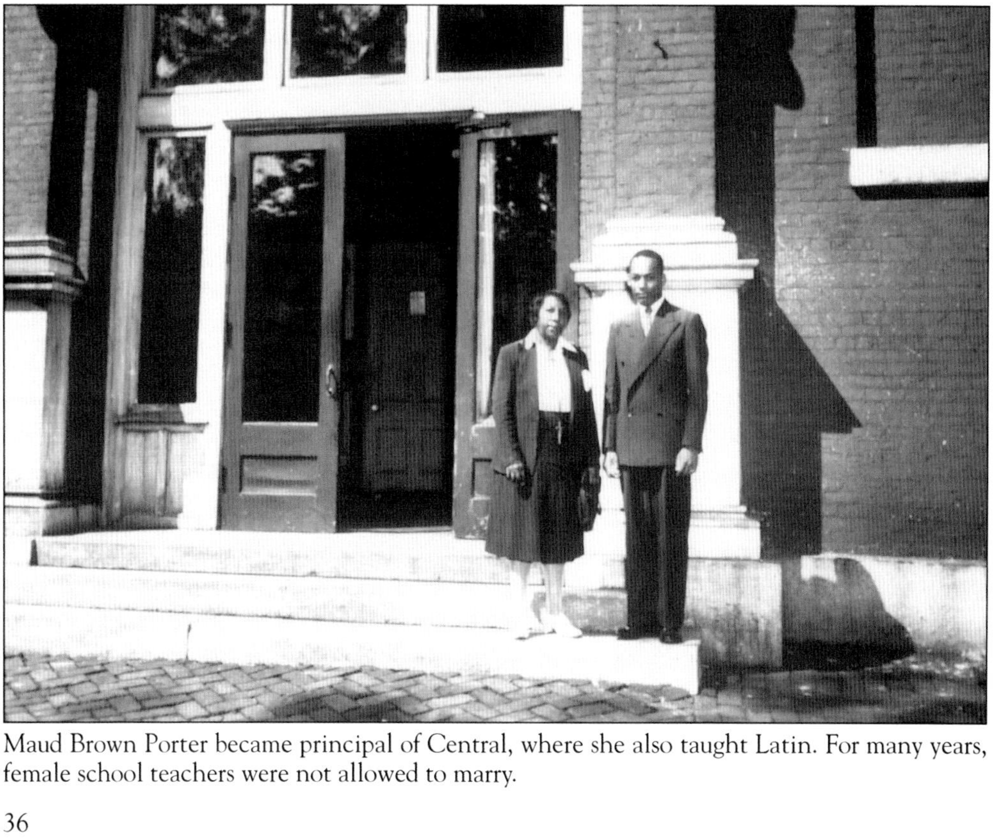

Maud Brown Porter became principal of Central, where she also taught Latin. For many years, female school teachers were not allowed to marry.

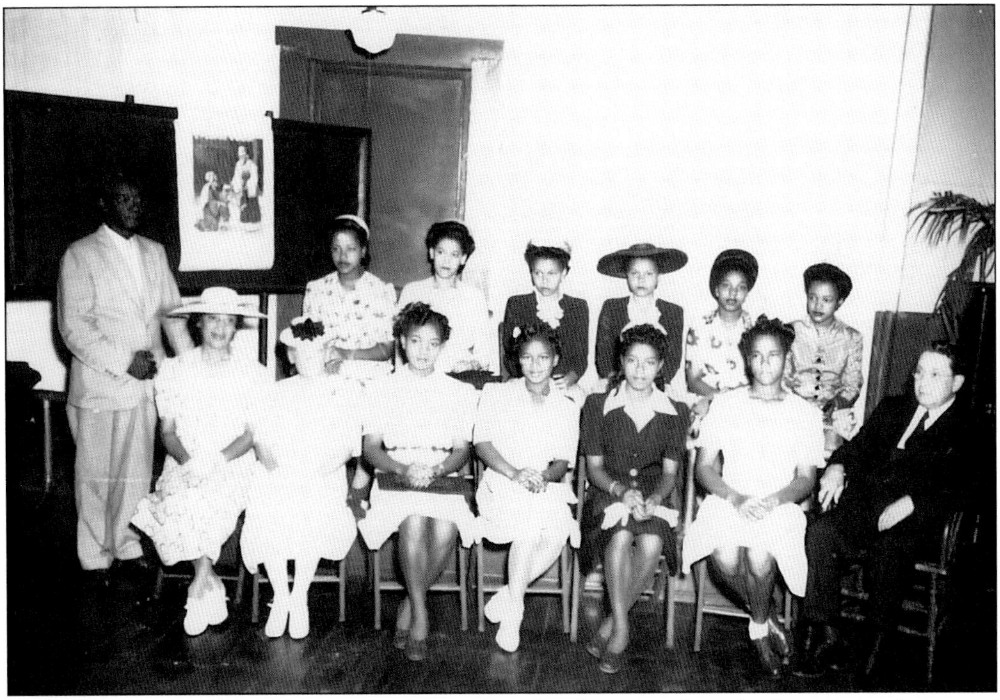

Mr. William A. Tisdale, a history teacher at the school, is seated on the far right with some of his students.

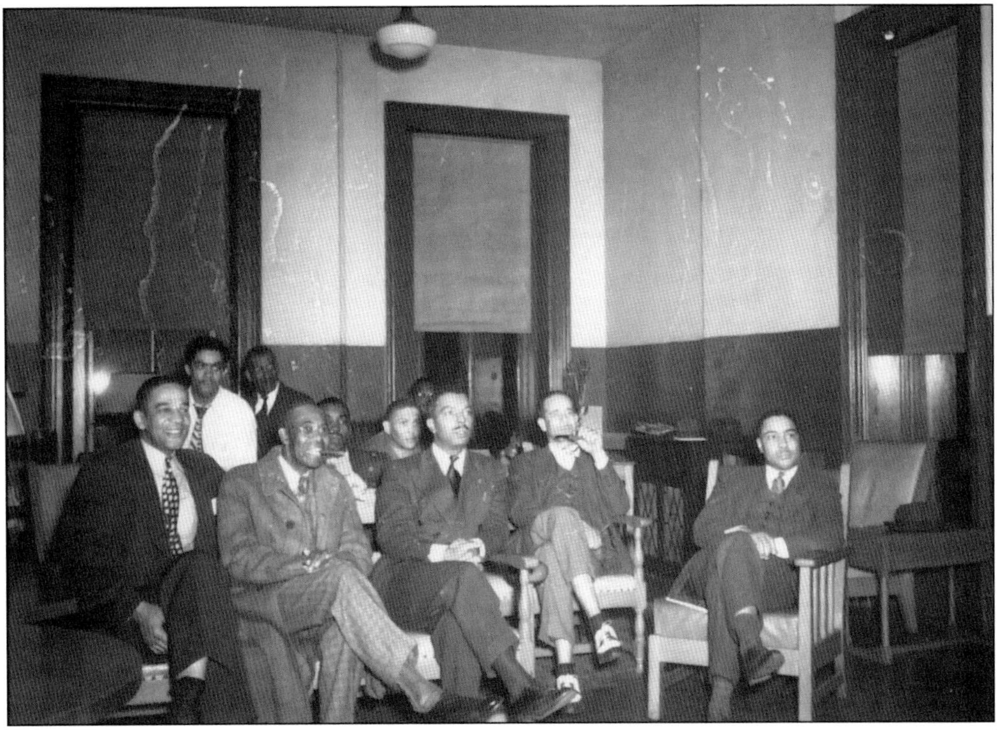

These Central faculty members, from left to right, are pictured as follows: Victor Perry, Carl Forbes, William Johnson, and Huston Baker.

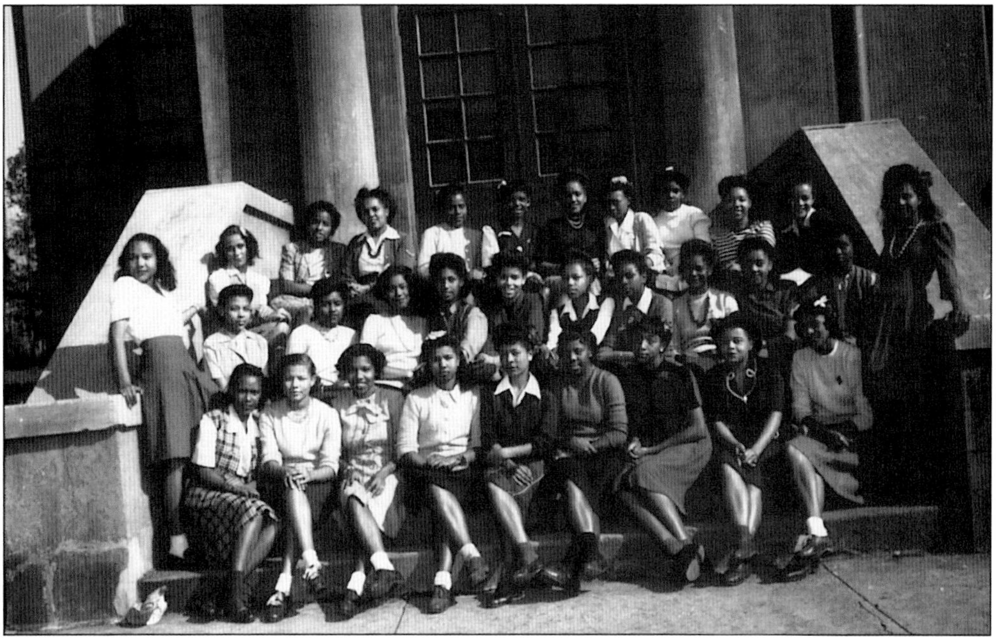

Students pose in front of the Ninth Street entrance to Central. (*c.* 1946.)

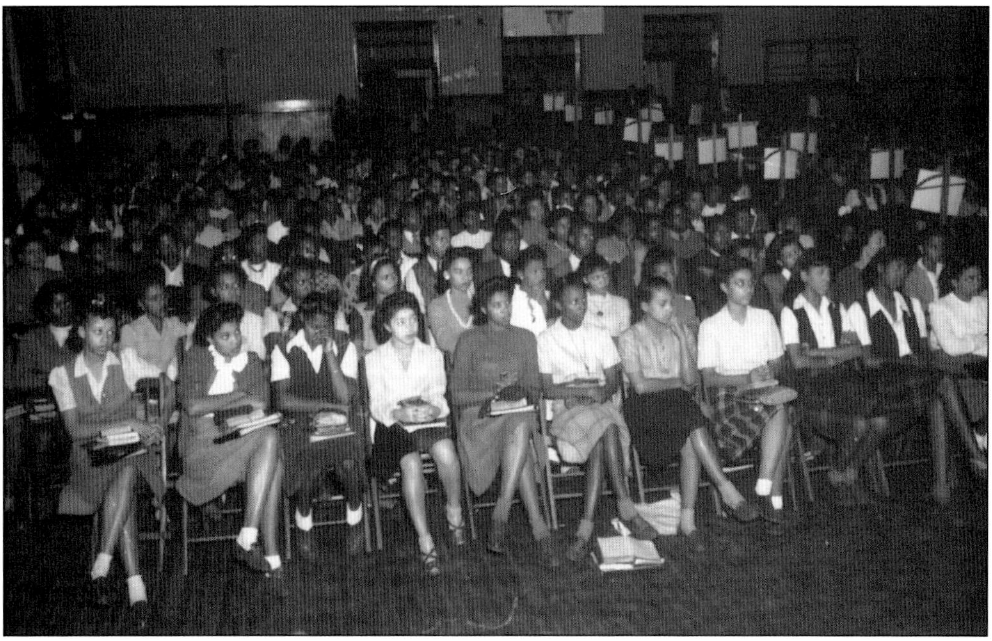

These Central students prepare for a graduation exercise assembly in the school's gymnasium.

Four

LOCAL FIREFIGHTERS

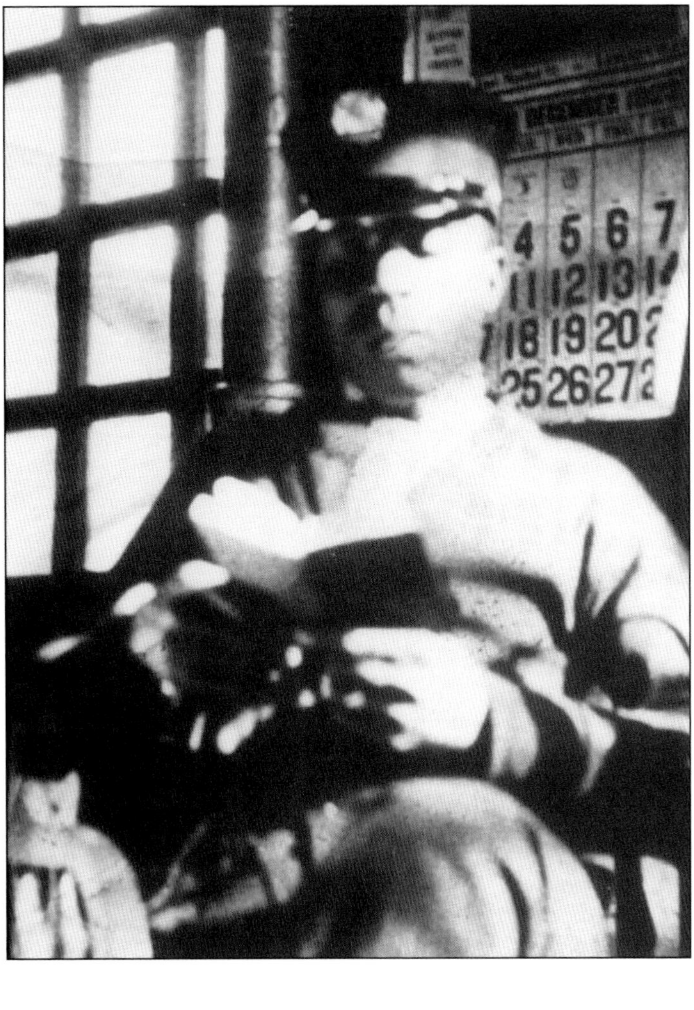

John W. Winston was hired December 4, 1924 by the new, all-black Engine Company No. 8. Notice the December 1923 calendar hanging in the background, which notes the date they went on line. Winston died in 1943.

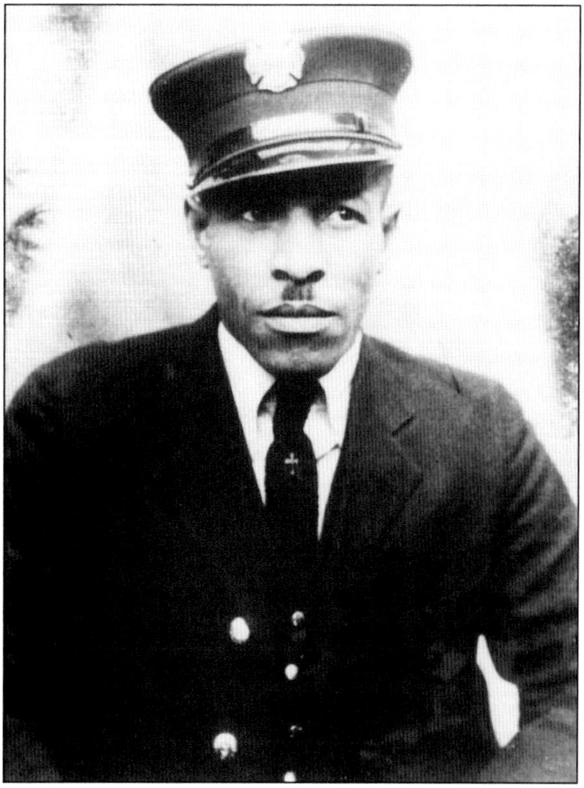

Antonio Blackburn worked for the Engine Company No. 8 firehouse, which was located at the corner of Thirteenth and Maple Streets. Blackburn was hired on March 15, 1924, and served as acting captain in 1928. He retired with a disability on February 1, 1950. (*c.* 1920s.)

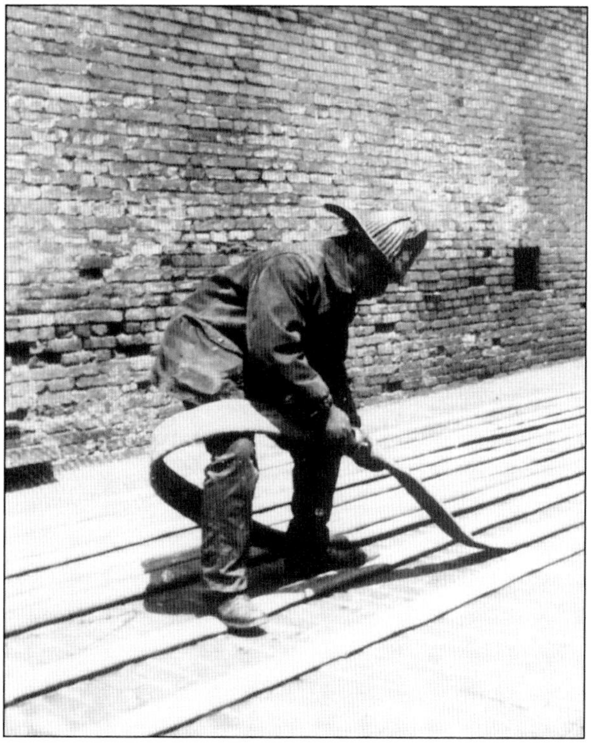

Horace Green of Engine Company No. 8 is seen in this early 1930s photograph checking firehoses. He was hired on October 9, 1923 as part of the first African-American recruits. Green died on October 28, 1939.

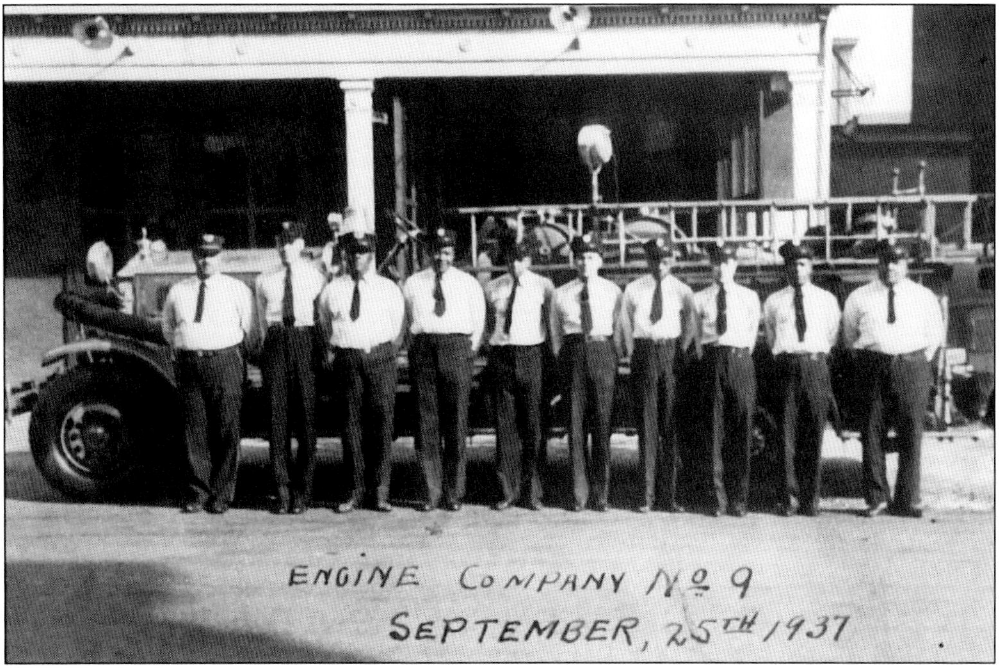

Pictured in this view, captured on film on September 25, 1937, are the newly hired firefighters at Engine Company No. 9 and those at Engine 8 who manned the second all-black firehouse in Louisville. They are, from left to right, as follows: Captain Alonzo Malone, Garland Kaufman, George Baldock, Jacob Collins, Eddie Bradfield, William T. Adams, Emanuel Terry, Reginald Talton, Roy Murphy, and Ramsey Jackson.

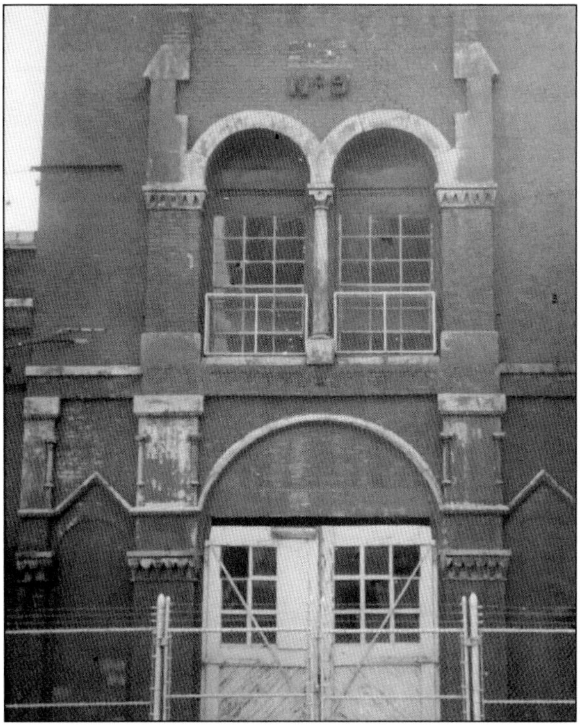

Engine Company No. 9 firehouse closed on October 17, 1941 to make way for the construction of President Franklin D. Roosevelt's New Deal Housing program in Louisville. It became the site of the Sheppard Square Public Housing project.

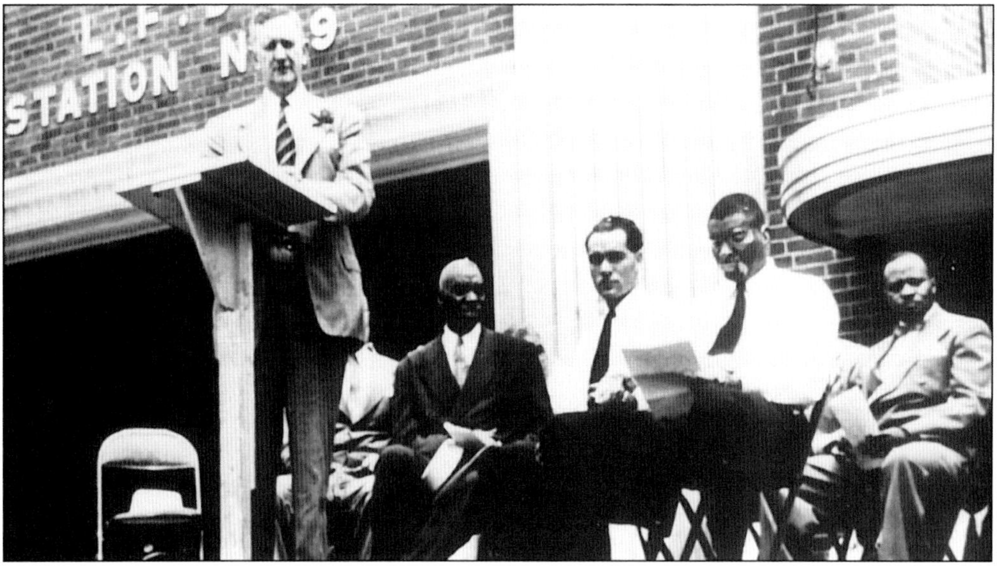

On July 15, 1946, a new firehouse was dedicated to the all-black Engine Company No. 9. Louisville Mayor E. Leland Taylor is at the podium, with Rev. Charles Owens of Lampton Baptist Church standing to his right. Others in attendance, from left to right, are as follows: Lt. Reginald L. Talton, Capt. Otis B. Smith, and Earle Pruitt (manager of Beecher Terrace Public Housing Projects and advisor to the mayor on race relations).

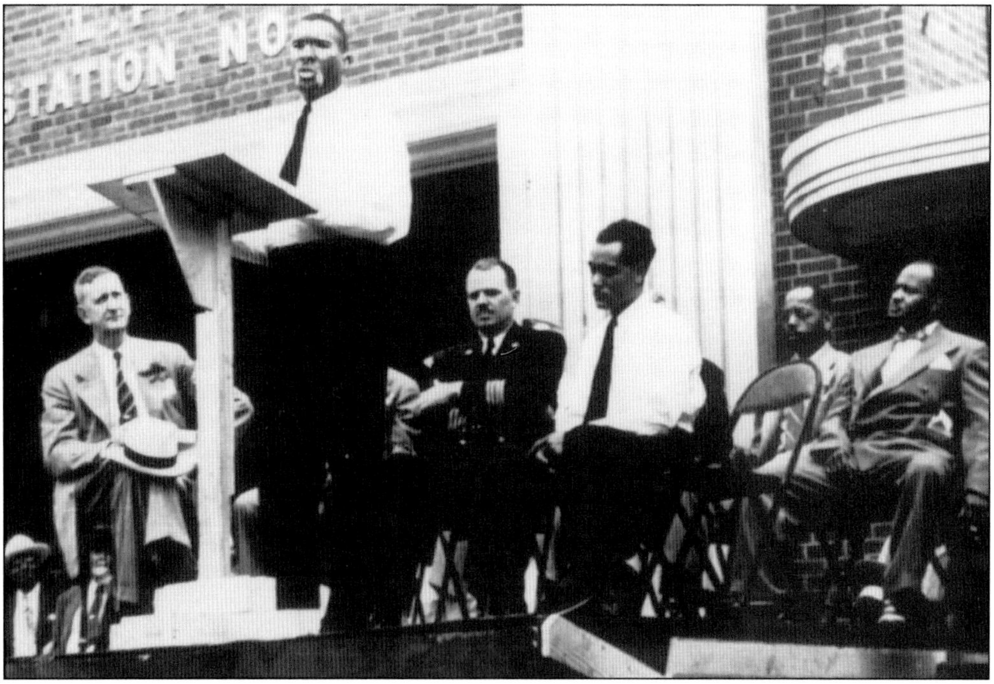

Pictured in this view, from left to right, are as follows: Mayor E. Leland Taylor (seated), Capt. Otis B. Smith (at podium), Fire Chief John Krusenklaus, Lt. Reginald Larry Talton, Des Moines W. Beard (manager of Sheppard Square Public Housing Project), and Earle Pruitt. Others in attendance (not pictured) include A.E. Meyzeek (O.P.A. information assistant) and a girls' choir directed by Iola Acton.

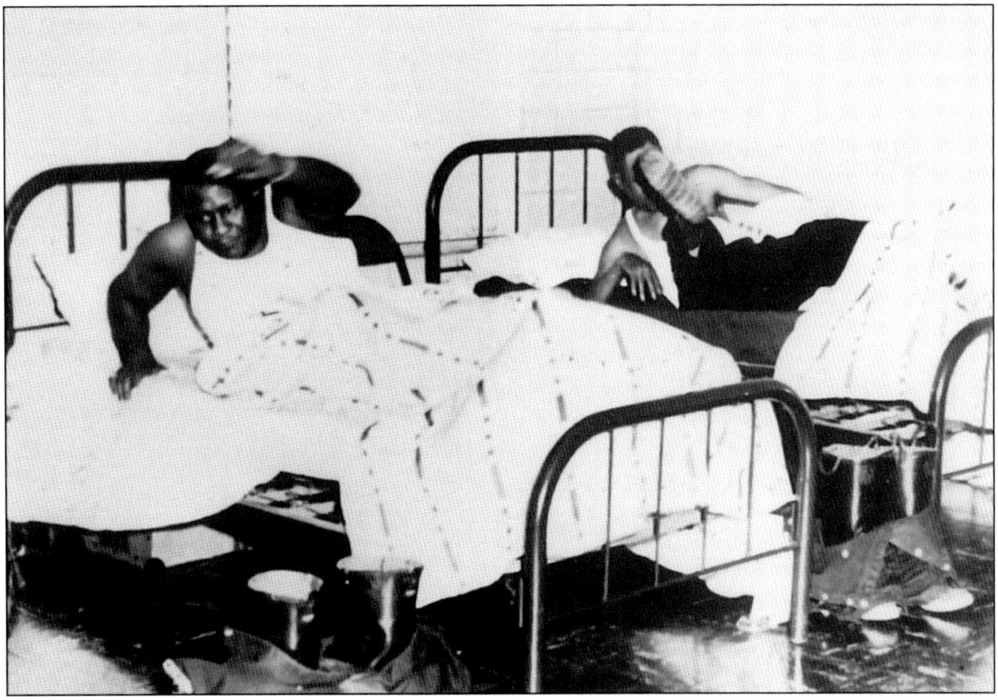

These firefighters are reacting to a fire alarm in the new Engine Company No. 9 station. Pictured from left to right are Jacob Collins and Kennedy Watson. (c. 1946.)

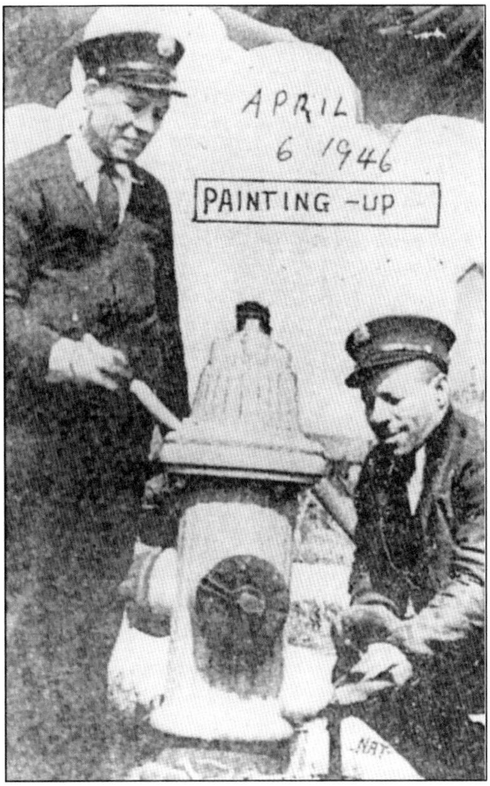

These firefighters are painting a fire hydrant and keeping it in good operation as part of their regular maintenance duties. Pictured in this April 1946 view are Kennedy Watson (standing) and Antonio Blackburn.

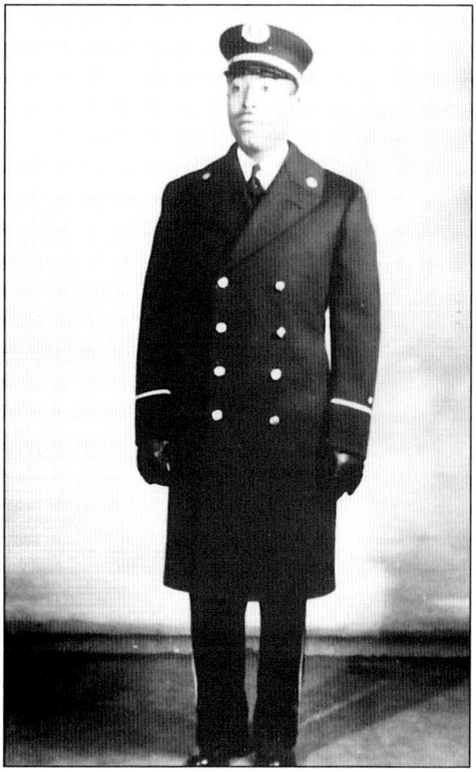

Lt. Paul Hopson was hired September 1937 on the second all-black Engine Company No. 9. He resigned in good standing on February 1, 1955 and moved to California because he was "unable to earn enough money." He could have been rehired if he had chosen to re-apply. Racial integration began in 1954 under Mayor Andrew Broaddus. No disruptive incidents were recorded.

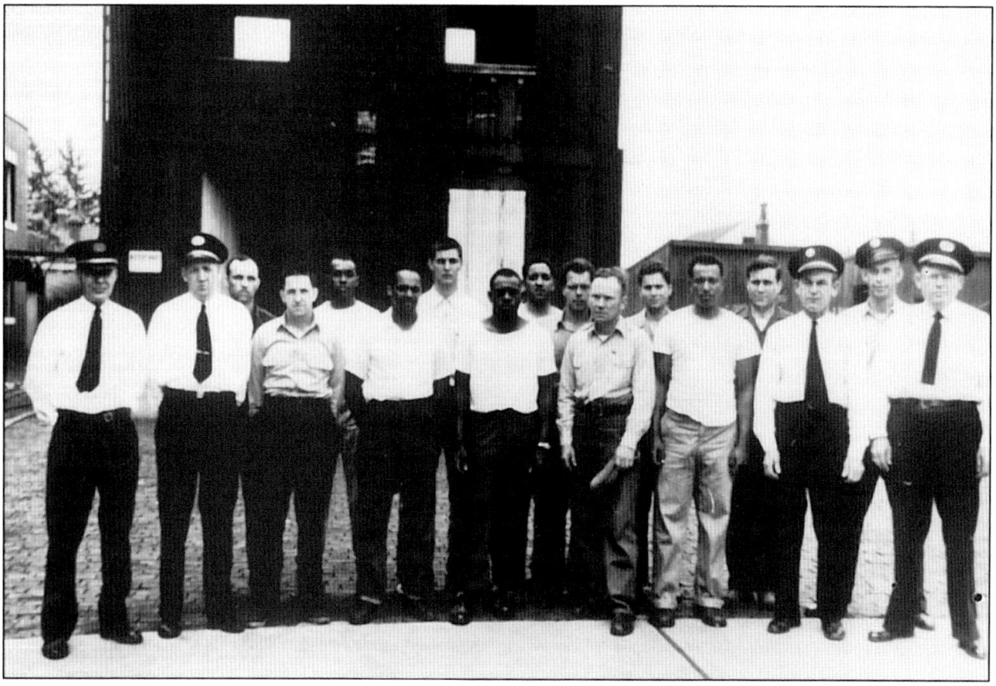

Pictured is the Fire Drill School class of June 27, 1954. Class members include Julius Gunter, Raymond Green, Sellis "Tony" Davis, Henry Maxwell, Robert Catlett, Leon Miller, ? Roscoe, and a man called "Rochester." Also pictured is Al Deppy (first officer on far left).

Roy Stanley (left) and Capt. Theodore Funk (right) are seen in this photograph of the Louisville Fire Department Headquarters. Stanley was one of two Blacks hired when the department was integrated in 1954.

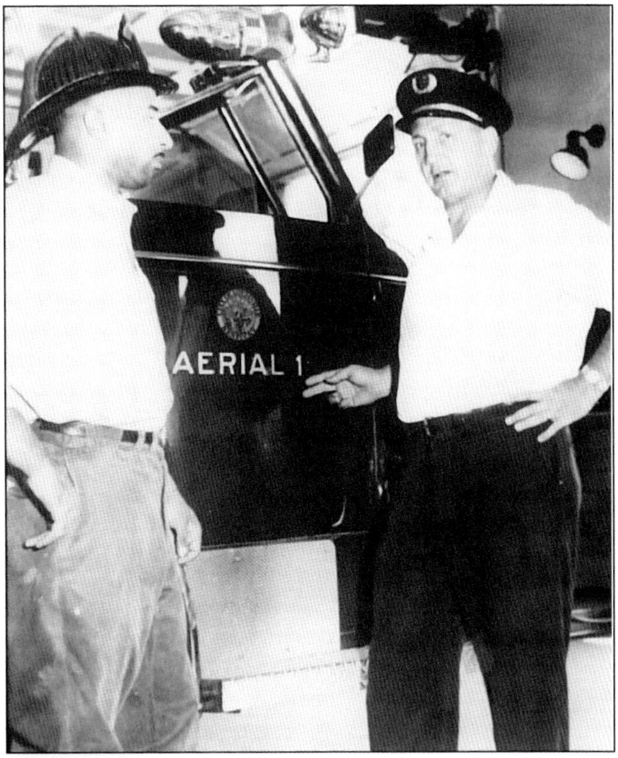

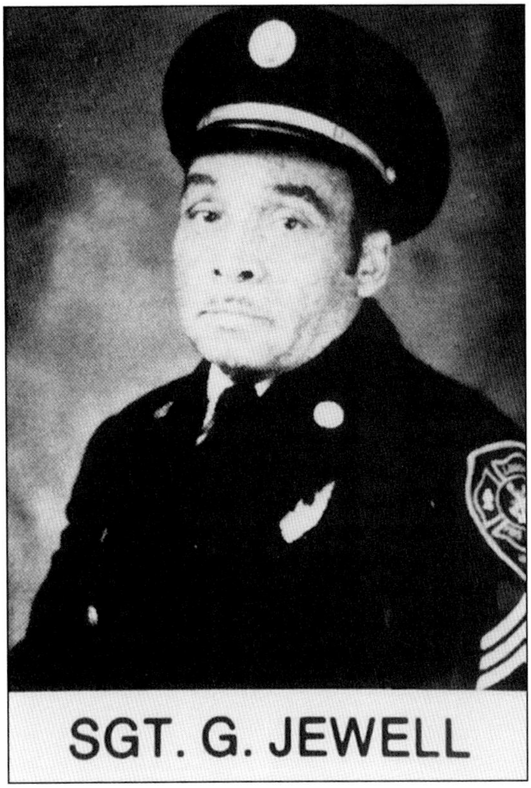

Sgt. George Jewell, pictured in this 1981 photograph, was hired in 1951 and retired on July 1, 1982. In August 1976, he became the first district chief's aide and driver. He was the first African-American driver of the chief of the Division of Fire in Louisville.

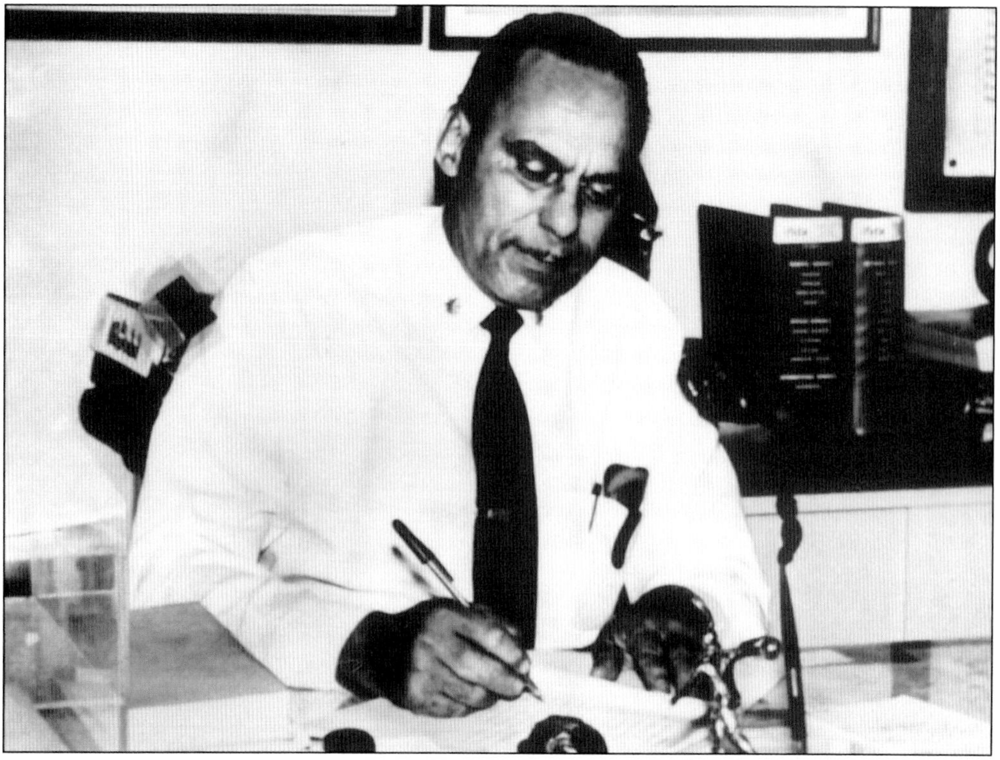

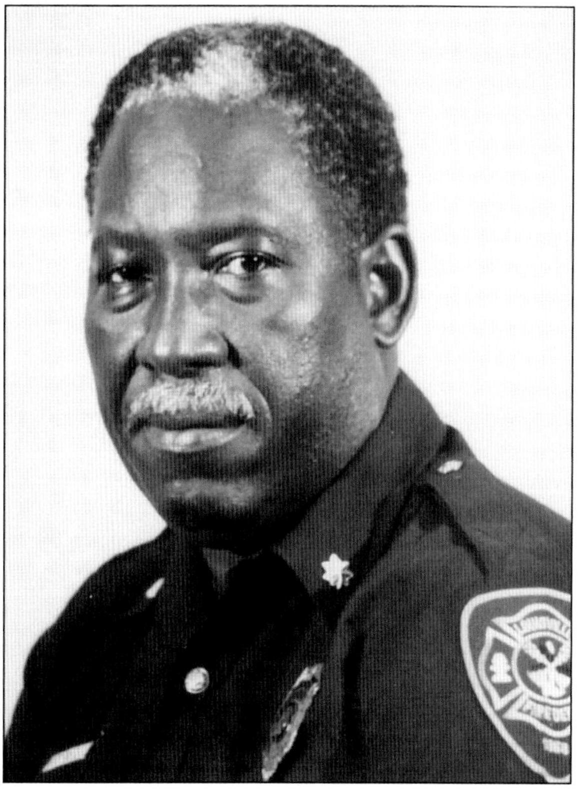

Pictured in this July 1967 photograph is Lt. Colonel William T. Adams. Adams was hired as one of the original members of the second all-black Engine Company No. 9 on July 17, 1937. He rose to the rank of lieutenant on October 17, 1939, became a captain on April 5, 1941, and was promoted to the position of assistant chief on July 1, 1967. He retired on March 27, 1974 and died of cancer in 1991.

Assistant Fire Chief Jesse West was hired by the Louisville Fire Department on October 1, 1959. He took a leave of absence to serve in the military from August 7, 1961 and was re-instated to the fire department on September 22, 1963. He retired on June 1, 1990.

Sgt. Benny Farrell, pictured in this 1981 photo, was hired in 1967 and became a founding member of the Black Professional Firefighters Association. He was a militant recruit who lobbied for more Black firefighters and officers. He retired on October 1, 1987.

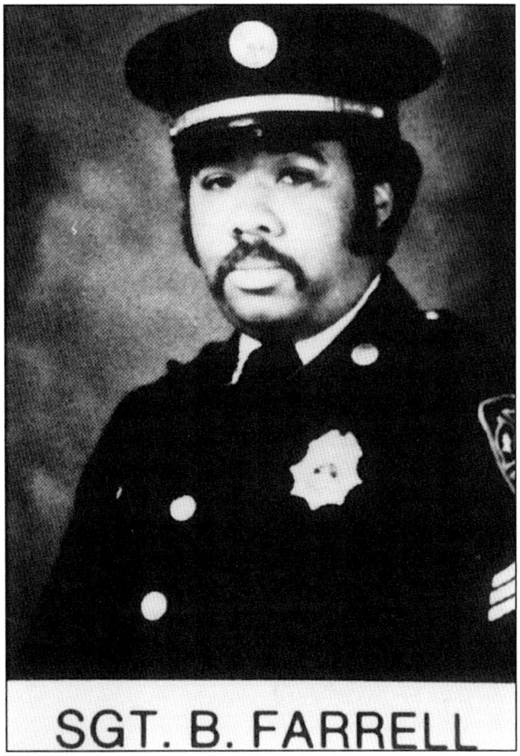

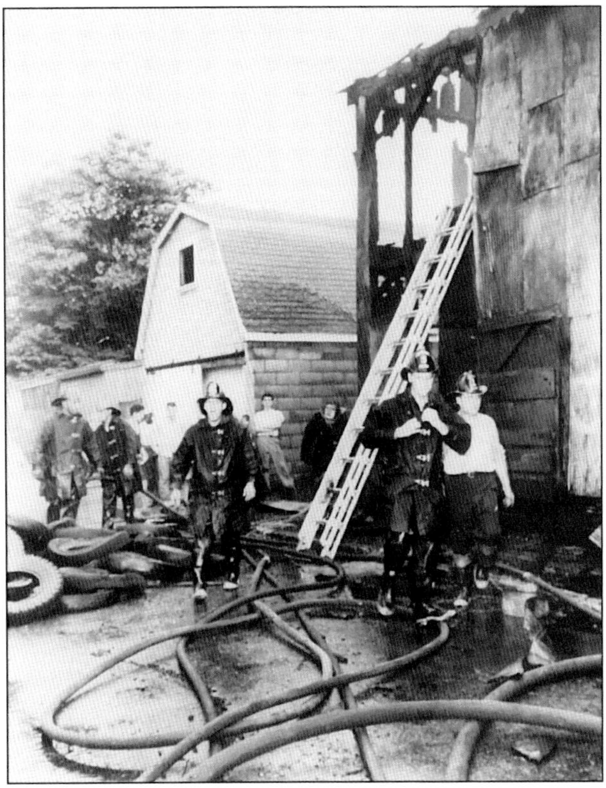

This tire store, located at Sixteenth Street and Broadway, was engulfed in flames in the summer of 1956. Lt. Logan Miller (far left) was a member of the Fire Prevention Bureau.

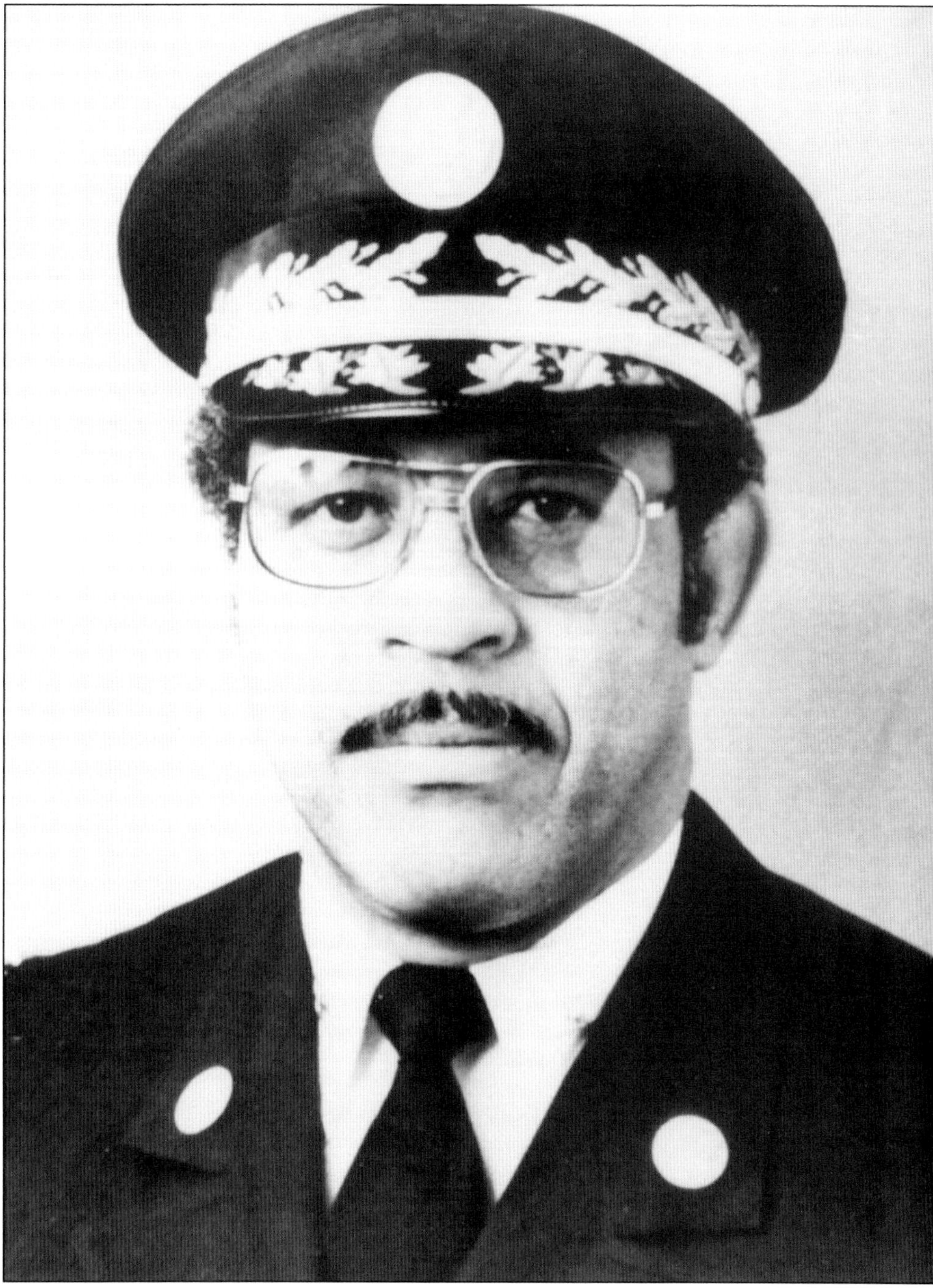

Larry Bonnafon joined the Louisville Fire Department in December 1955 and, at age 18, became the youngest recruit. He worked his way up the ranks and became the first and only black fire chief. He served in that capacity from 1979 until he retired in 1986.

Five

World War II and the Fight for Democracy

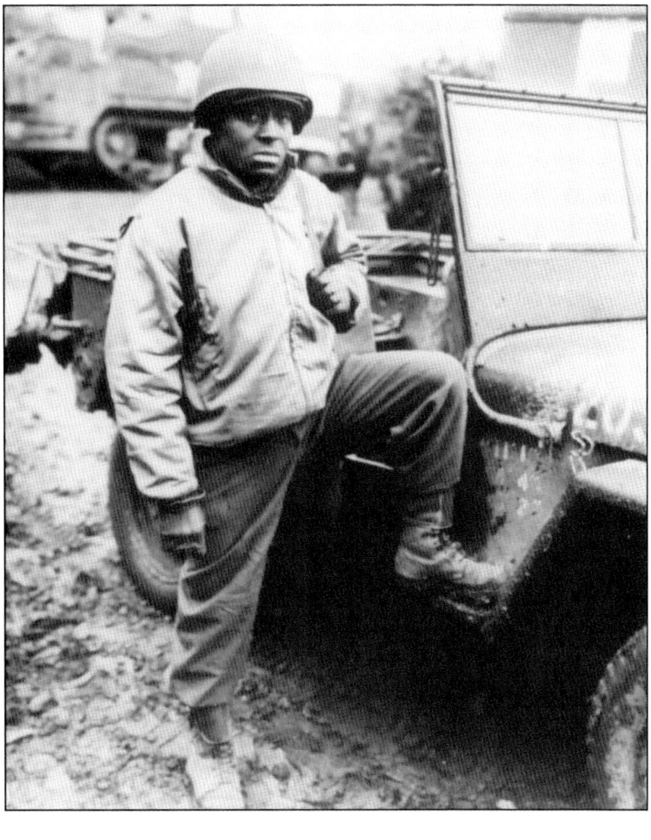

Warrant Officer Clarence I. Gobold of the 761st Tank Battalion at Fort Knox, Kentucky, earned a battlefield promotion to second lieutenant for his simultaneous handling of battalion adjutant and personnel officer.

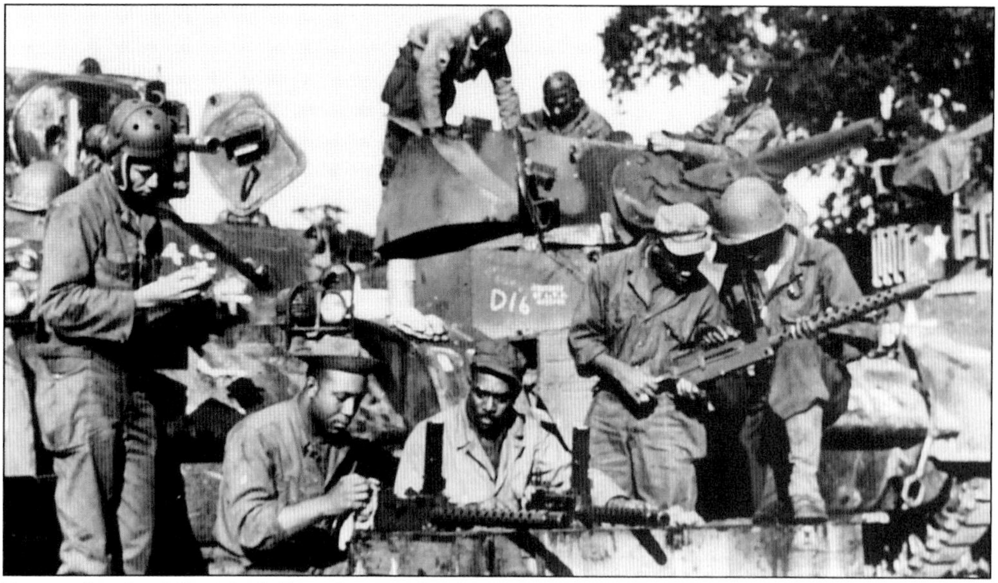

Pictured is the 761st Tank Battalion at the front in Europe, checking their tanks and guns.

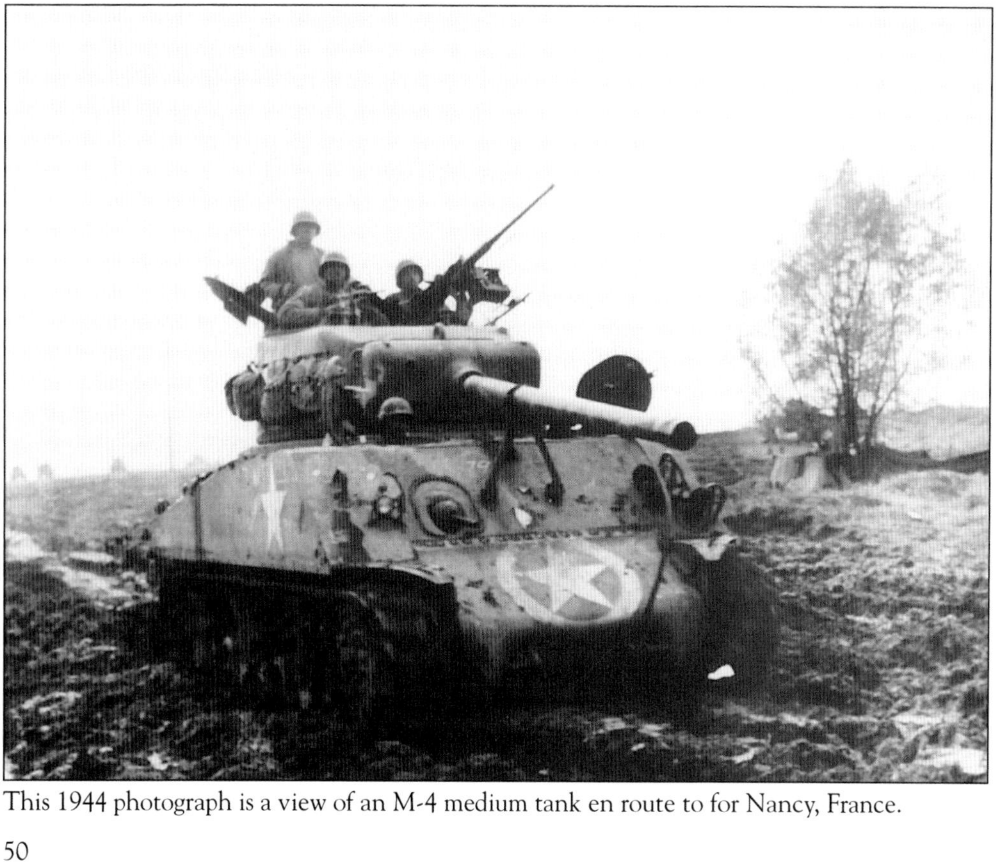

This 1944 photograph is a view of an M-4 medium tank en route to for Nancy, France.

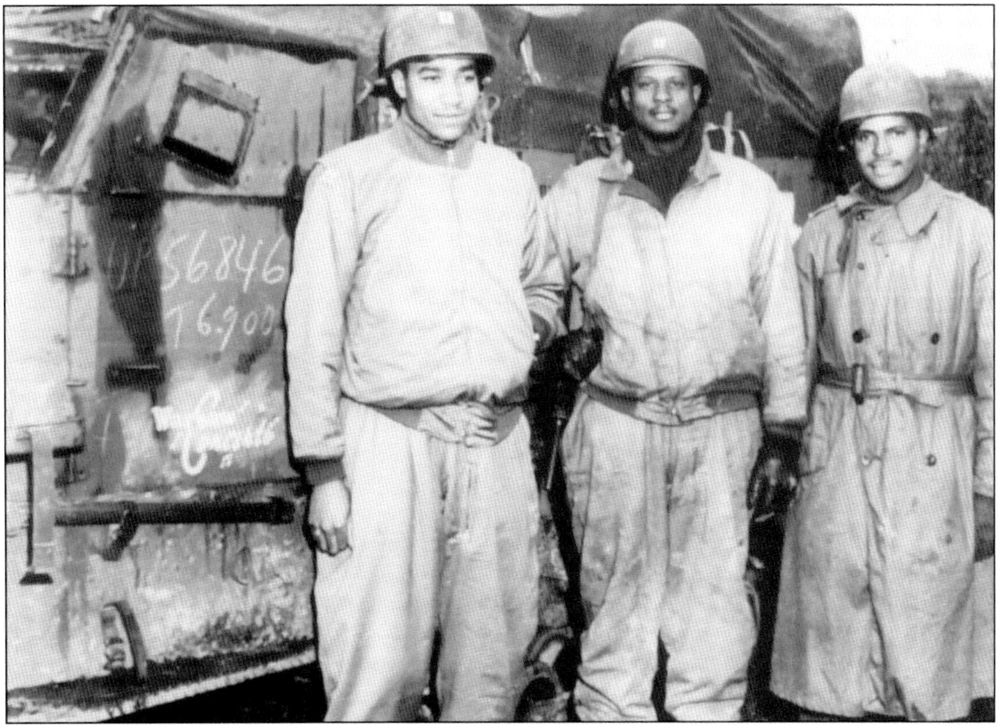

In this November 1944 photograph, some of the officers of the 761st Medium Tank are, from left to right, as follows: Captain Harrison, Captain McHenry, and Lieutenant Lightfoot.

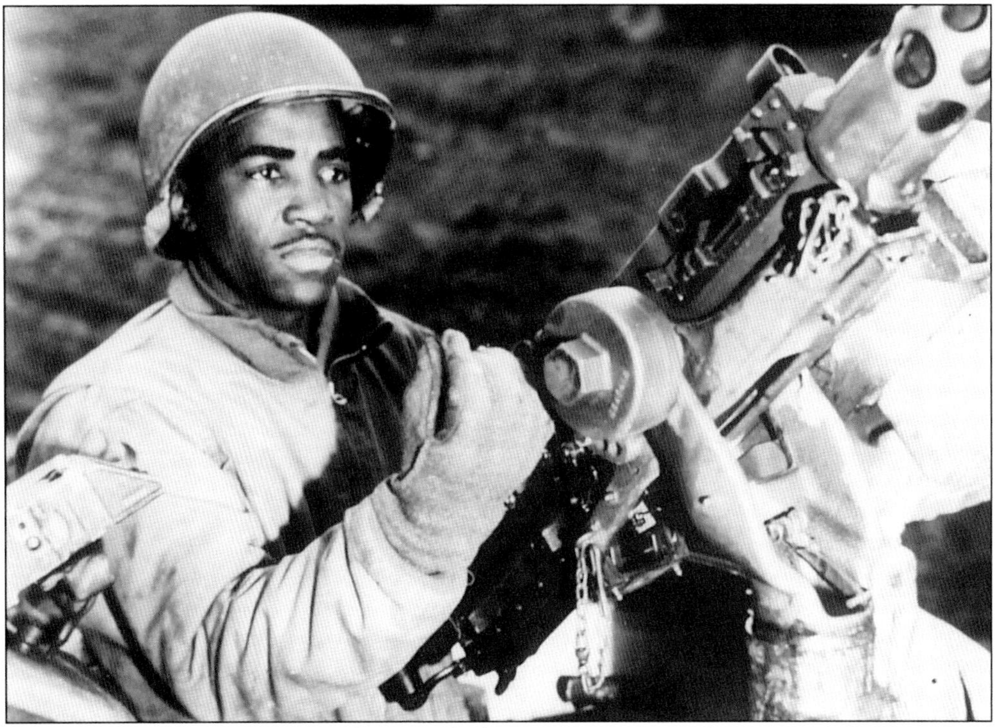

Pictured is Private L.C. Byrd, as photographed in France in 1944.

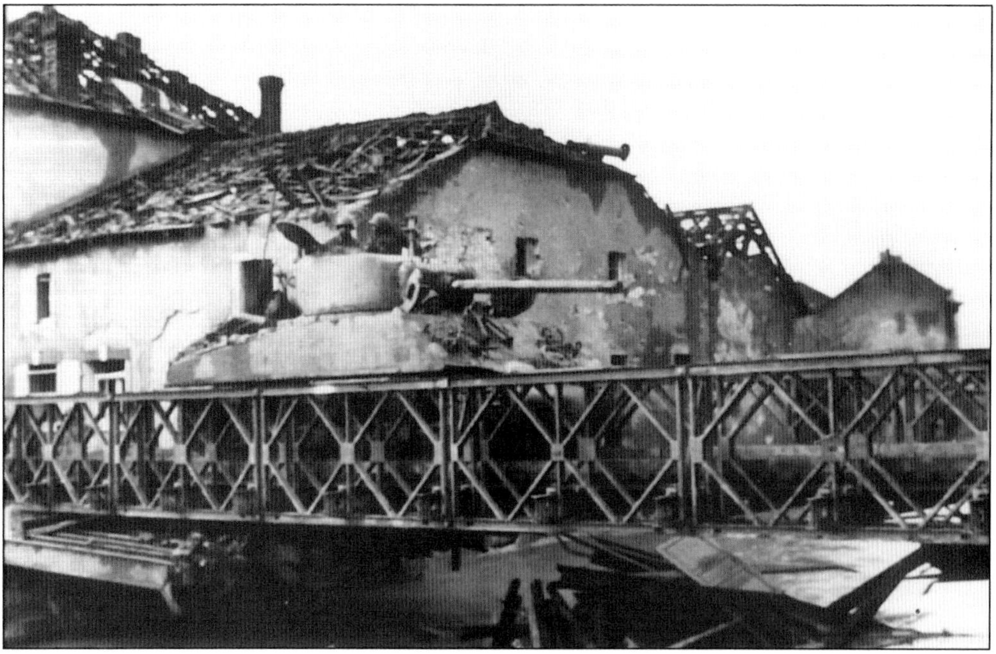

In this November 1944 view, a tank from Company A (761st Tank U.S. Third Army) is seen moving up to a forward position in the combat zone as it crosses the Bailey Bridge in the town of Vic-Ser-Seille.

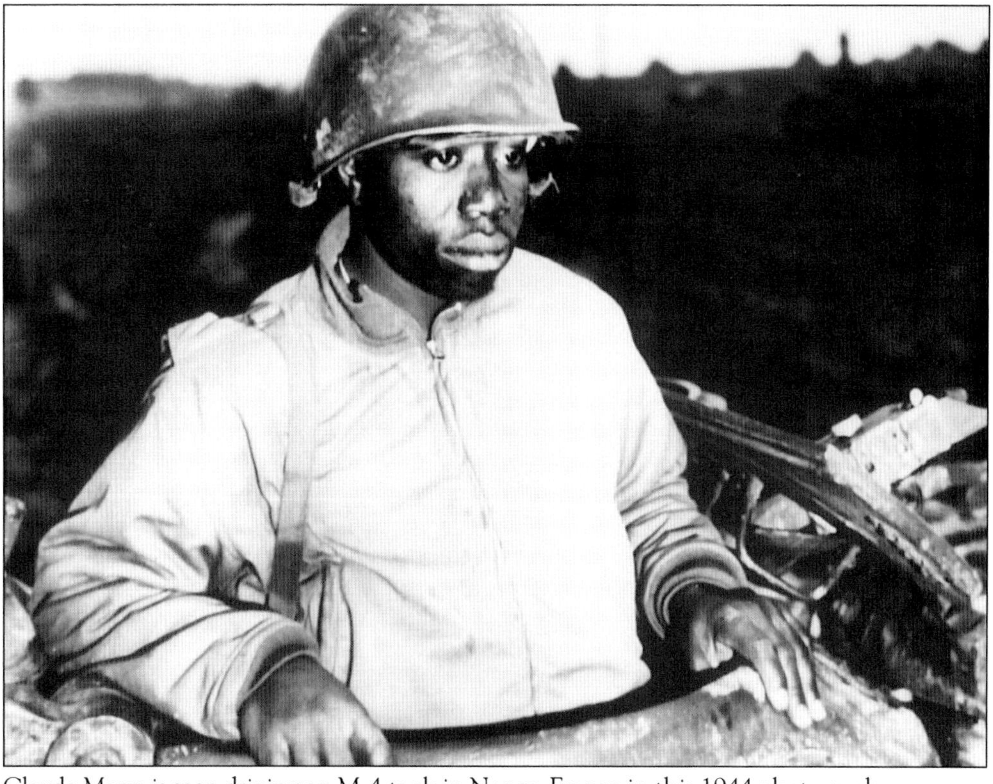

Claude Mann is seen driving an M-4 tank in Nancy, France in this 1944 photograph.

Private Ernest A. Jenkins is being decorated with the award of the Silver Star, given by George S. Patton Jr.

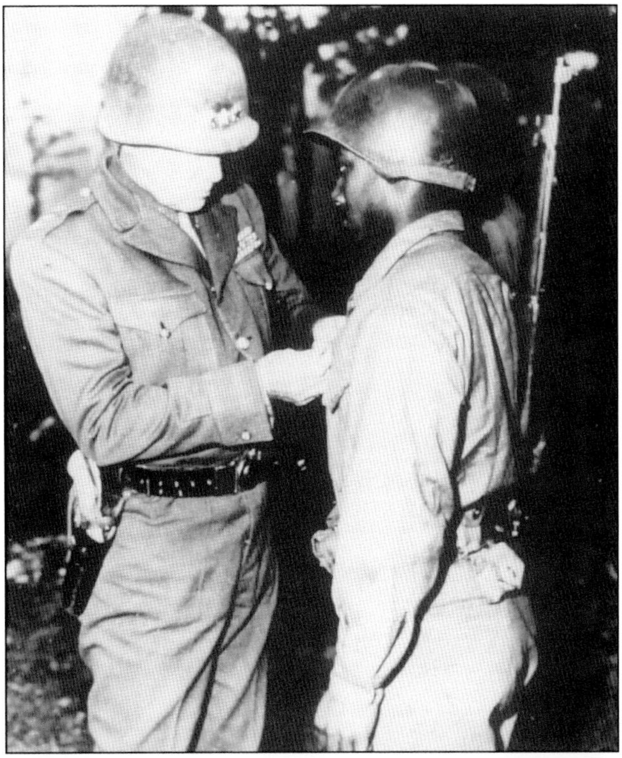

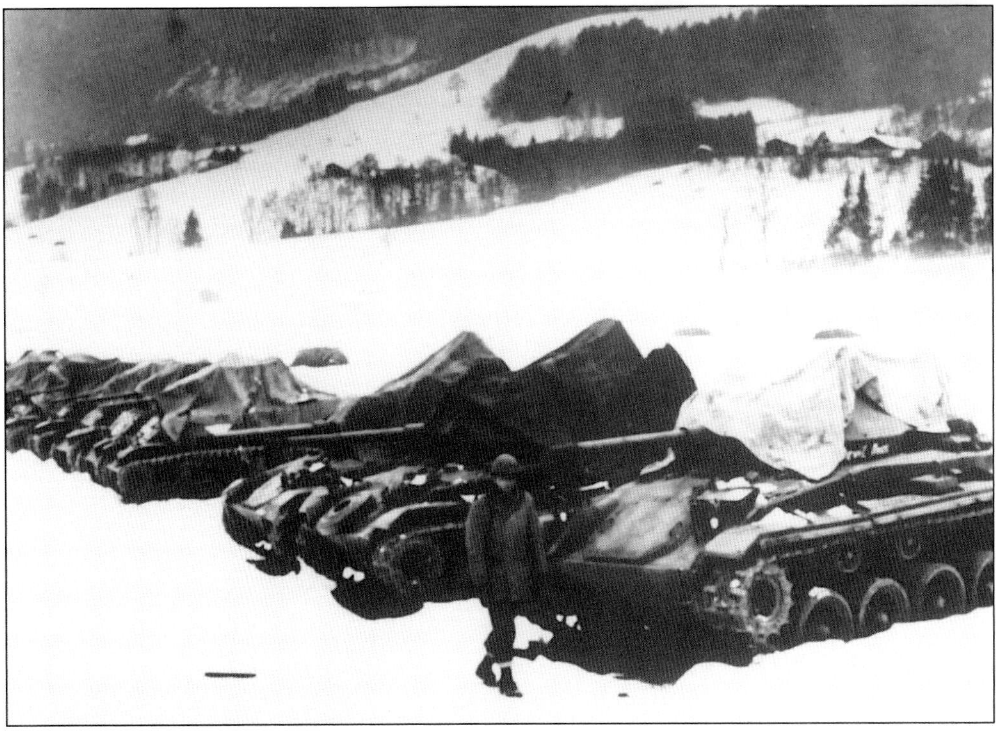

In this January 1946 photograph, taken in Munich, Germany, Private Eugene Hamilton guards the tank park of the 761st Tank Battalion.

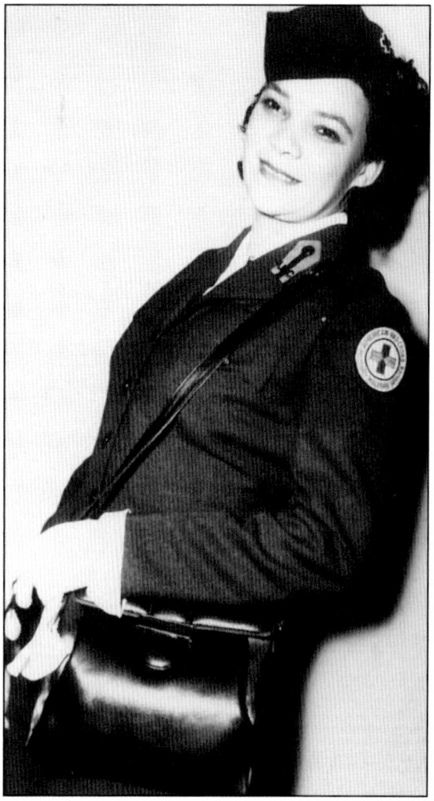

Marguerite Davis Stewart of Louisville is a graduate of Fisk University who served as a Red Cross professional. She trained in Washington, D.C. during WW II.

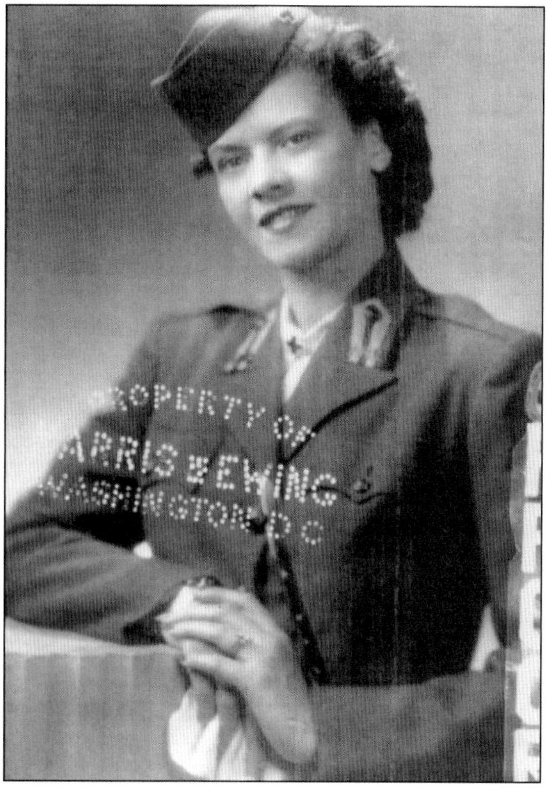

Marguerite Stewart directed a service club which met at both Bowman Field and at Fort Knox. She also served in Asia and later retired with a distinguished record.

Six

A Community of Faith

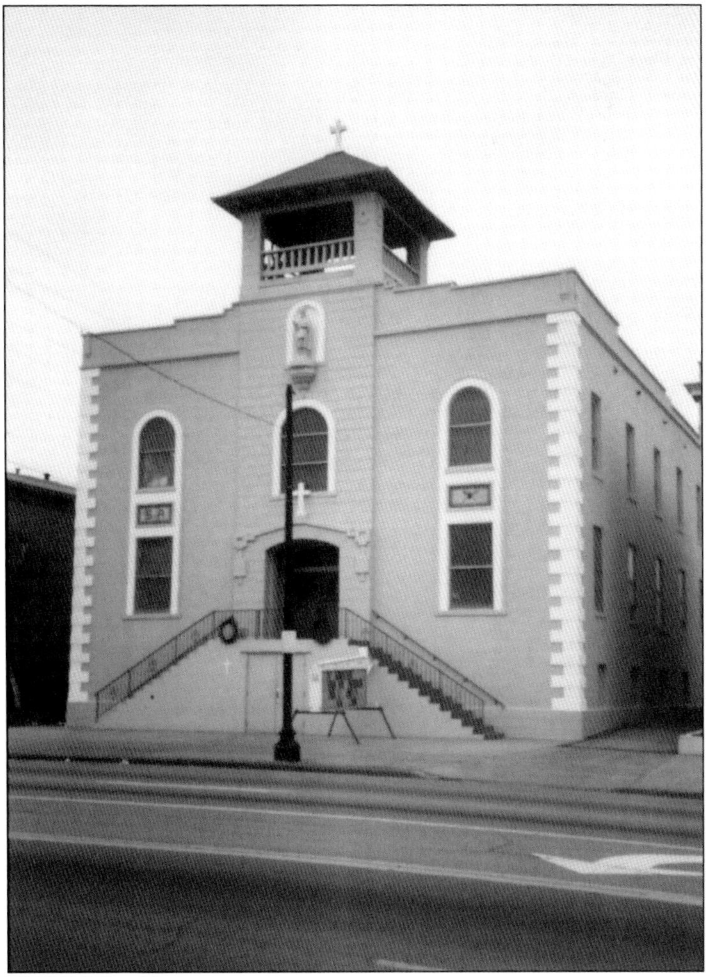

On July 10, 1869, Bishop McClosky's committee decided to build Saint Augustine Catholic Church on Broadway, near Fourteenth Street. About 75 Catholics marched on February 20, 1870, from their temporary services in the basement of the cathedral to their own church. Rev. John L. Spalding presided over the church, which was next-door to his home. Mass was set aside for white Catholics until Sacred Heart Church was built in 1873.

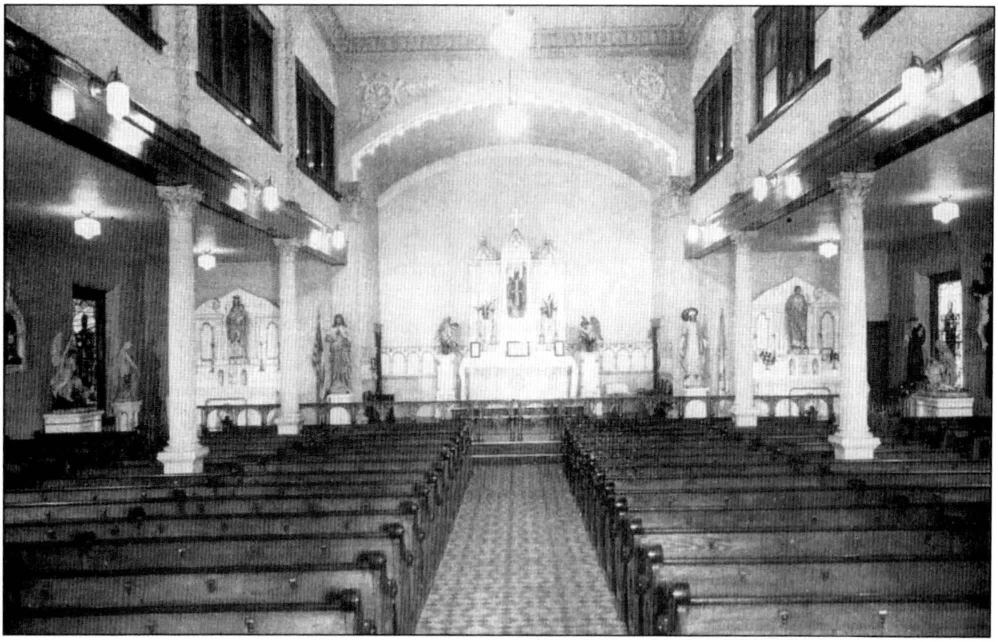

Pictured in this 1945 photograph is an interior view of St. Augustine Church.

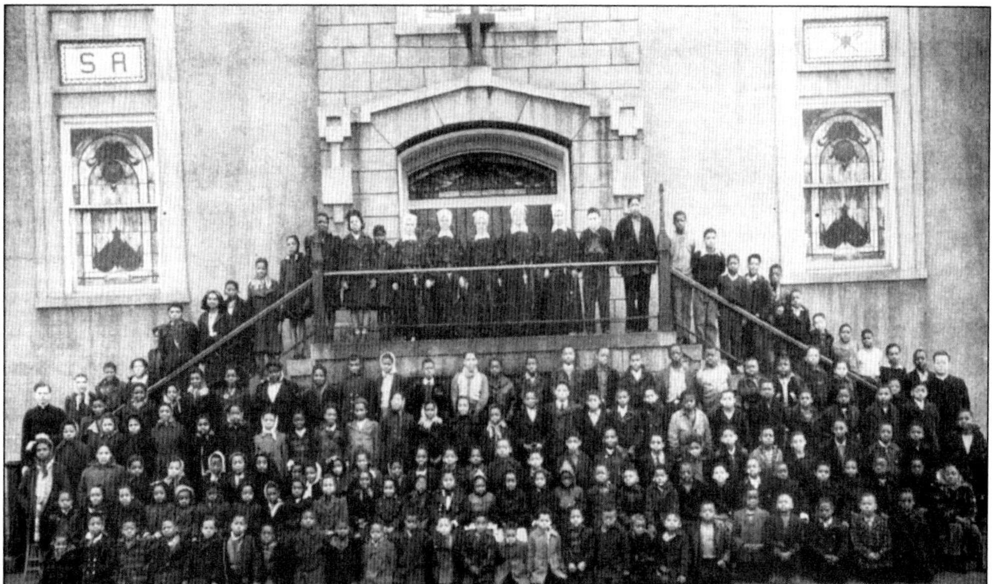

Pictured in this 1945 view are the children of St. Augustine School in grades kindergarten through eight. Hundreds of men from St. Augustine served in the United States Armed Forces during WW II, and many of these pictured were their children.

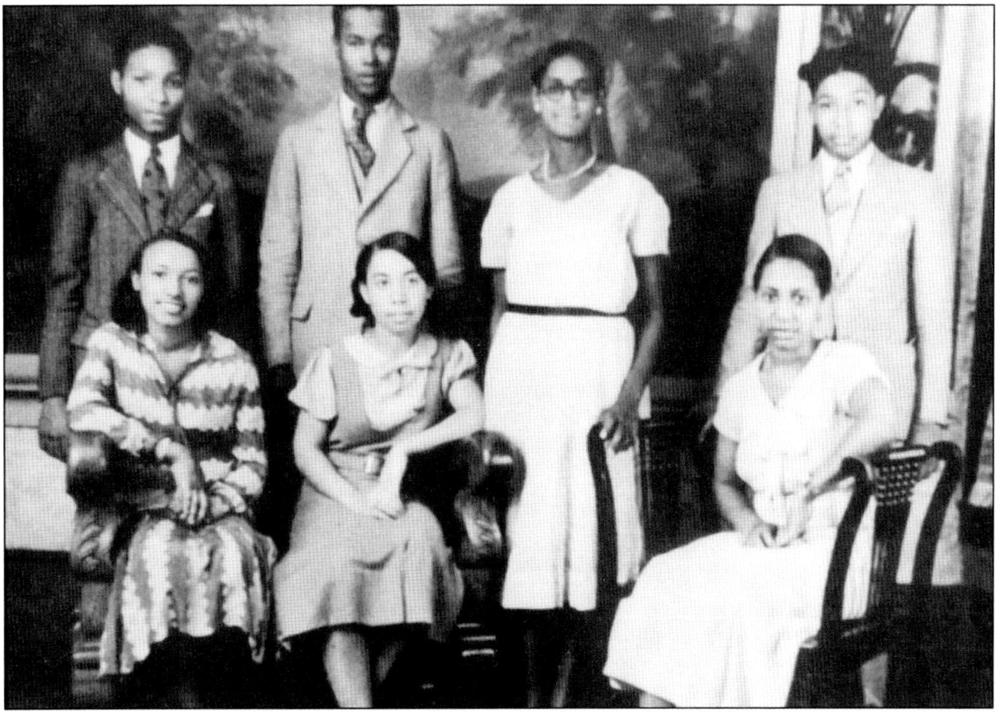

This is a view of the Catholic High School's class of 1933. Catholic High School was founded in the fall of 1921 with four students. Classes were taught by the Sisters of Charity, along with one lay teacher. Pictured from left to right are as follows: (seated) Edith Casey, Constance Davis, Mary Ann Wakefield; (standing) Joseph Hayden, Albert Mulligan, Elizabeth Burks, and Frank Edelen.

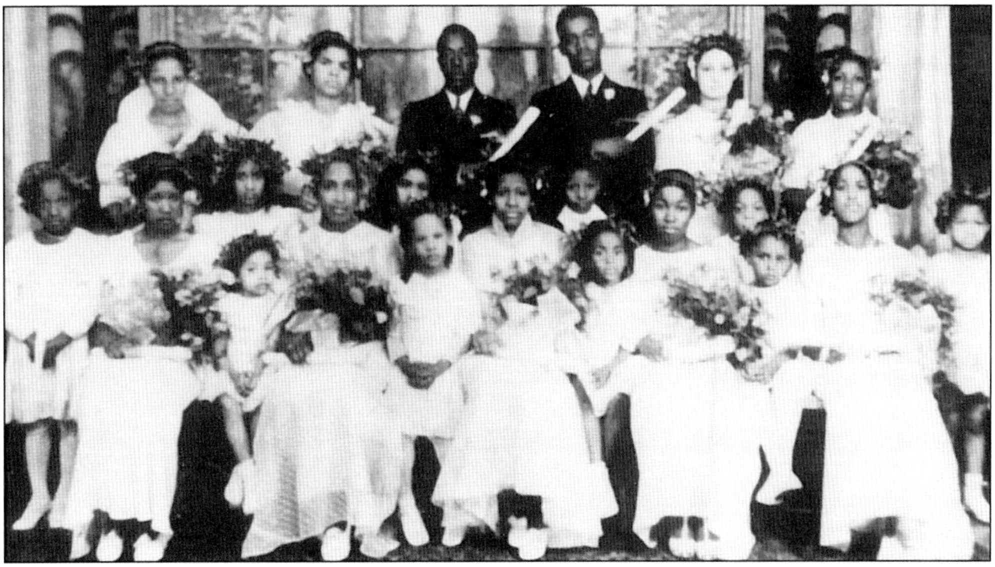

Pictured is the Catholic High School class of 1935. Class members, from left to right, are as follows: (seated) Marie Ross, Anna Lee Rodgers, Mauguerite Edelen, Lucille Mulligan, and Marie Burks; (standing) Helen Casey, Julia Gowdy, Eddie Elery, George Edelen, Donna Summerville, and Henrietta Reed.

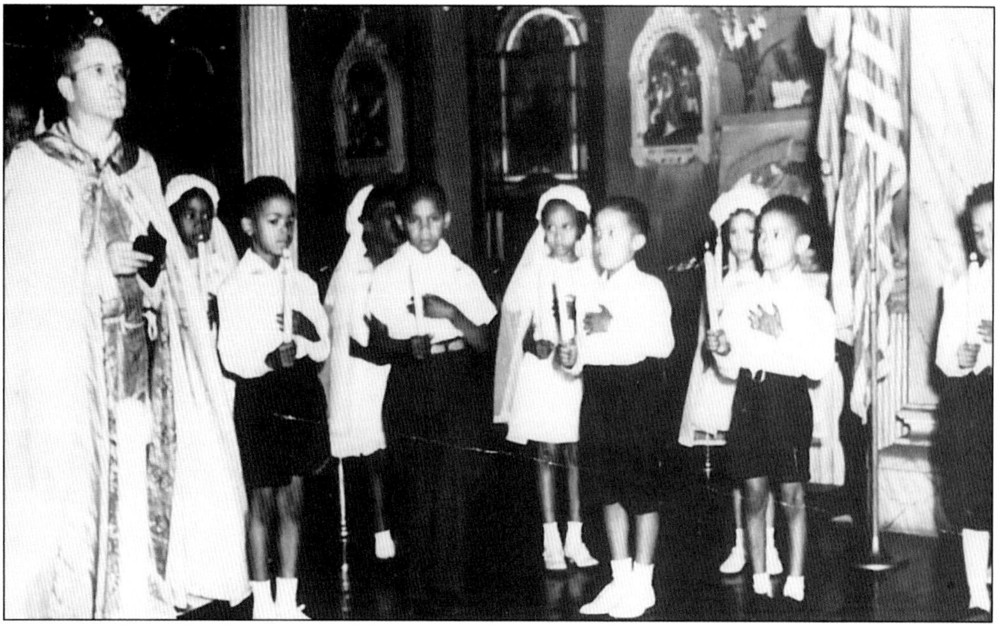

In this May 1943 photograph taken at St. Augustine, Father William D. Hines approaches the altar as the children follow to renew their baptismal vows before receiving their First Holy Communion.

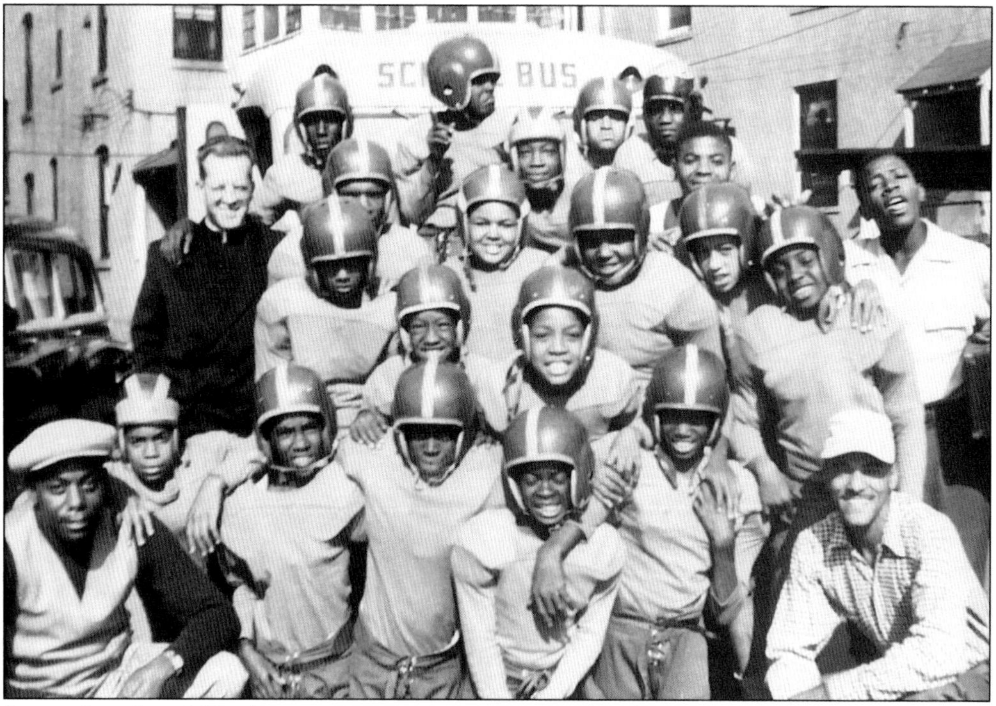

Pictured in this 1950s photo view is St. Augustine's grade school football team. Pictured, from left to right, are as follows: (front row) Coach Charles Thomas (far left) and Assistant Coach Newt McCravey (far right); (back row) Father Dennis Hines (far left) and Thompson (a Central High School football player who helped the team, far right).

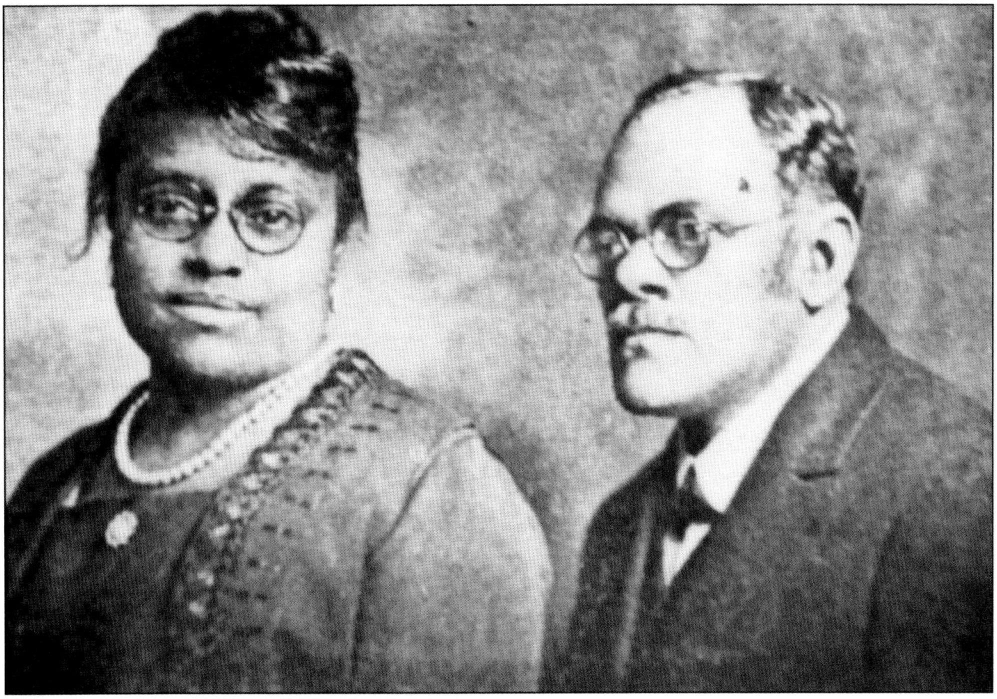

In 1900, Rev. George C. Clement became pastor of the old Twelfth Street Church. He is pictured with his wife, Emma Clarissa Clement.

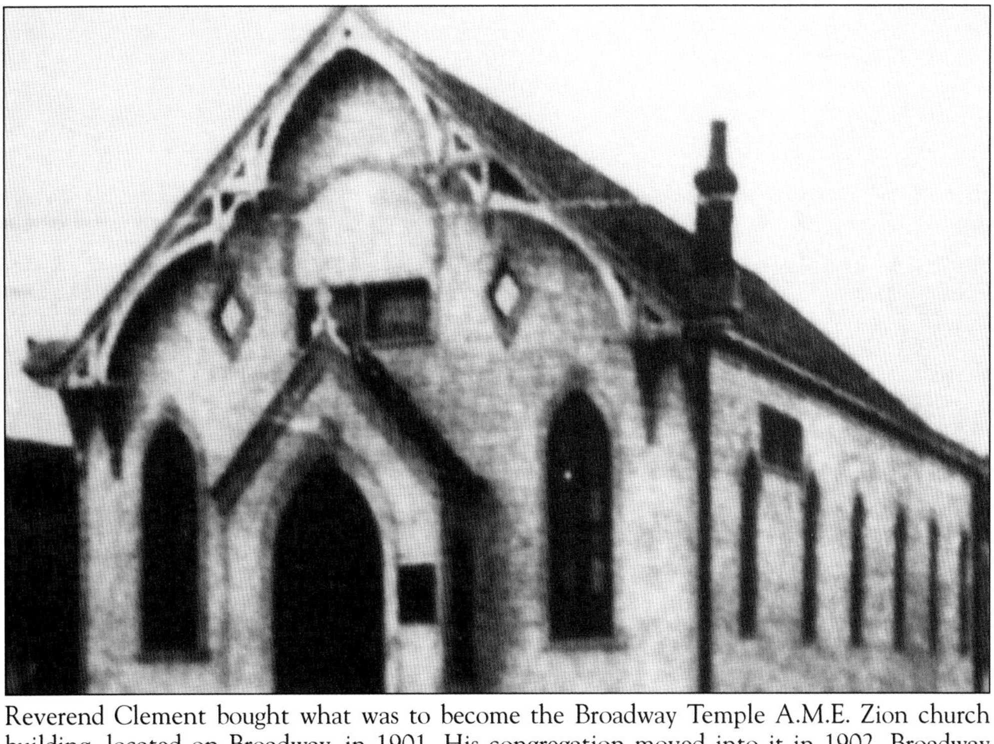

Reverend Clement bought what was to become the Broadway Temple A.M.E. Zion church building, located on Broadway, in 1901. His congregation moved into it in 1902. Broadway Temple was organized in 1867.

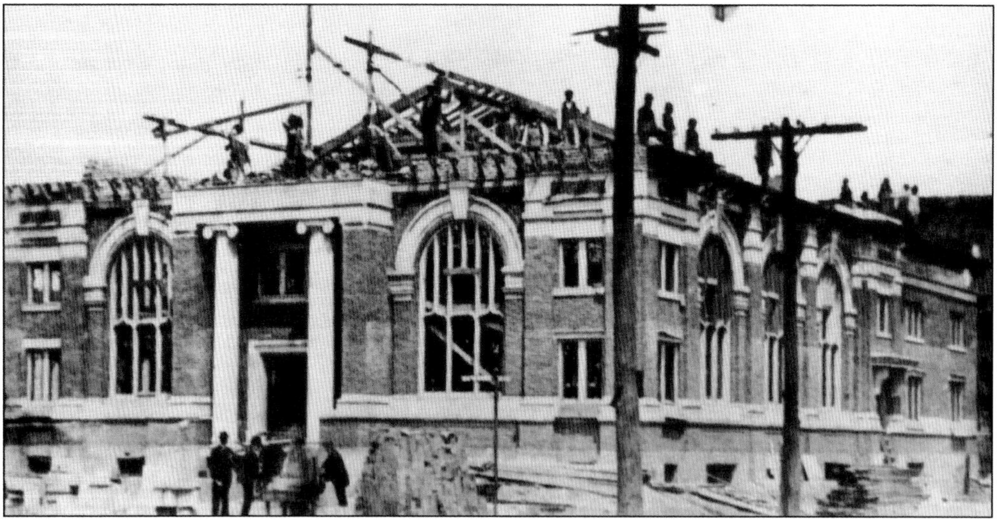

Seen in this 1915 view is the construction of the new Broadway Temple A.M.E. Zion Church, located at 662 South Thirteenth Street. The church was built by Samuel Plato, an African-American contractor.

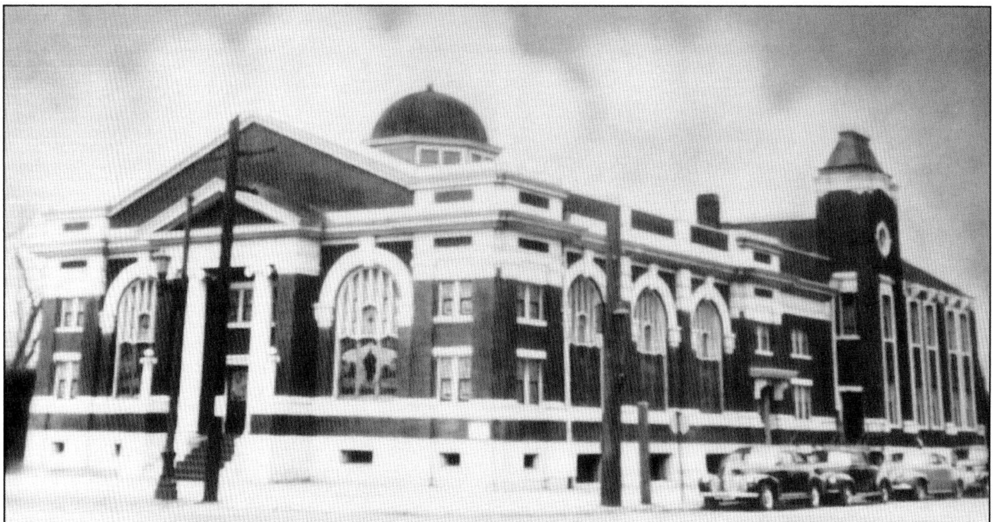

The Broadway Temple, as pictured in this c. 1930s photograph, has stained-glass windows that also list church members as benefactors per window.

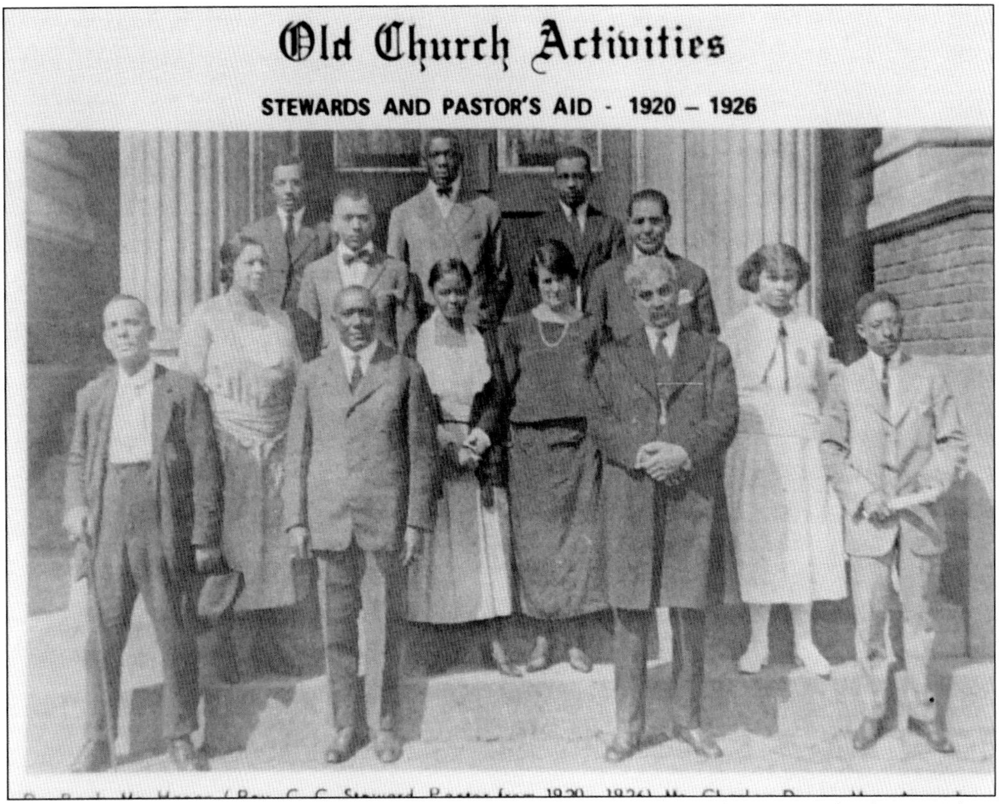

Pictured is C.C. Steward (pastor) and his Pastor's Aid group at Broadway Temple. (c. 1923.)

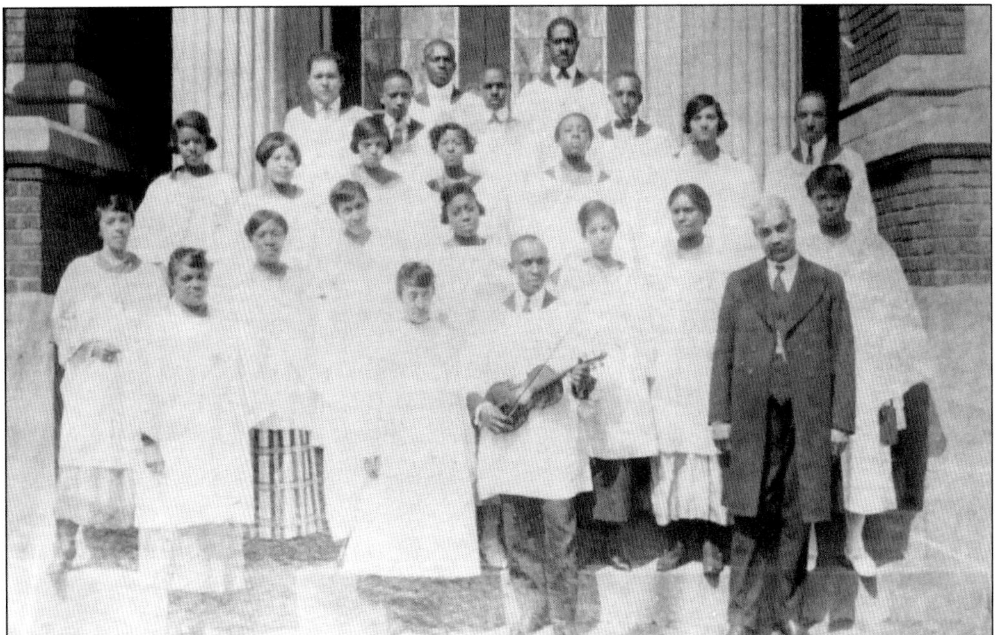
Pastor C.C. Steward, along with the church choir and violinist, poses for this photograph at Broadway Temple. (c. 1923.)

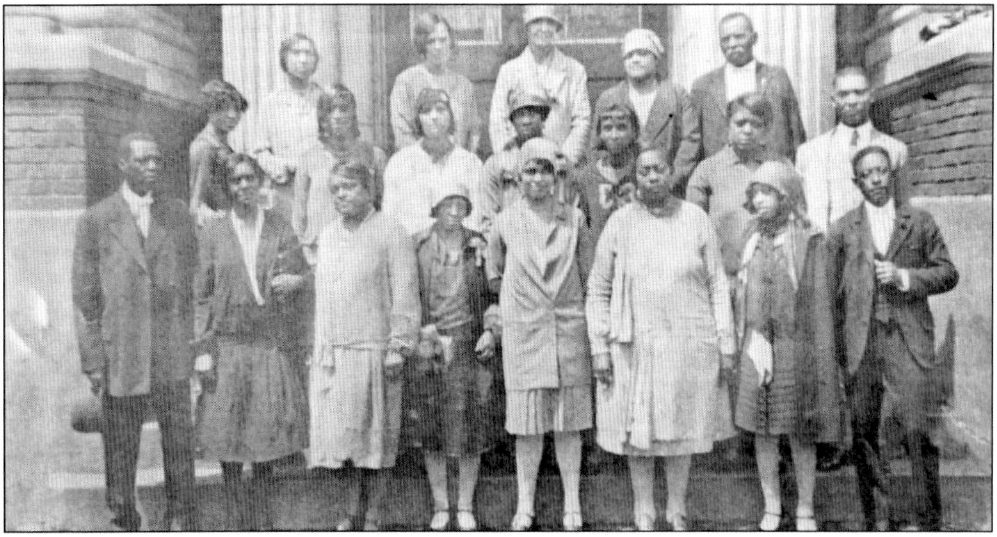

Pictured in this *c.* 1926 view are Sunday school officers at Broadway Temple.

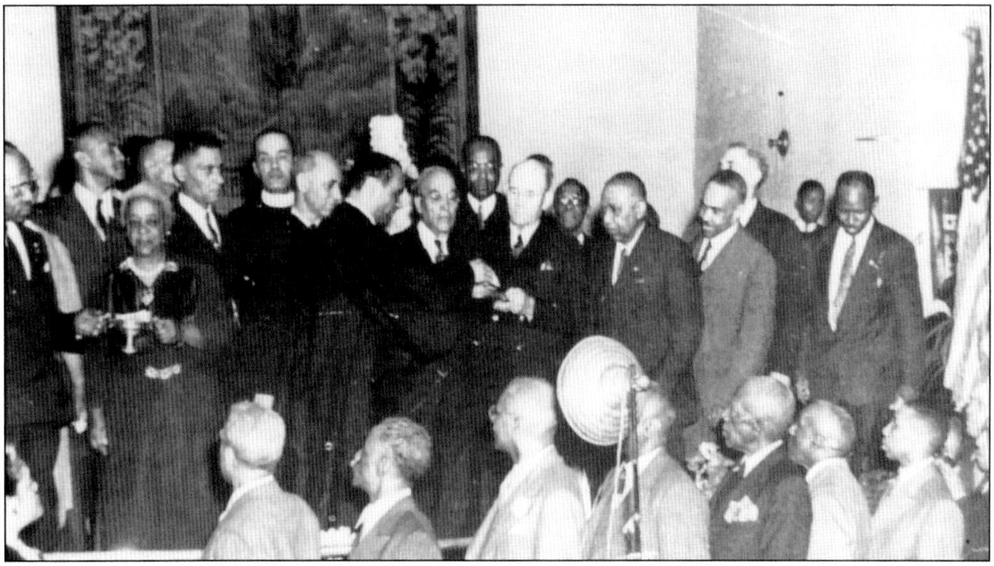

Pastor Raymond L. Jones is pictured in this photograph, which was made on Easter Sunday on April 9, 1944 at Broadway Temple. They also held a solemn and symbolic "Mortgage Burning" to celebrate having paid off the church mortgage.

This photograph was made at the African Methodist Episcopal Zion Church's 33rd Quadrennial General Conference in Louisville, held May 5–19, 1948.

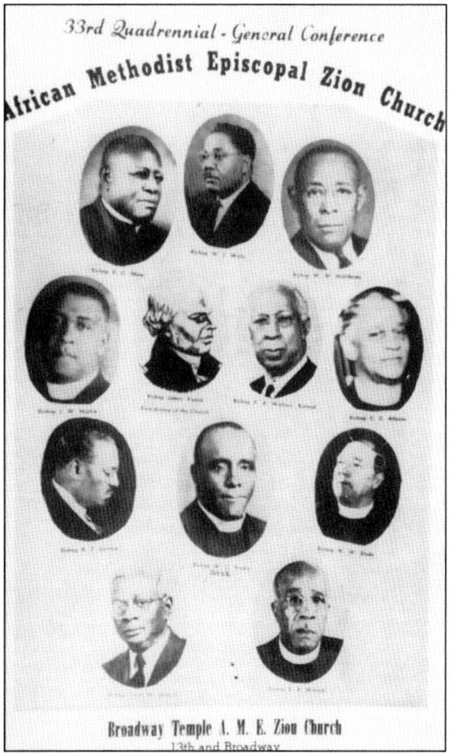

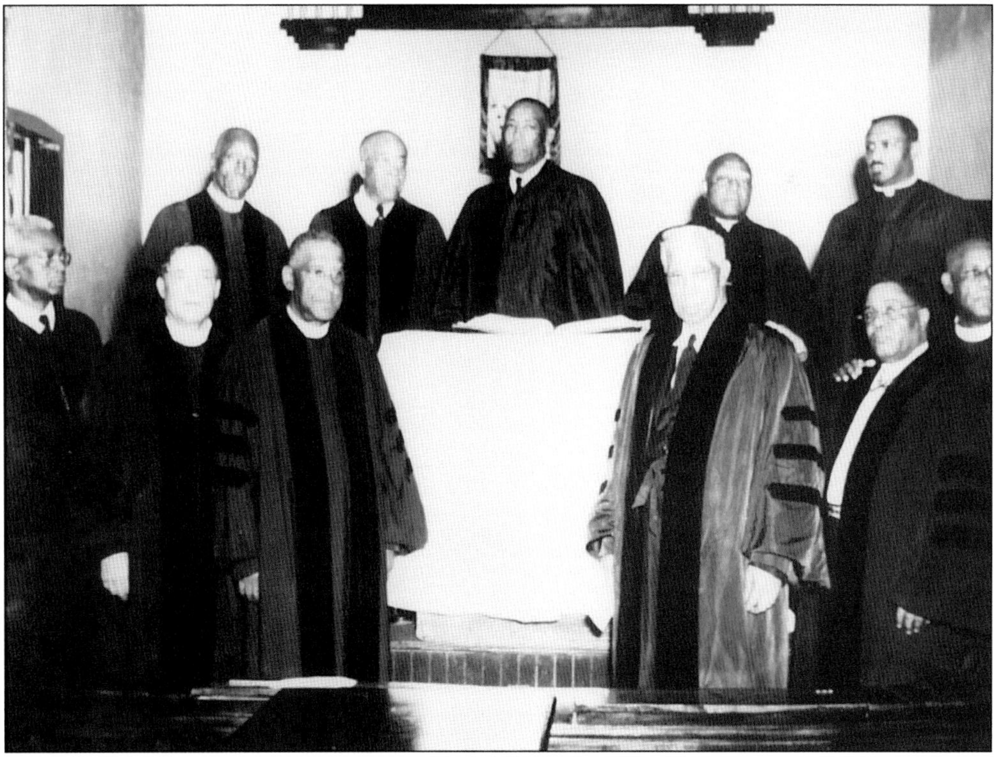

African Methodist Episcopal Bishops attended the General Conference.

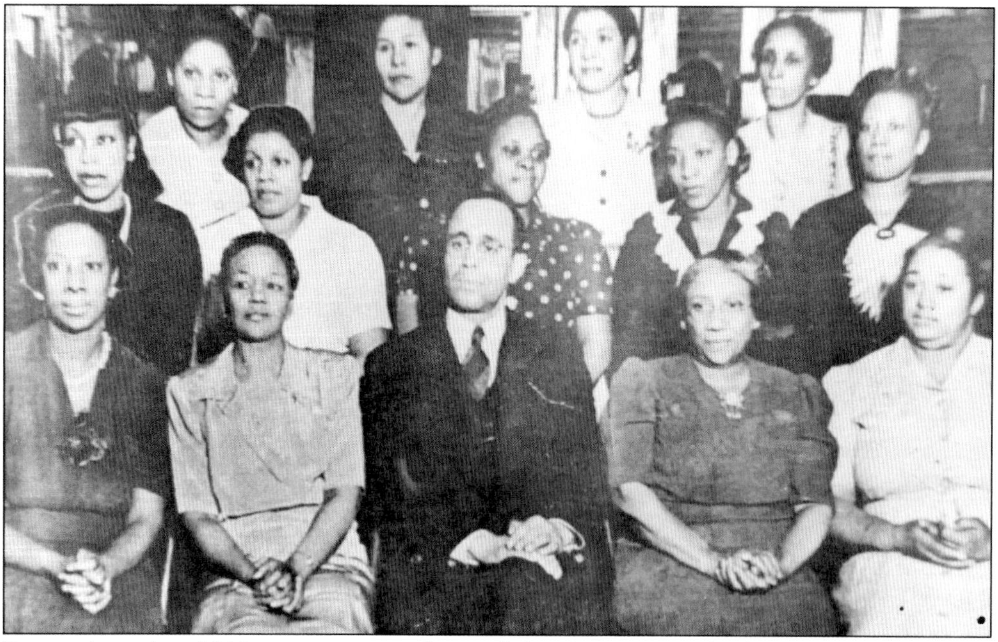

Pictured in this 1948 view are members of the Annie M. Blackwell Club with Rev. Raymond L. Jones.

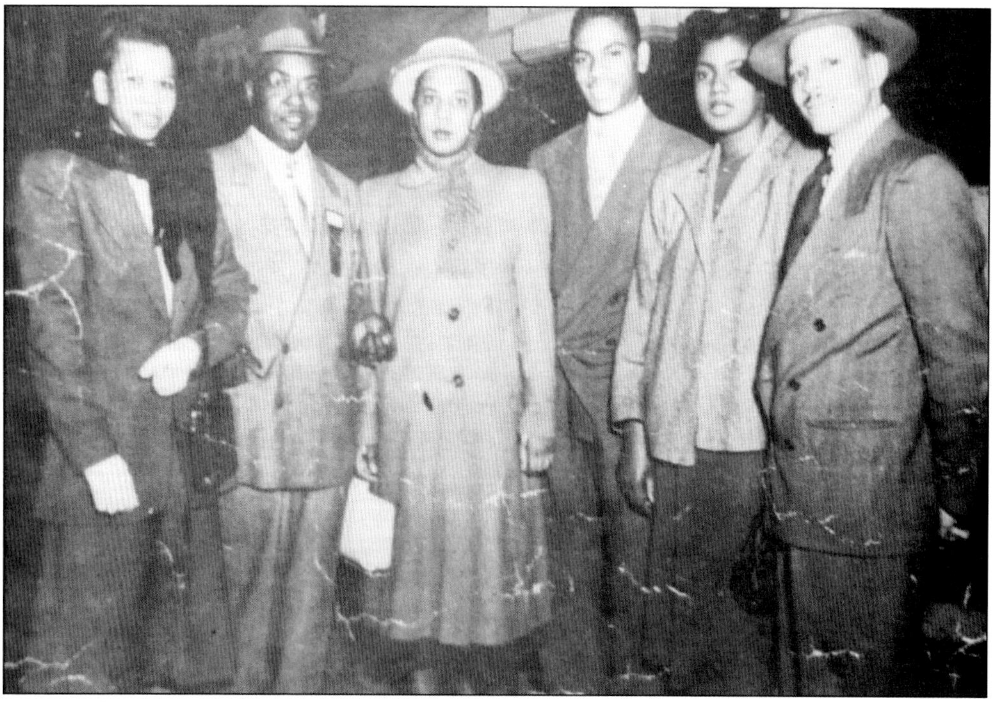

Some of the attendees at the 1948 General Conference of the A.M.E. Zion Church at Broadway Temple are, from left to right, as follows: Adele Sigar, Rev. John H. Miller, Mrs. Bernice Miller, Mr. Gordon, Phyllis Ellis, and Rev. William Carl Audrey.

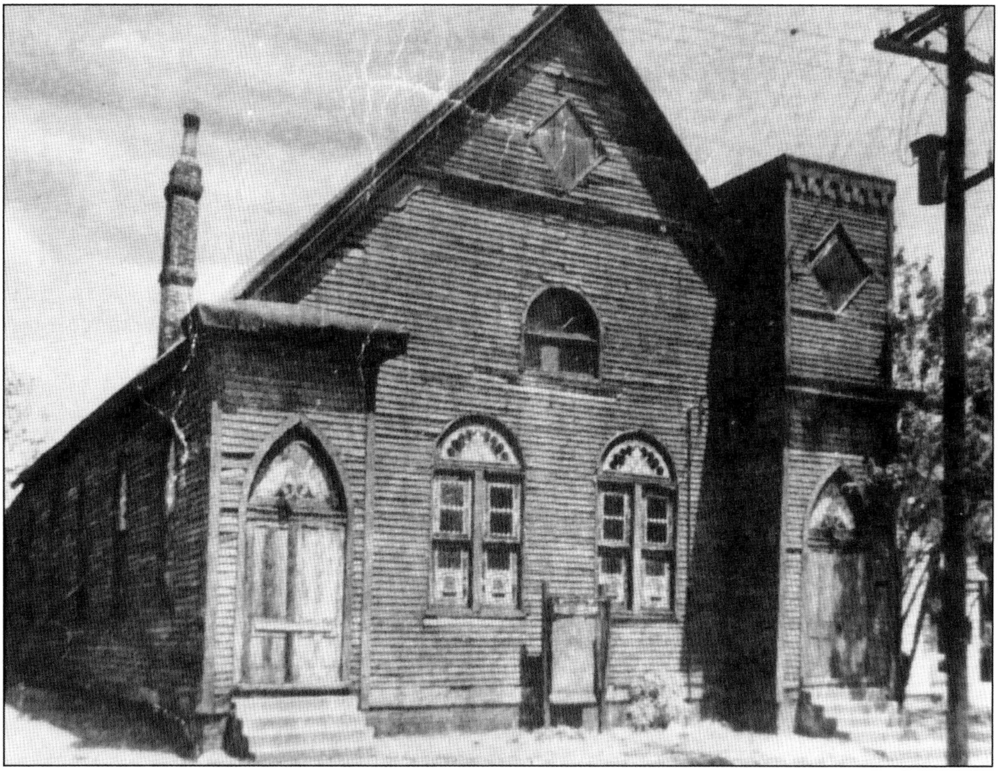

Centennial Olivet Baptist Church, located at 1519 West St. Catherine Street, was founded in 1870.

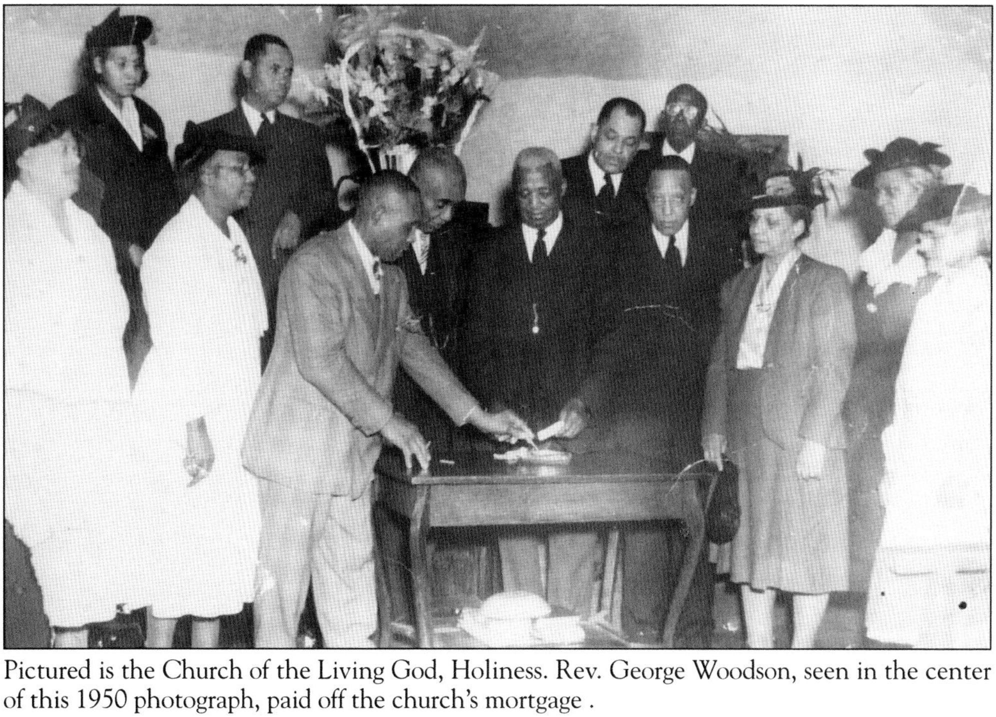

Pictured is the Church of the Living God, Holiness. Rev. George Woodson, seen in the center of this 1950 photograph, paid off the church's mortgage .

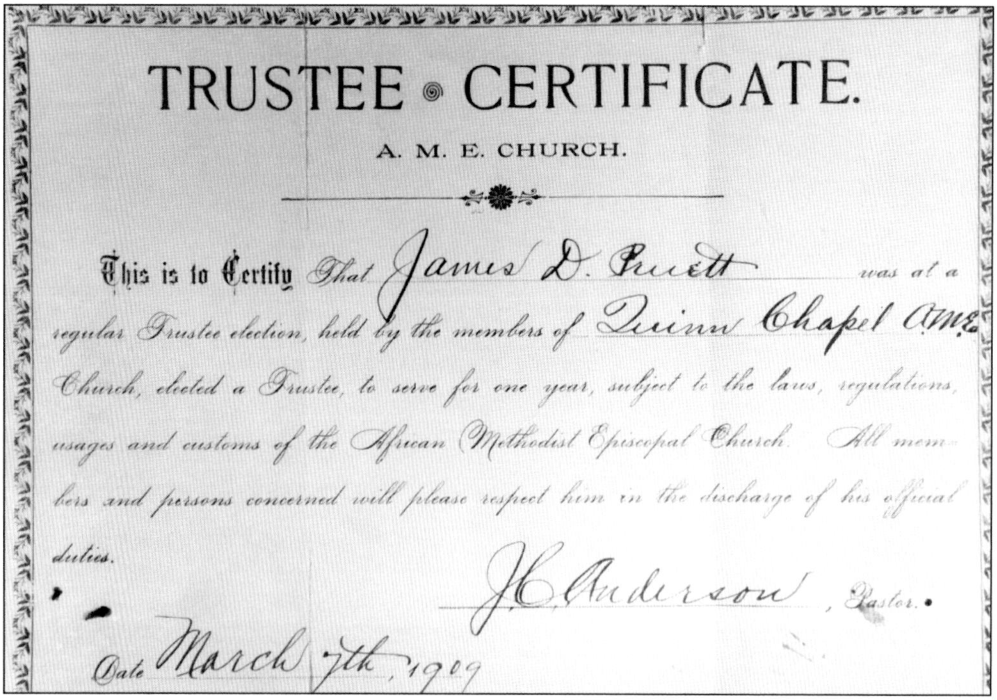

TRUSTEE CERTIFICATE.

A. M. E. CHURCH.

This is to Certify That James D. Pruett was at a regular Trustee election, held by the members of Quinn Chapel A.M.E. Church, elected a Trustee, to serve for one year, subject to the laws, regulations, usages and customs of the African Methodist Episcopal Church. All members and persons concerned will please respect him in the discharge of his official duties.

J.H. Anderson, Pastor.

Date March 7th, 1909

This trustee certificate, dated March 7, 1909, was awarded to James D. Pruitt, a member of Quinn Chapel A.M.E. Church.

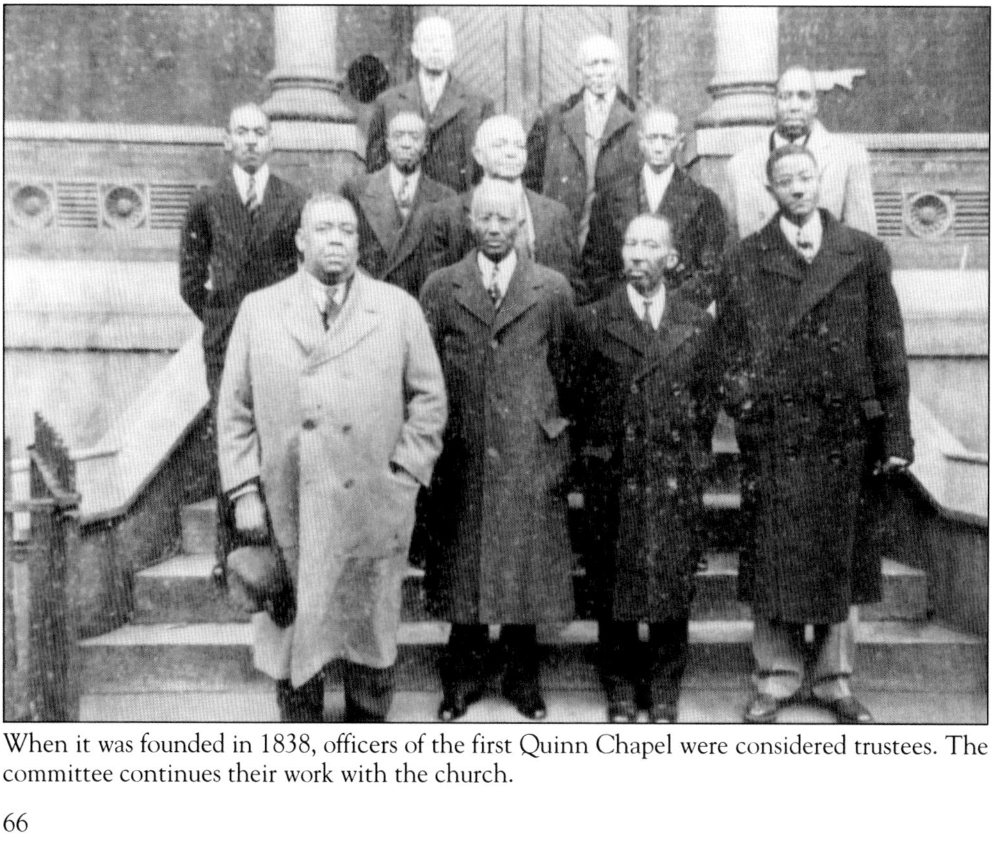

When it was founded in 1838, officers of the first Quinn Chapel were considered trustees. The committee continues their work with the church.

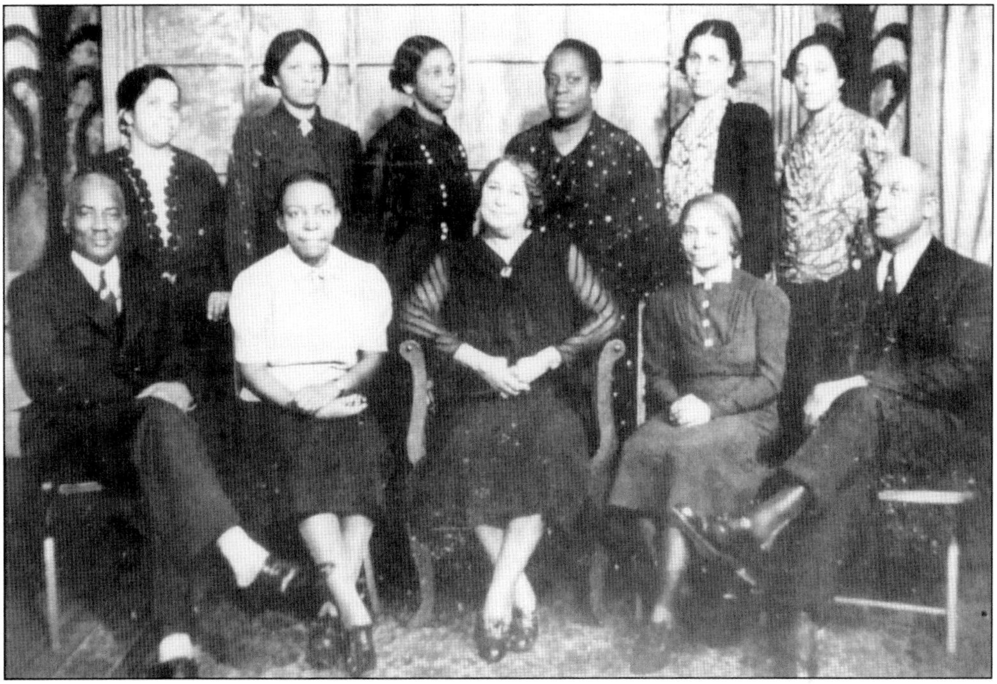

The Sunday School Guild was organized under the pastorate of Rev. J.T. Morrow. It secured chairs for the children's Sunday School.

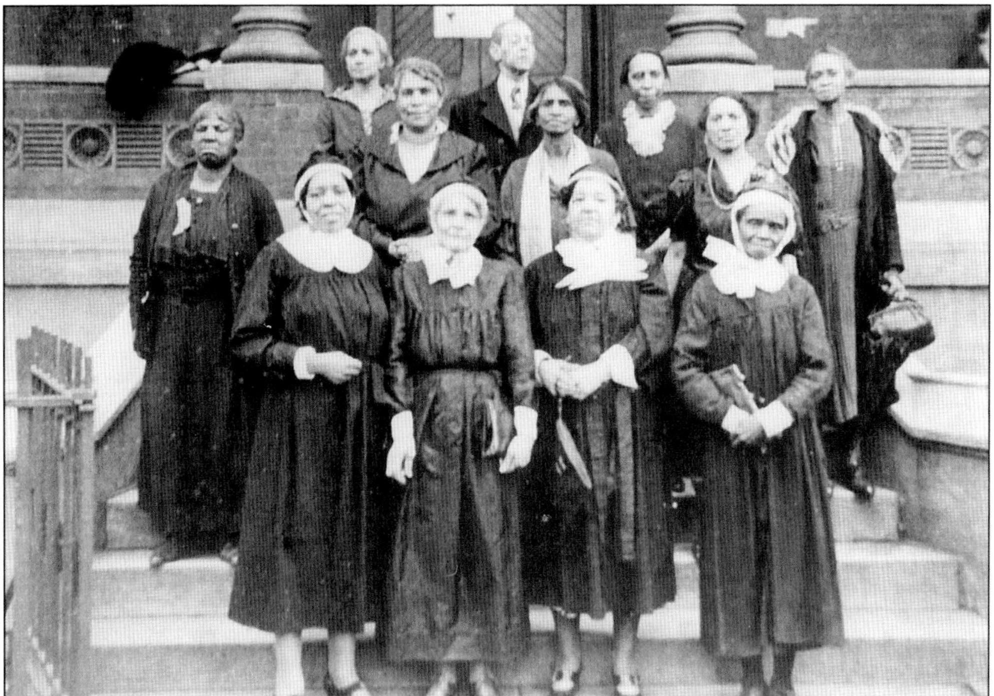

The Presiding Elders Cabinet was organized in 1925 by Pastor R.C. Henderson, who appointed Mrs. Bessie Pennick to be president.

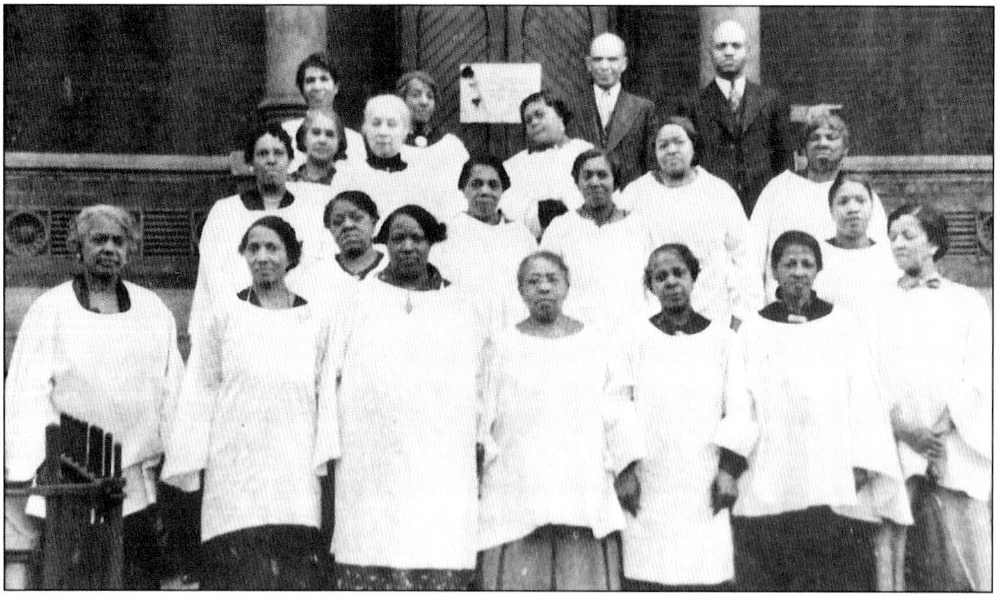

The Gospel Chorus was founded by Rev. R.C. Ransom Jr. on November 26, 1937 in the dining room of Quinn Chapel. The chorus performed in the church, the community, and in suburban towns.

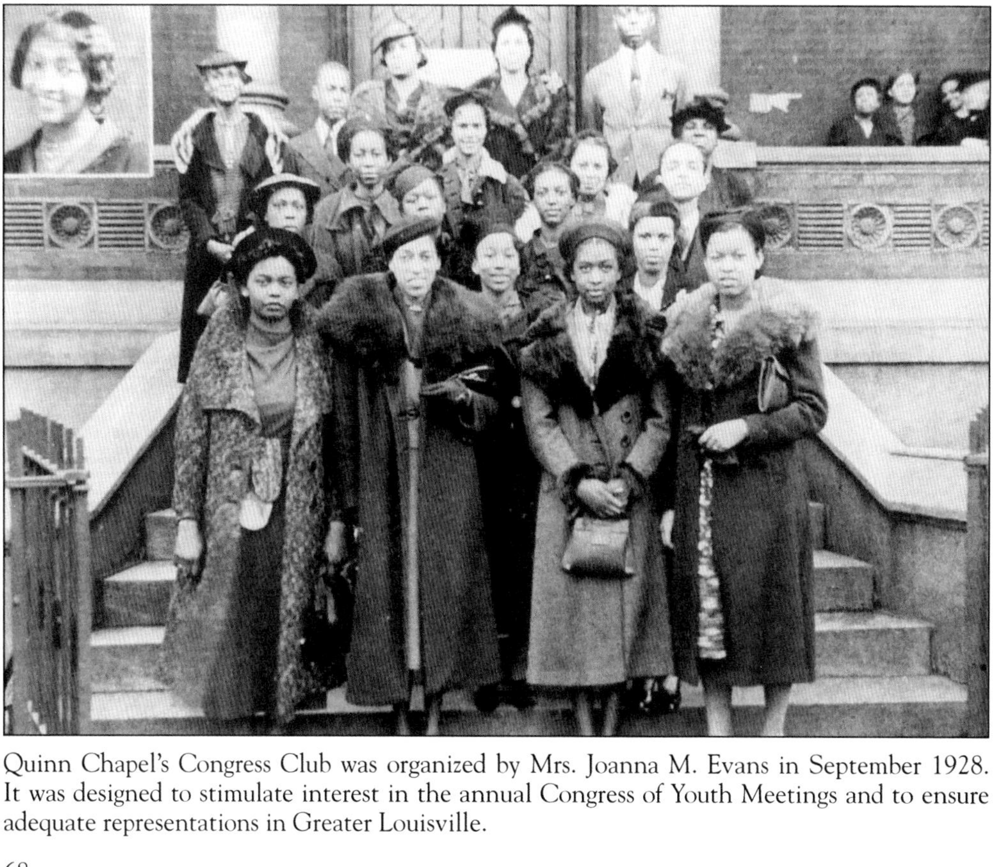

Quinn Chapel's Congress Club was organized by Mrs. Joanna M. Evans in September 1928. It was designed to stimulate interest in the annual Congress of Youth Meetings and to ensure adequate representations in Greater Louisville.

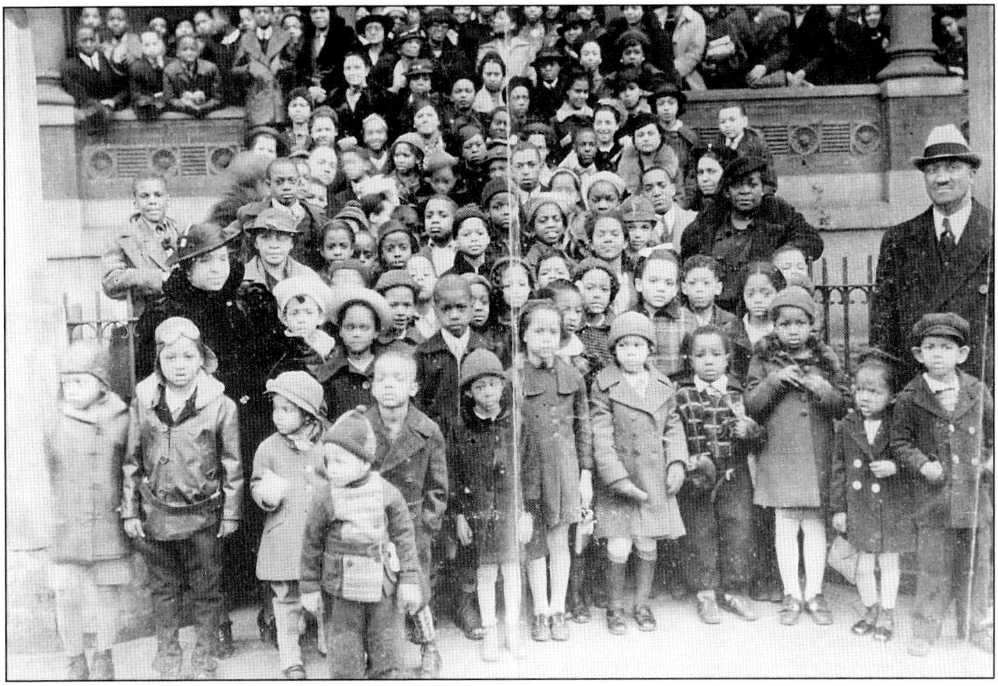

The Quinn Chapel A.M.E. Sunday school poses in front of the church in this 1938 photograph.

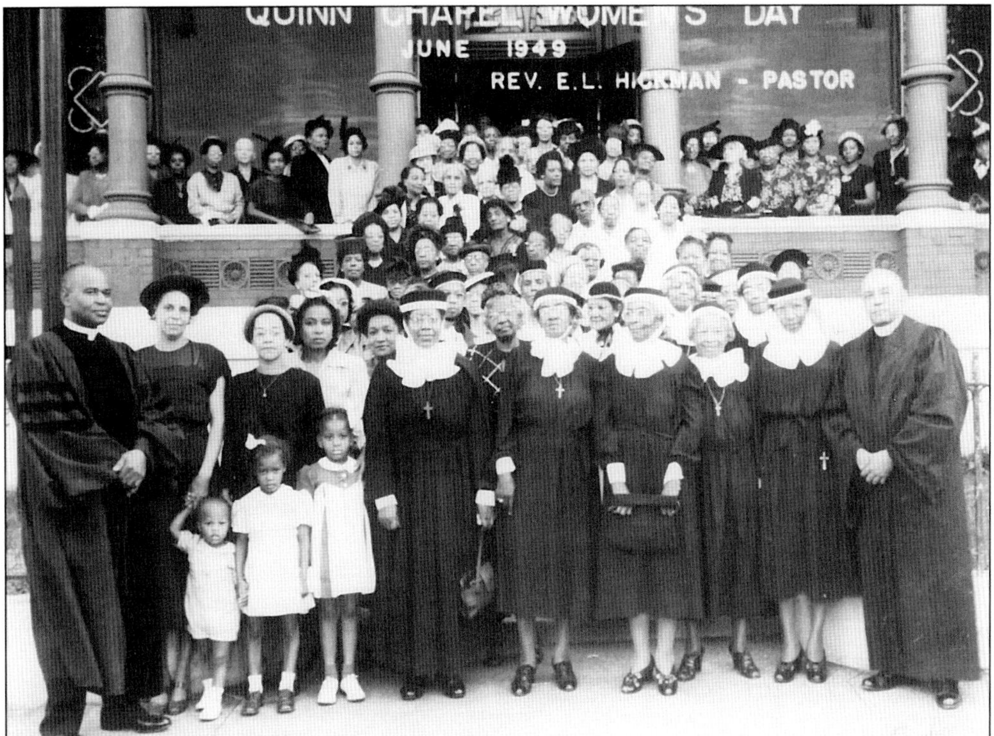

In this photograph of Quinn Chapel A.M.E., the caption reads as follows: "Quinn Chapel Women's Day, June 1949, Rev. E.L. Hickman—Pastor."

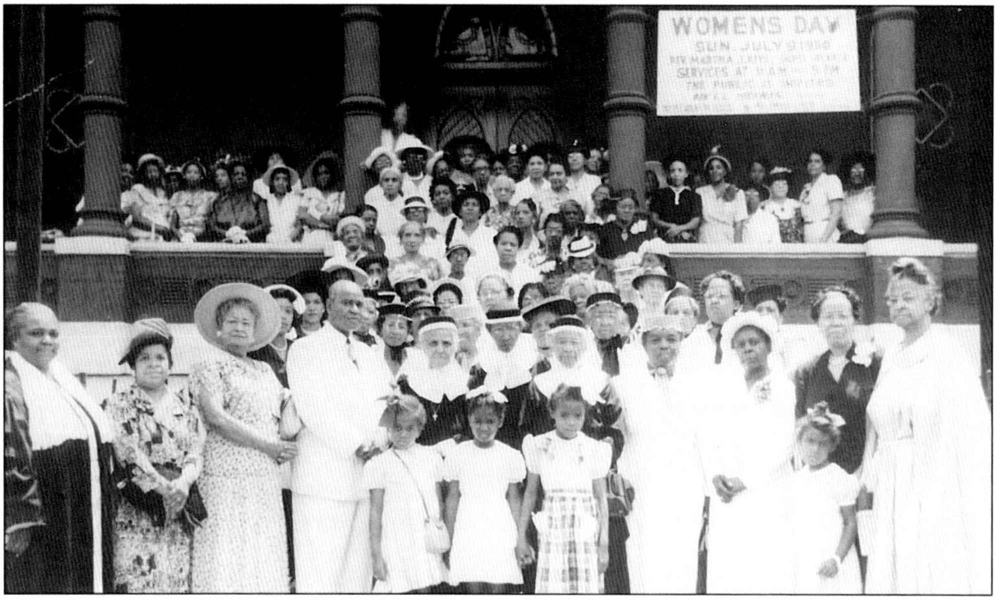

Church members are gathered in front of a Quinn Chapel A.M.E. banner, which reads as follows: "Women's Day Sun. July 9, 1950. Rev. Martha J. Keys, Guest Speaker. Services at 11a.m. and 5p.m. The public is invited. Rev. Ernest Lawrence Hickman, Pastor. Mrs. M.B. Robinson, General Chairman. Mrs. Emma L. Reid, Co-chairman."

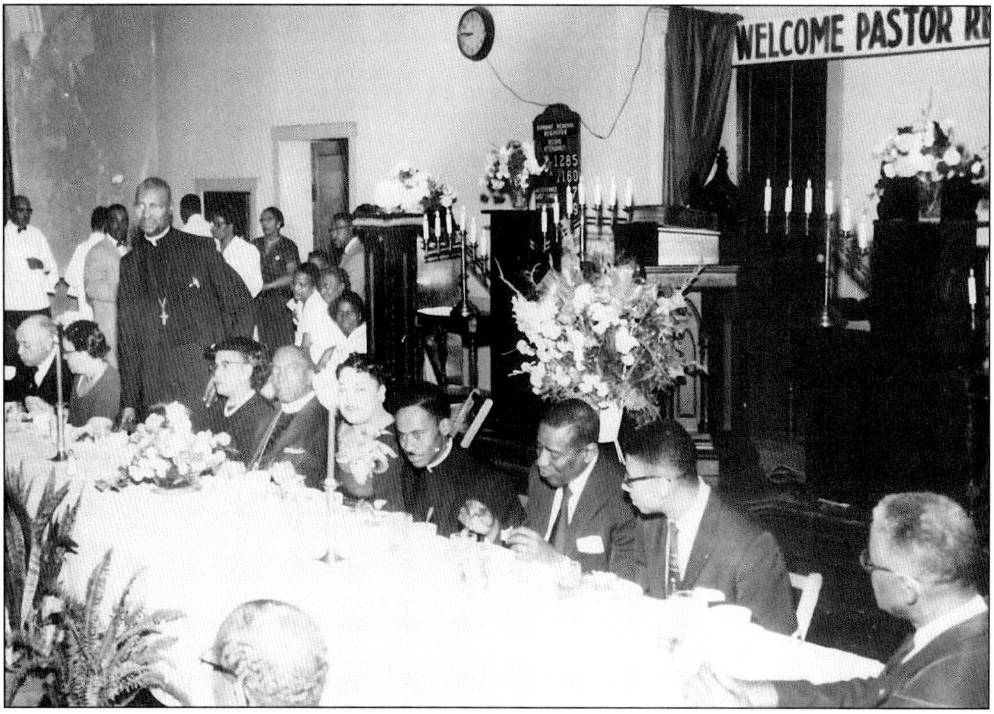

In this view of the Quinn Chapel A.M.E. banquet room, the sign on the wall reads "Welcome Pastor Reid." Men and women of the church are seen eating while the minister and a waiter stand on the far right. Many members of the wait staff were members of the chapel's congregation.

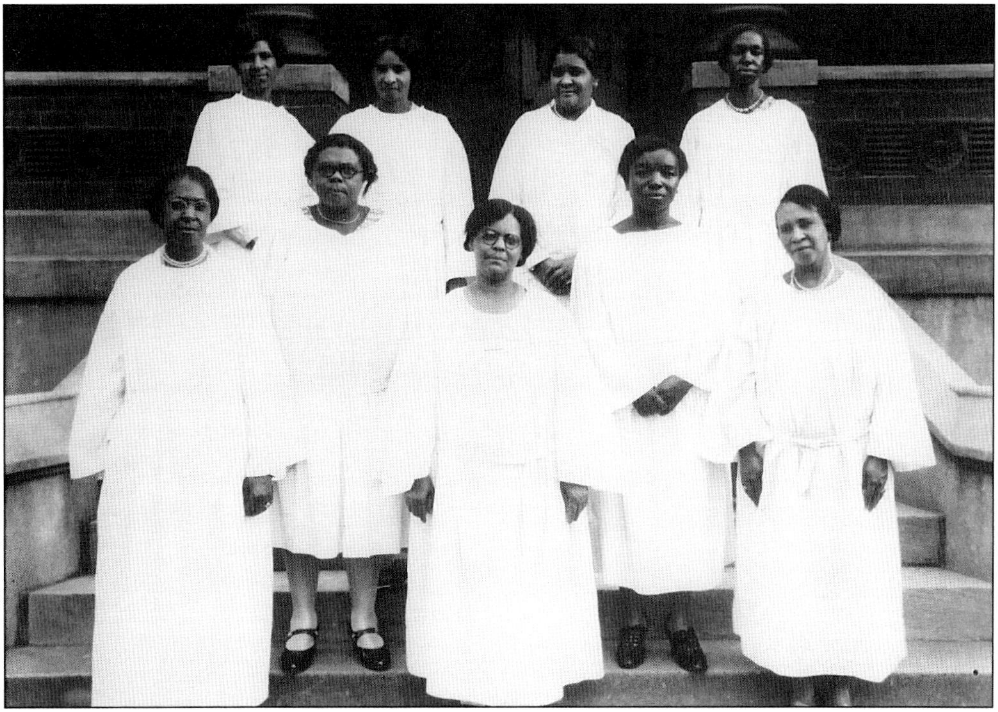

The members of the Quinn Chapel A.M.E. Gospel Choir are pictured from left to right as follows: (front row) Carrie Brown, Emma Manning, unidentified, Anna Lyons, and Flora Gaiter; (back row) Emily Ward, Katie Franklin, Laura Hines, and Mary Parker. (*c.* 1925.)

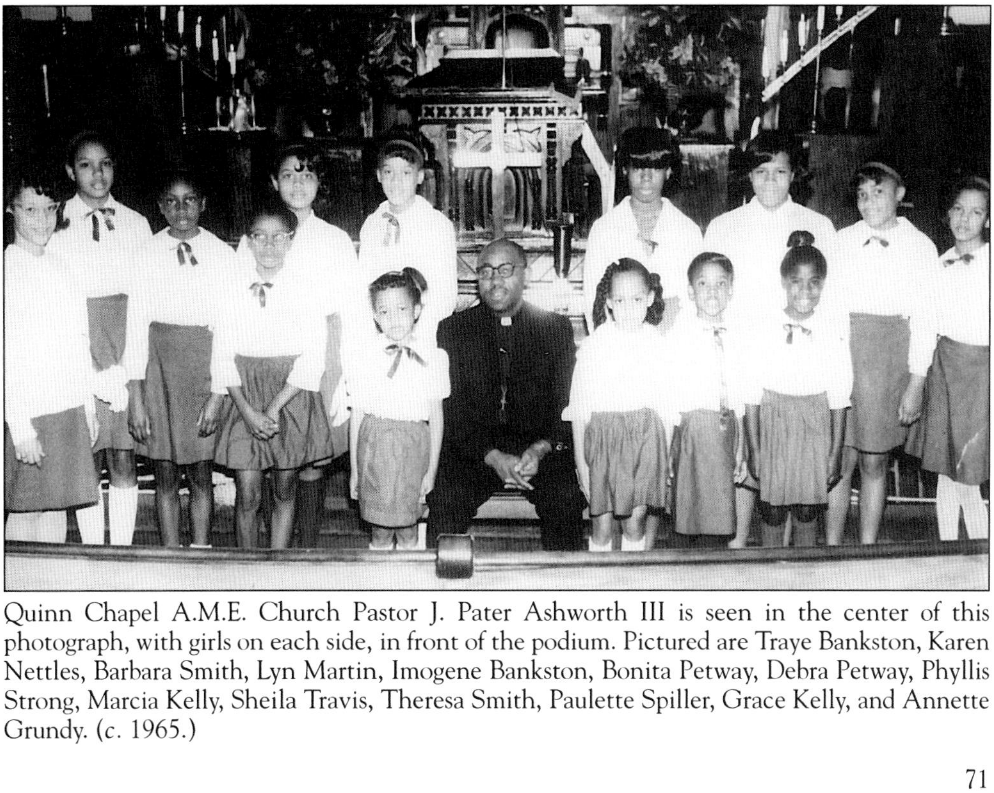

Quinn Chapel A.M.E. Church Pastor J. Pater Ashworth III is seen in the center of this photograph, with girls on each side, in front of the podium. Pictured are Traye Bankston, Karen Nettles, Barbara Smith, Lyn Martin, Imogene Bankston, Bonita Petway, Debra Petway, Phyllis Strong, Marcia Kelly, Sheila Travis, Theresa Smith, Paulette Spiller, Grace Kelly, and Annette Grundy. (*c.* 1965.)

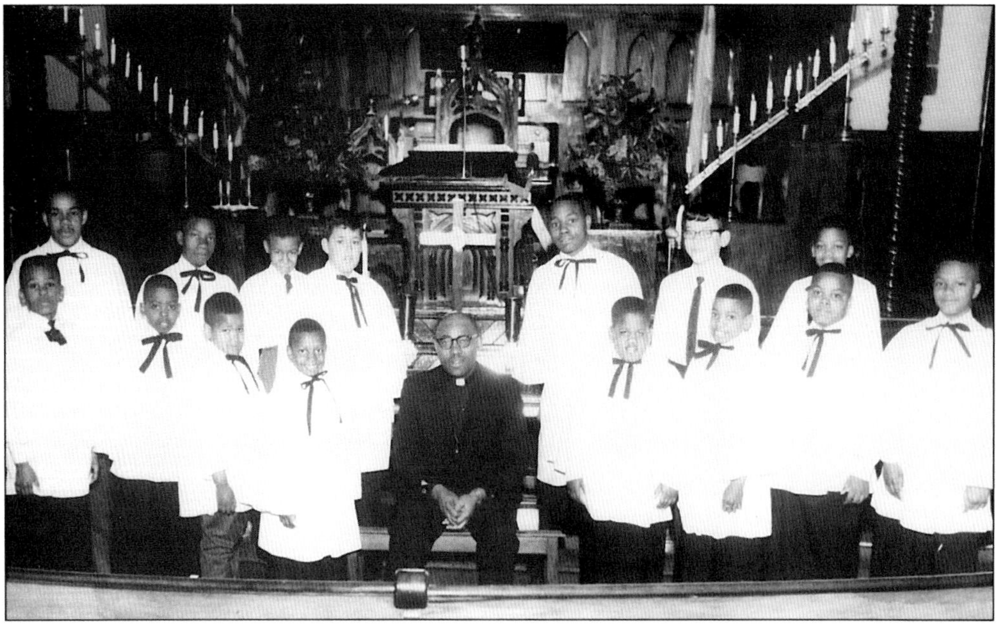

In this photograph, the Quinn Chapel A.M.E. Pastor is seen in the center with altar boys on each side, in front of the podium. Pictured from left to right in this view are as follows: (first row) unidentified, Michael Smith, Billy Davis, Dwayne Petway, Reverend Ashworth, Stewart Wilson, David Smith, Kent Coleman, and George Demeree Jr.; (second row) Percy Bankston, Ralph Petway, Ernest Kelly III, Peter Ebbs, unidentified, Jerry Brown, and Terence Gank. (*c.* 1965.)

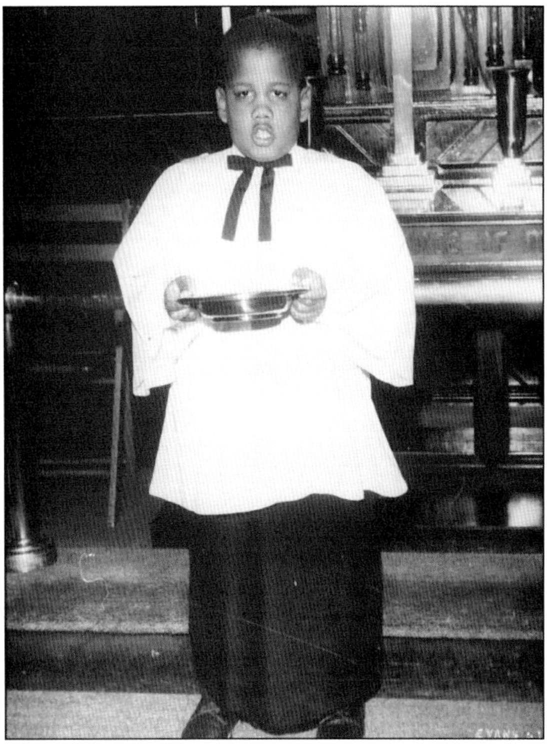

In this photograph, Stewart Wilson is one of the altar boys.

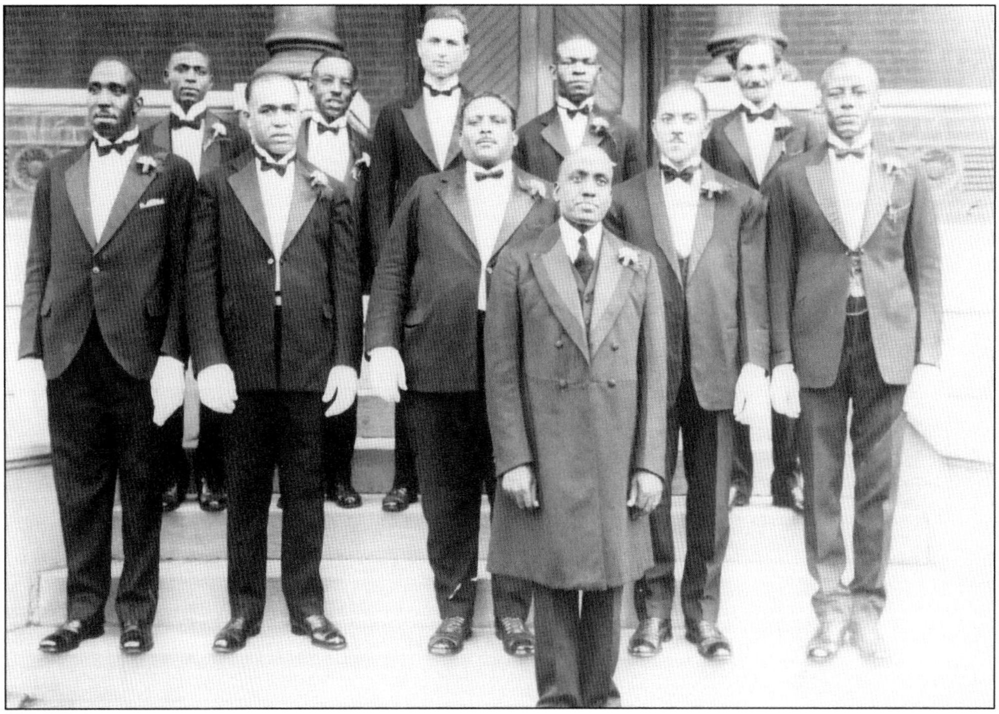

Many of the men at this 1955 Quinn Chapel A.M.E. Church function served as waiters for the event.

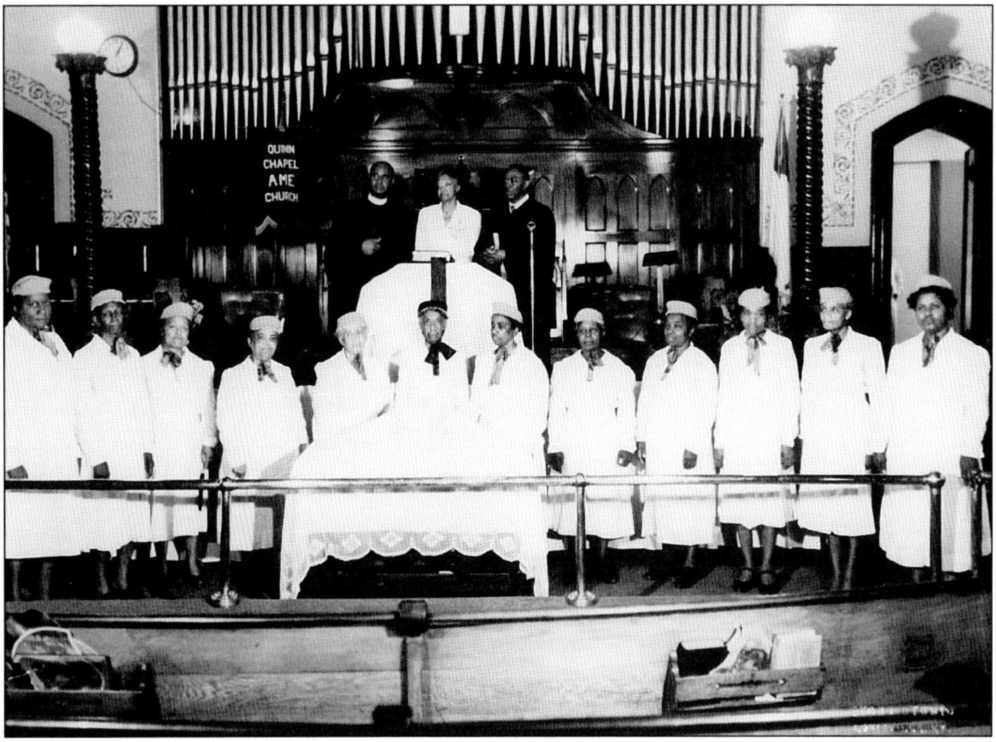

Pictured is a view of Quinn Chapel A.M.E. during a Holy Communion.

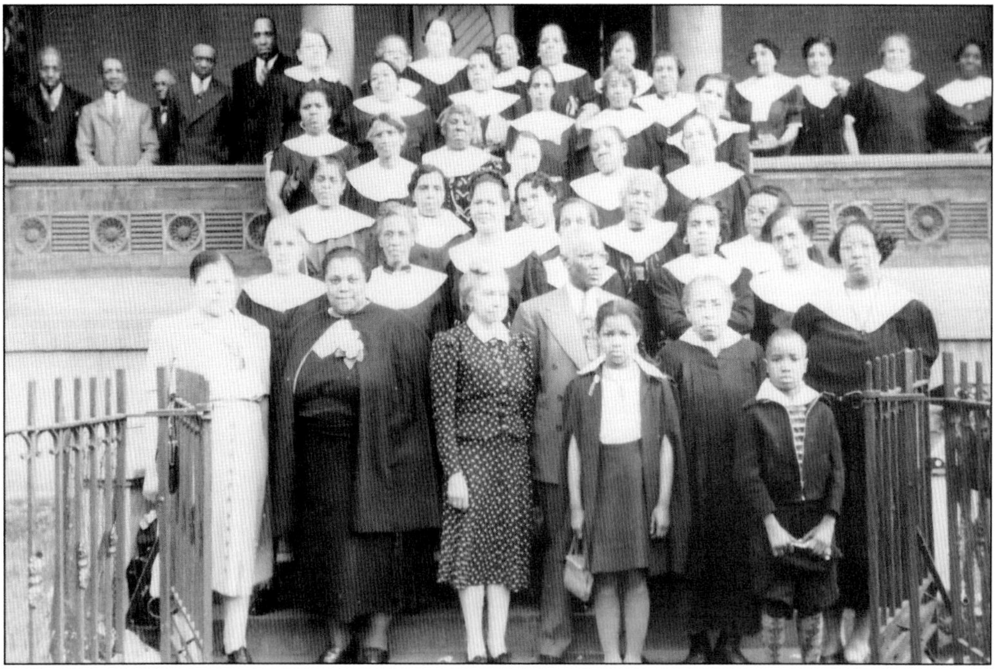

In this photograph, made April 15, 1941, the Quinn Chapel A.M.E. women's choir is seen in front of the church, and the members of the men's choir stand on the left. Pastor Green H. Jenkins and his wife are in front, with a girl and a boy.

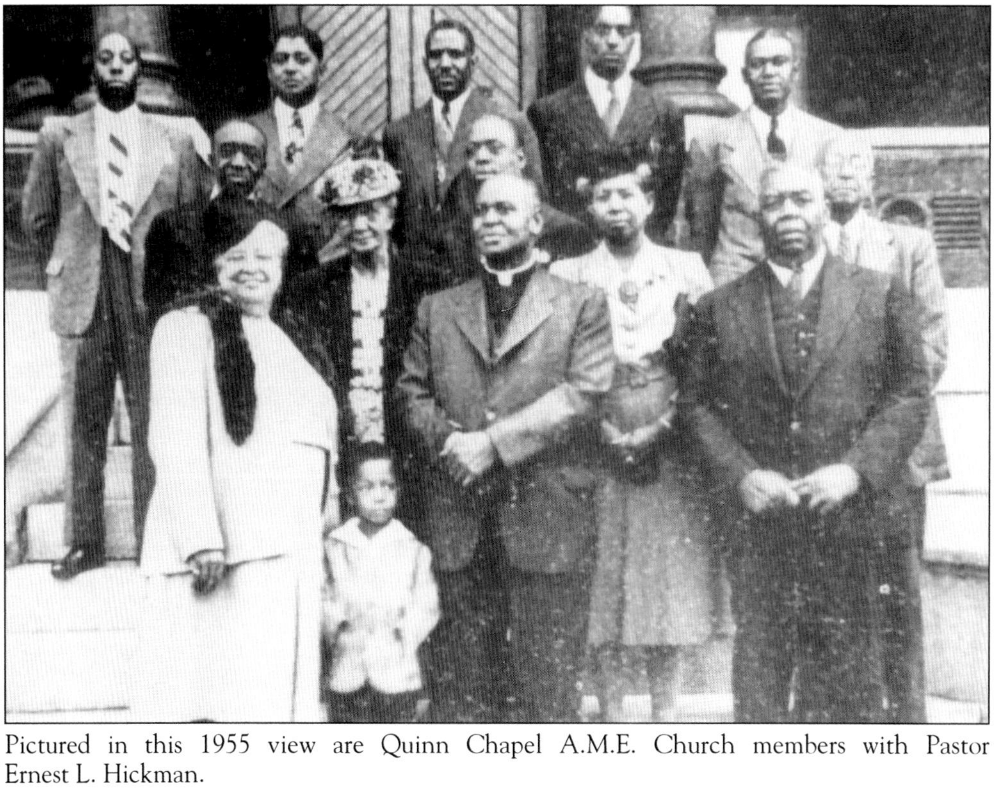

Pictured in this 1955 view are Quinn Chapel A.M.E. Church members with Pastor Ernest L. Hickman.

Seven

Lodges and People of Pride

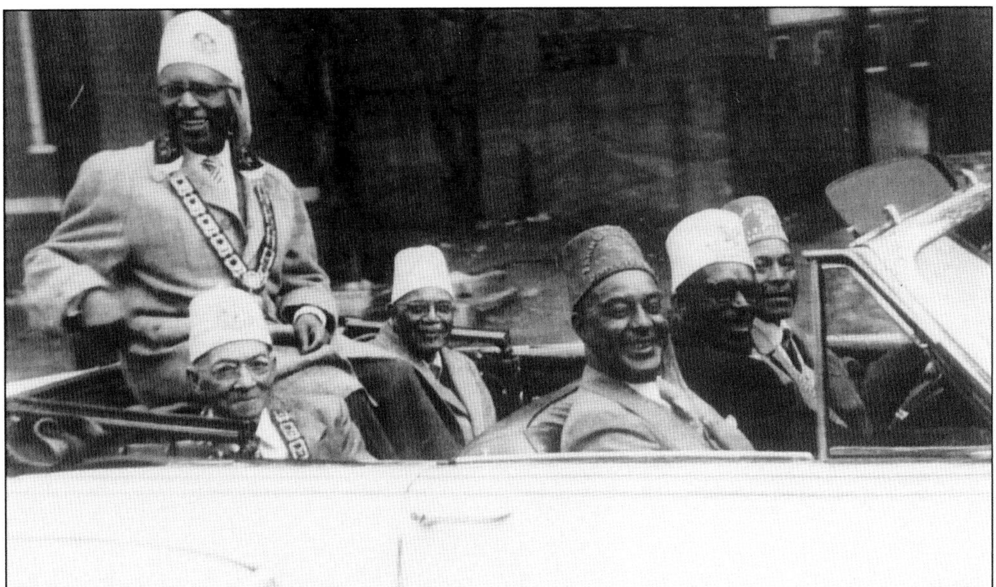

Louisville once had three to five African-American parades every Sunday during the summer because there were so many lodges. Lodge members marched in a variety of locations. The Improved Benevolent and Protective Order of Elks of the World (I.B.P.E.L.W.) was particularly active. Pictured is the Blue Grass Lodge of the Elks, I.B.P.E.L.W. Robert "Rivers" Williams is seen in this 1948 photograph driving his Cadillac down Chestnut Street. Fred L. Stith, grand exalted ruler in the lodge, is seated in the back seat. Clifford Wilcox is seated in the front seat (middle) and to his right is Ben P. Wells, a tailor.

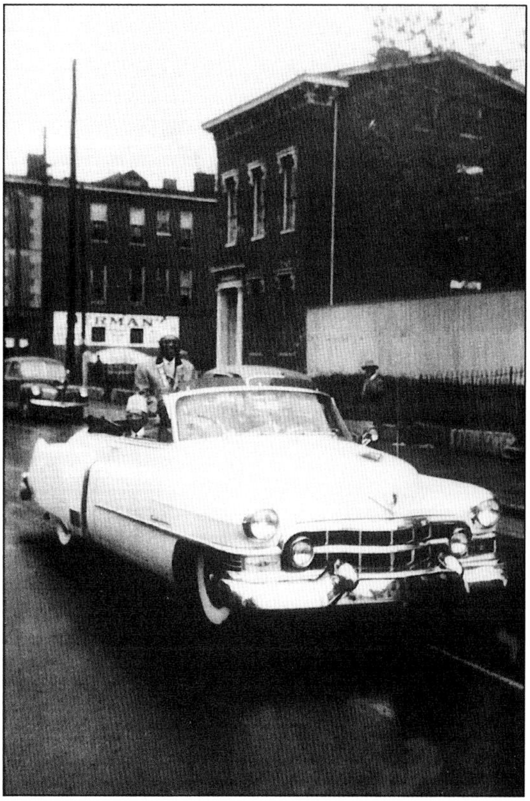

Robert Williams is pictured driving his Cadillac with Blue Grass Elks officers as passengers. Williams owned and operated the Top Hat nightclub, which was a very popular night spot.

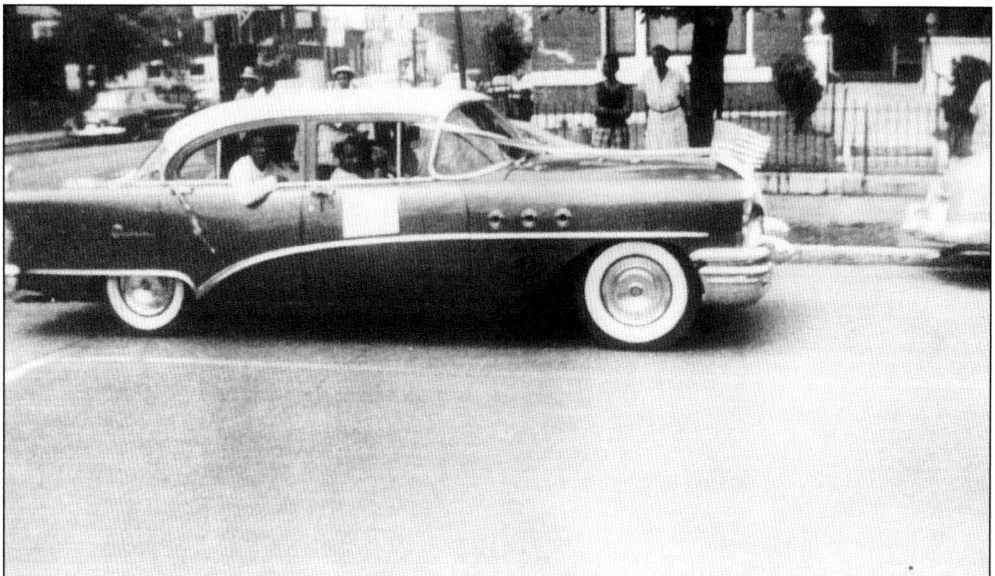

In this photograph taken during a parade, lodge members ride by in a Buick, proudly displaying the United States flag on the hood of the car.

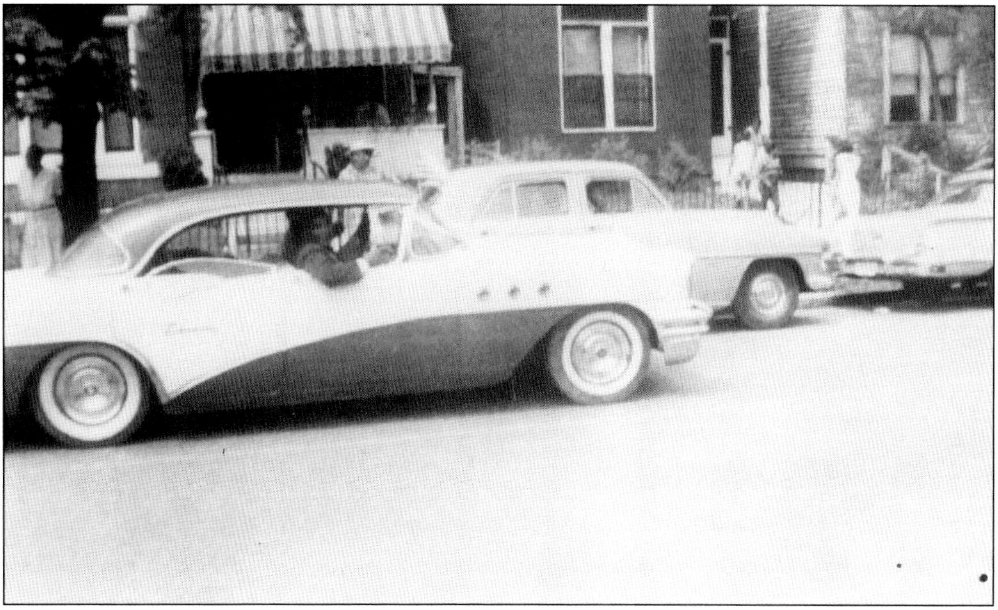

Another group of lodge members rides by in a Buick as onlookers watch the parade.

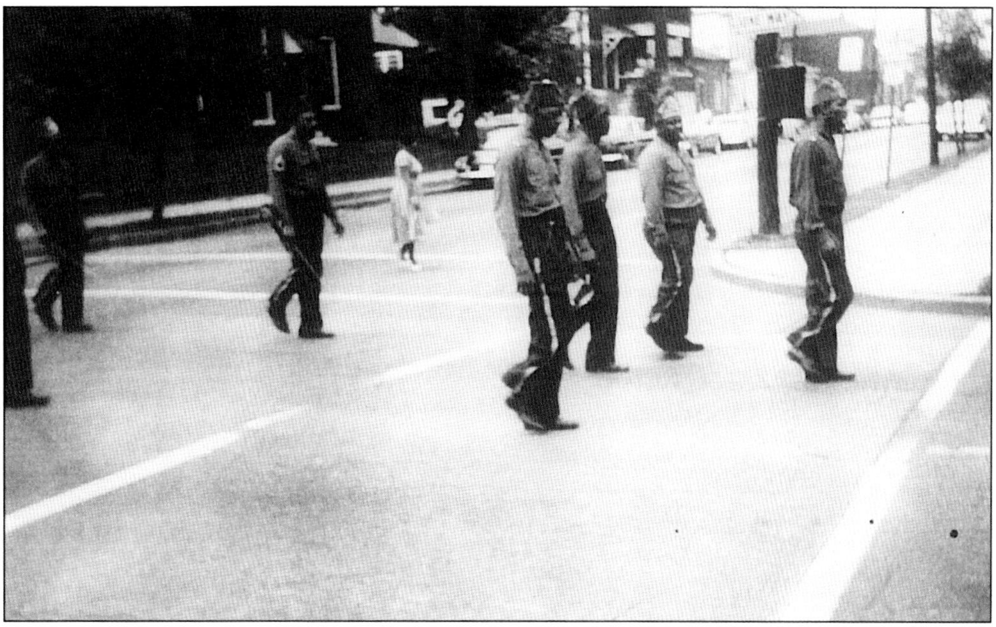

In this view, lodge members march in formation along Chestnut Street.

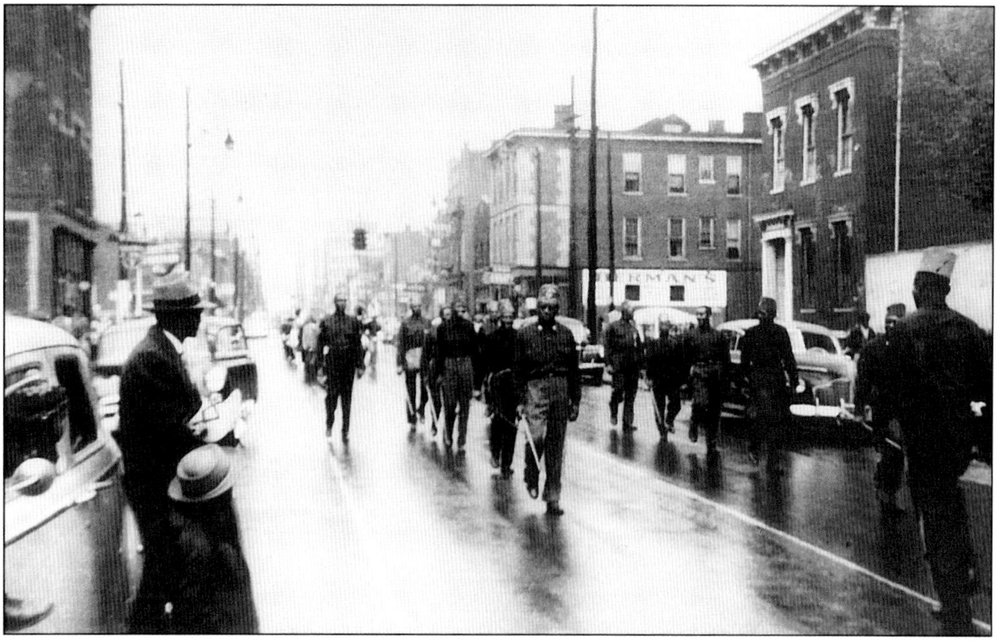

These lodge members, clad in their uniform of striped pants, and shirts and lodge hats, march by proudly, carrying walking canes.

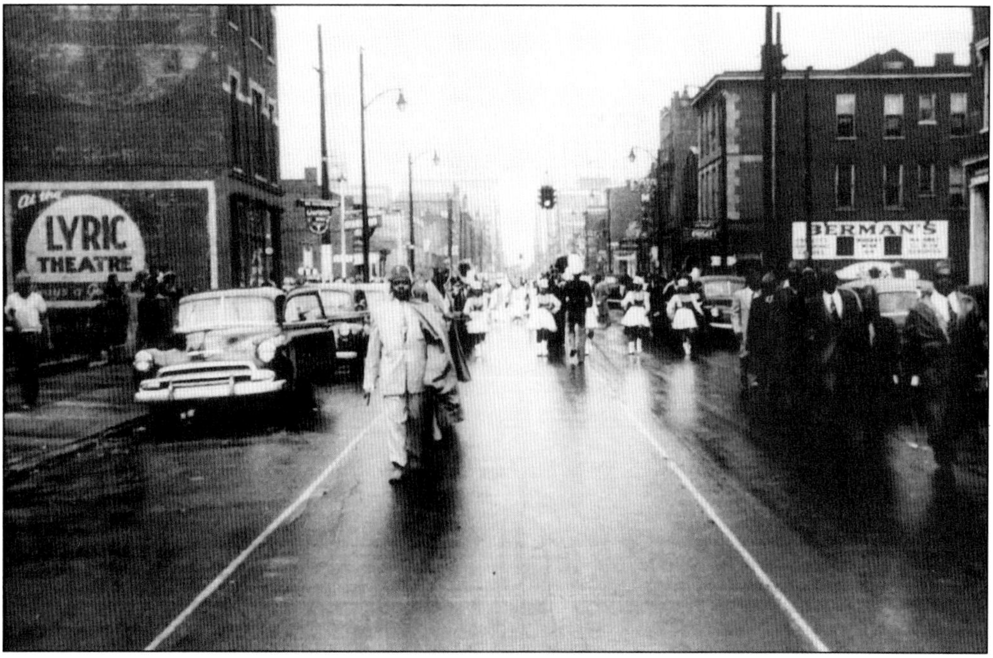

Pictured is a group of well-dressed lodge members wearing their traditional hats and capes.

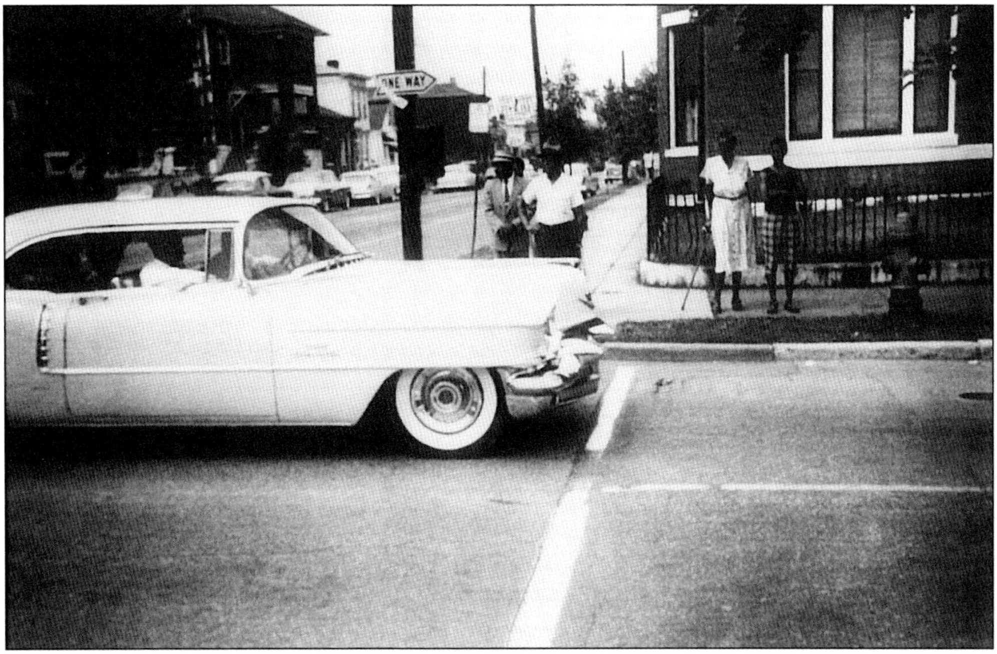

These lodge members are riding in a Cadillac, which is probably one of Rivers's cars.

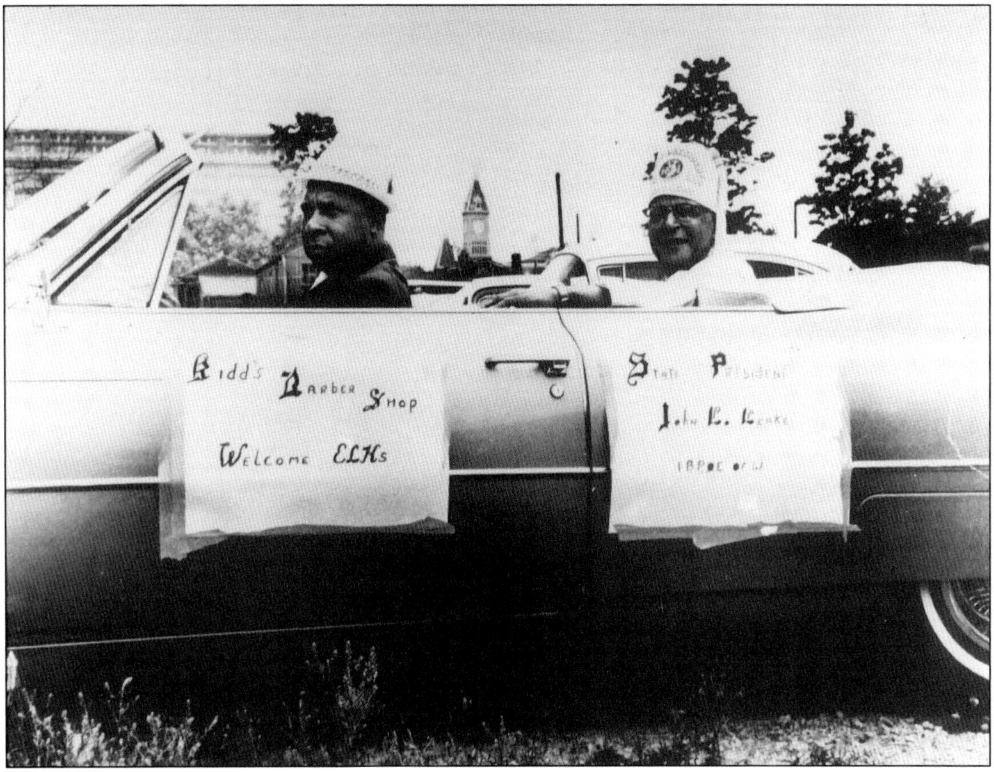

In this parade view, photographed years later, John L. Leake, Kentucky president of the I.B.P.E.L.W., is seated in the back seat of the car. He is wearing his Elks cap and uniform. Bidd's Barber Shop welcomed the Elks.

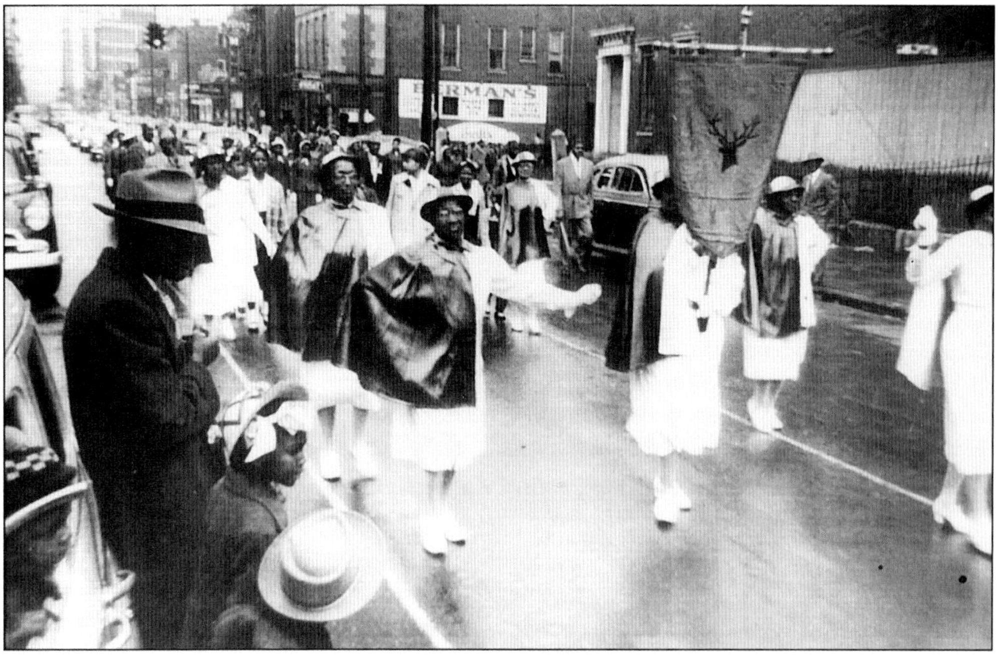

The female auxiliary of the Elks, known as the "Daughter Elks," march with the Elks banner. In this 1948 view, Everett Martin (left) watches the parade with two children, one of whom is his son.

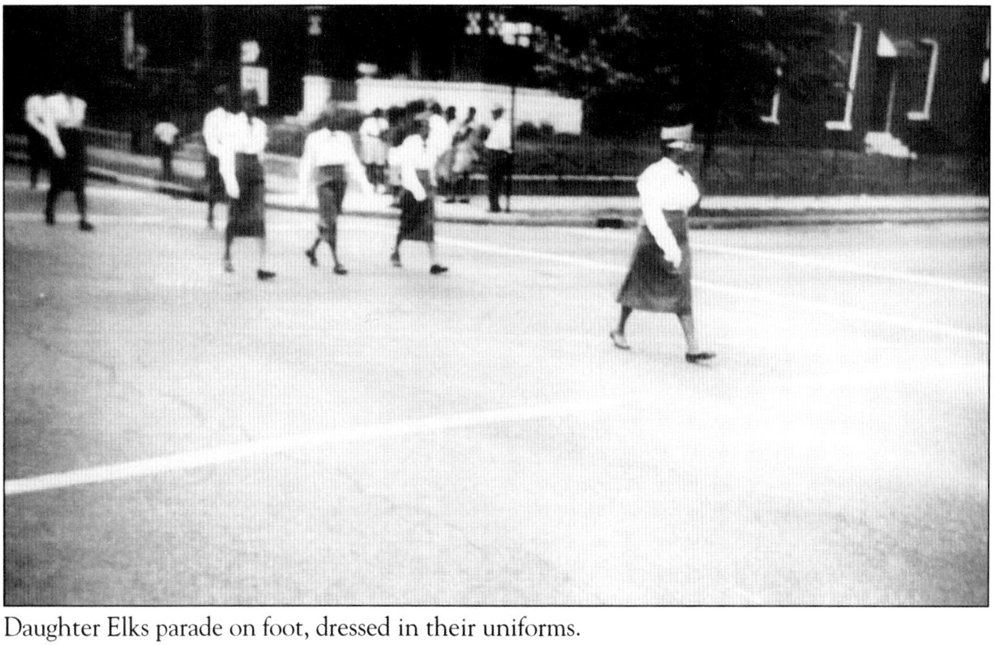

Daughter Elks parade on foot, dressed in their uniforms.

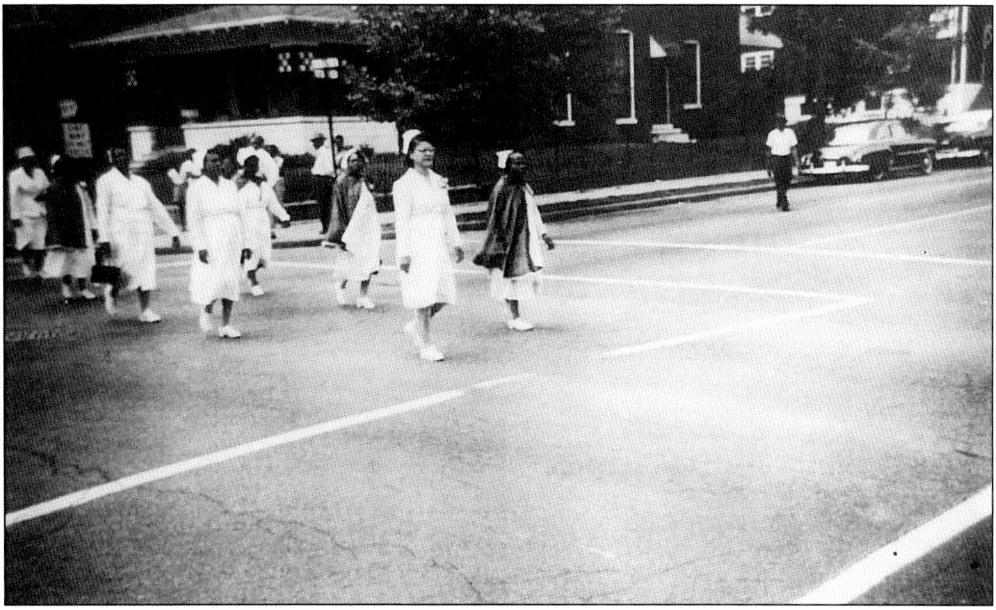

The women in white, brown, or dark uniforms were lodge auxiliary women or Daughter Elks. One of the groups pictured is a Lexington-based lodge. This may be the nurses unit. Many of the Daughter Elks had first aid training but few were trained nurses.

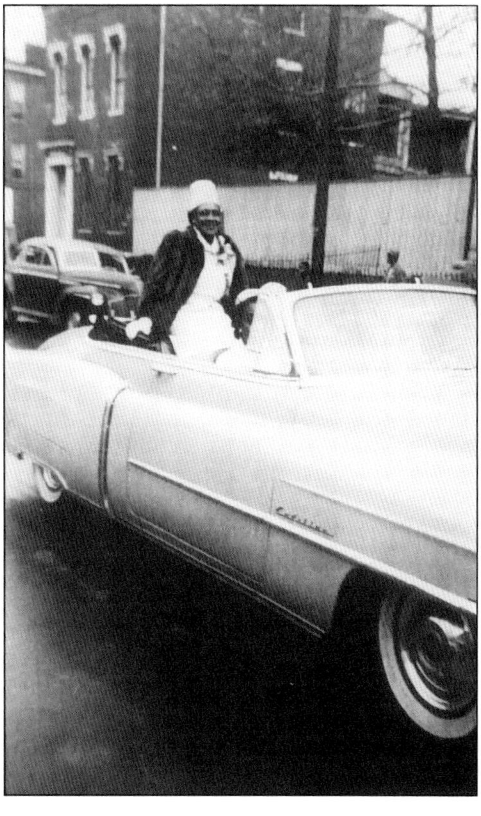

Daughter Elk Lillian B. Morris, wearing a mink coat and seated in the back seat, was Kentucky state president of the women's group.

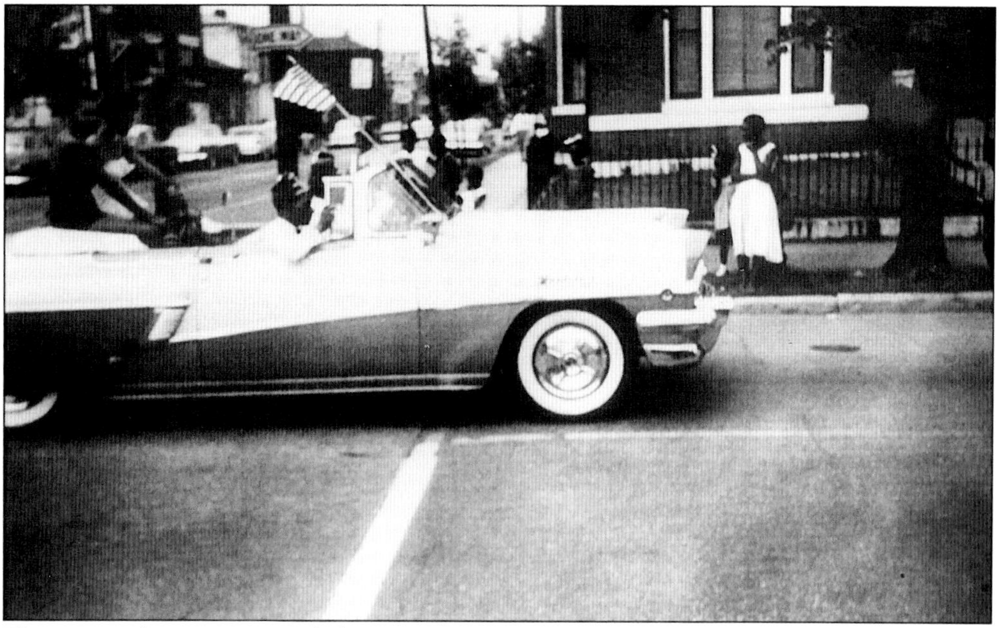

These young beauty queens ride by in an open-top car, displaying a U.S. flag.

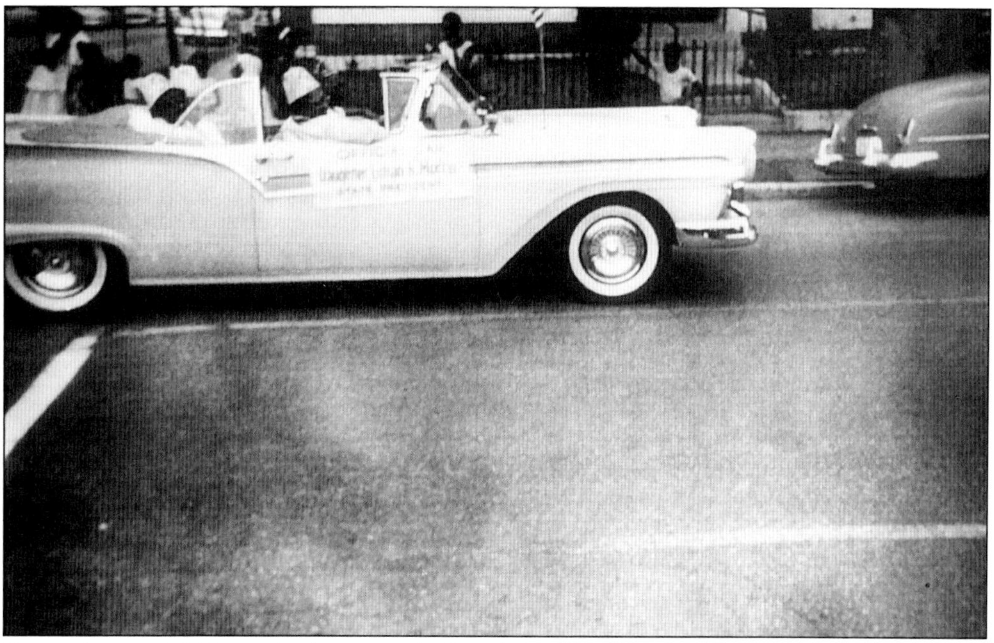

Pictured in this 1948 parade photo are the Daughter Elks officers in their car.

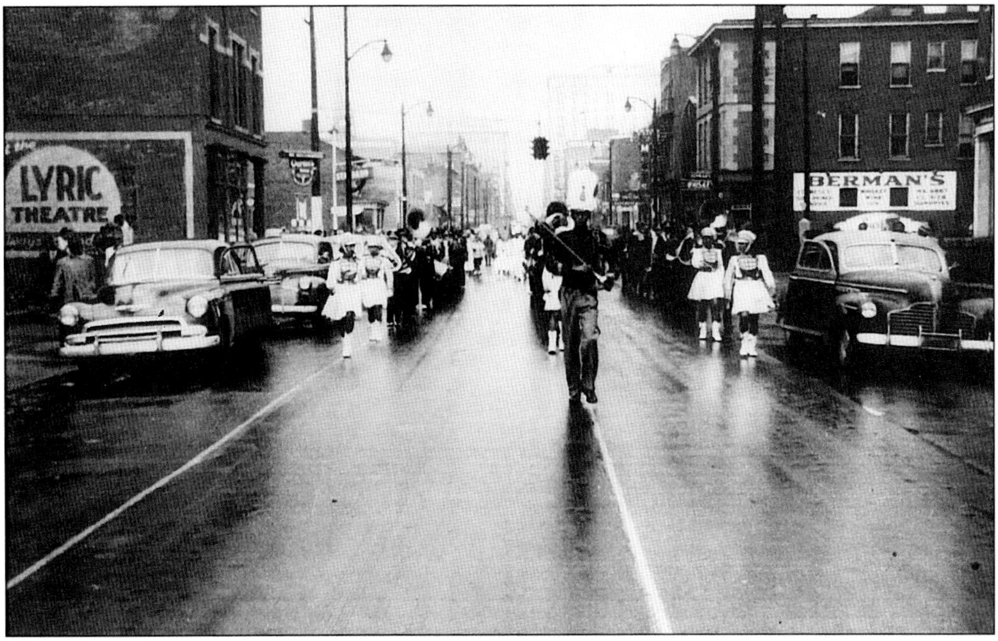

Central High School's Marching Band often marched during these events. The Elks made financial donations to the band fund at Central High School. (1948.)

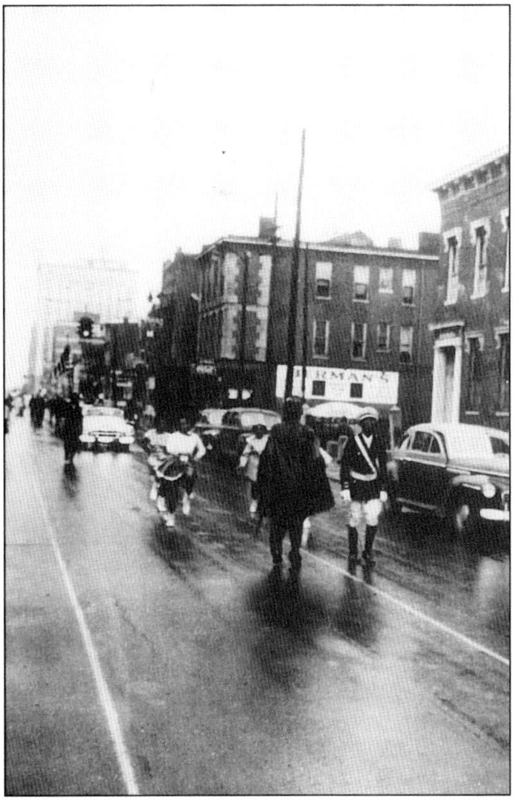
Pictured are the Junior Elks auxiliaries (or a middle school's marching band members). The drill master seen here is attired in full uniform, with regalia and boots. (c. 1948.)

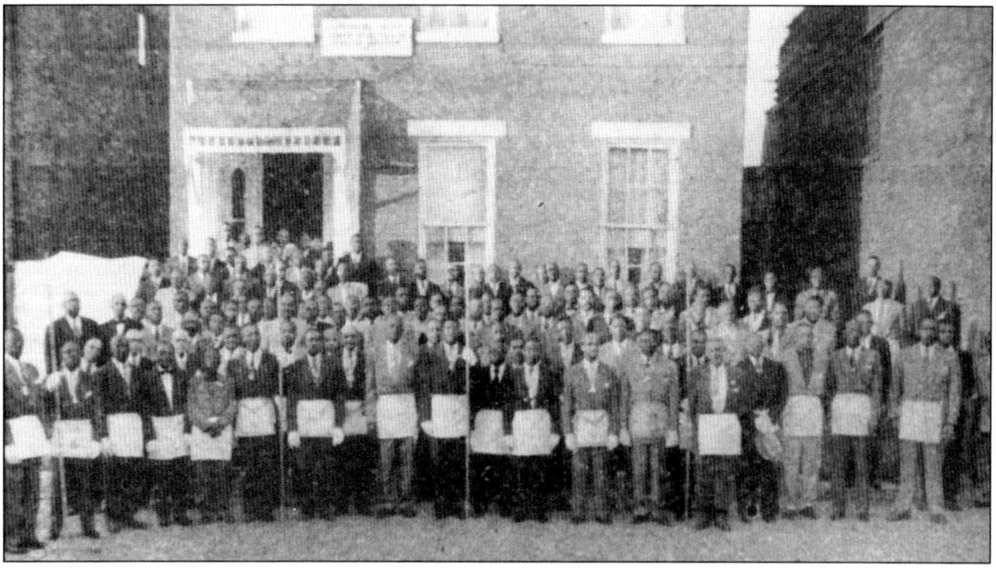

The officers of the Southern Cross Lodge No. 39 pictured in this 1955 view are attending a Prince Hall affiliation meeting at Quinn Chapel A.M.E. Church in Louisville.

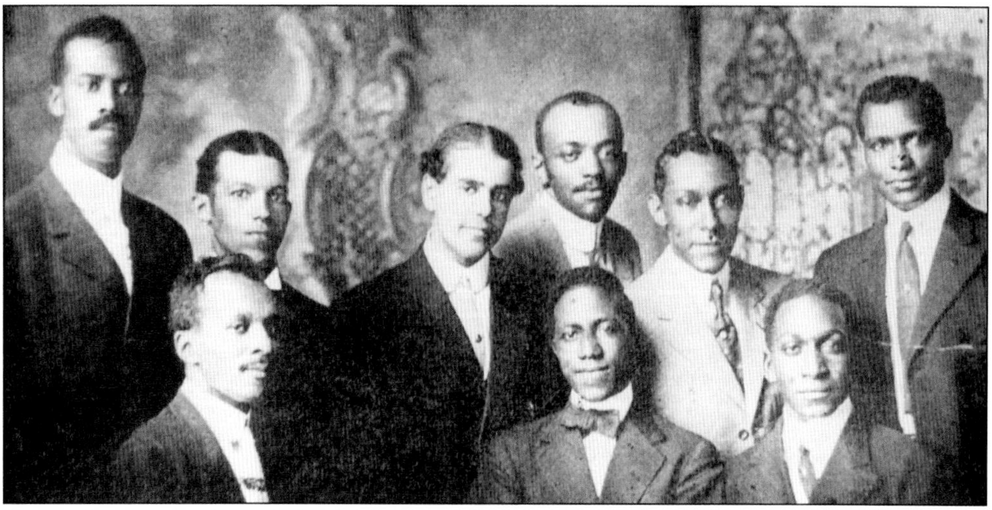

These charter members of the Alpha Lambda Chapter of Louisville were a part of the first graduate chapter of Alpha Phi Alpha, Inc. The organization, which was founded on April 11, 1911, was originally called the University Club. Members met at the Western Branch Library.

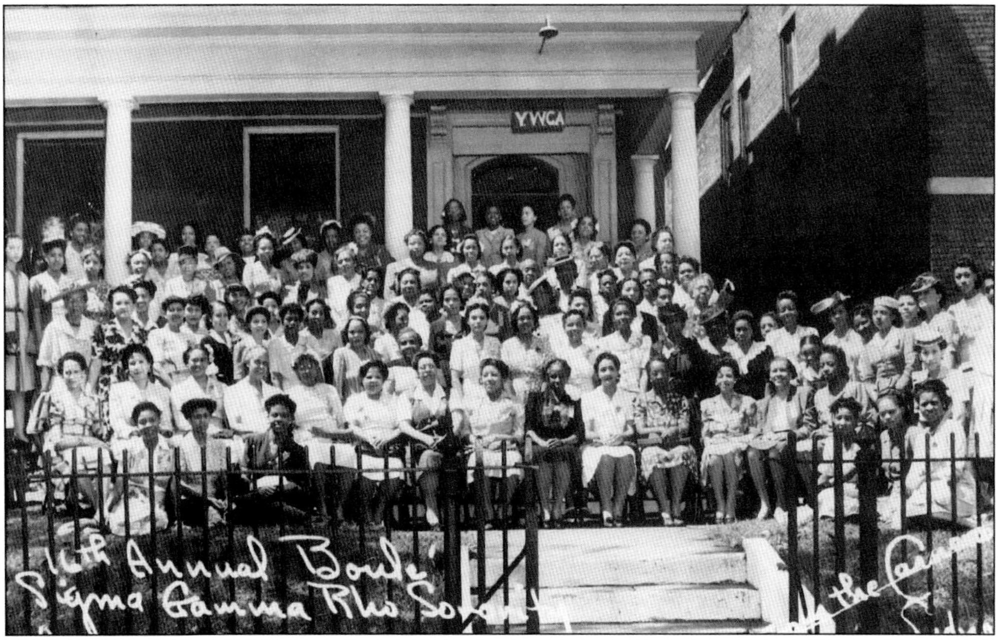

This August 1944 photo is a view of Sigma Gamma Rho Sorority's 16th Annual Ball, which was held at the old, segregated YWCA in Louisville.

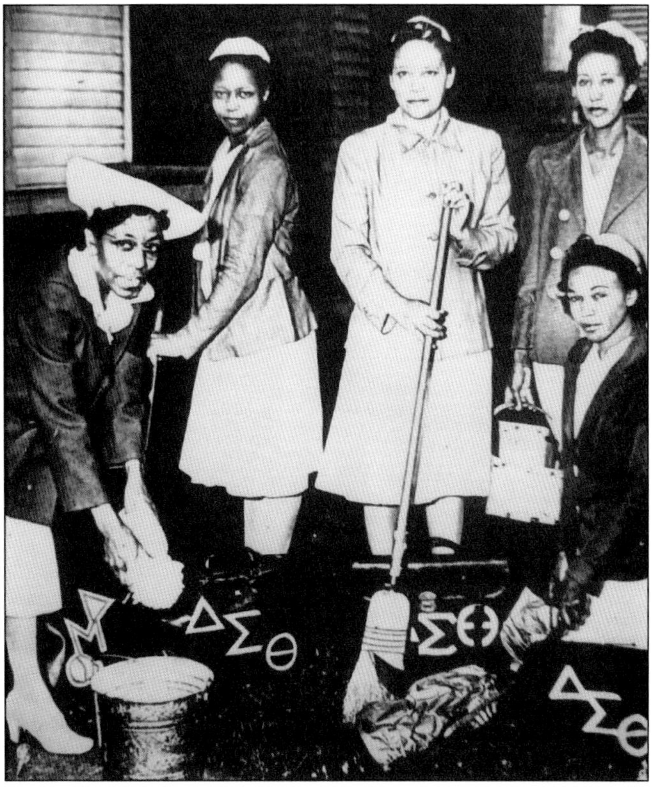

Louisville's Delta Sigma Theta Sorority stands at the corner of Sixth and Walnut Streets, cleaning sidewalks as part of their initiation. (*c.* 1952.)

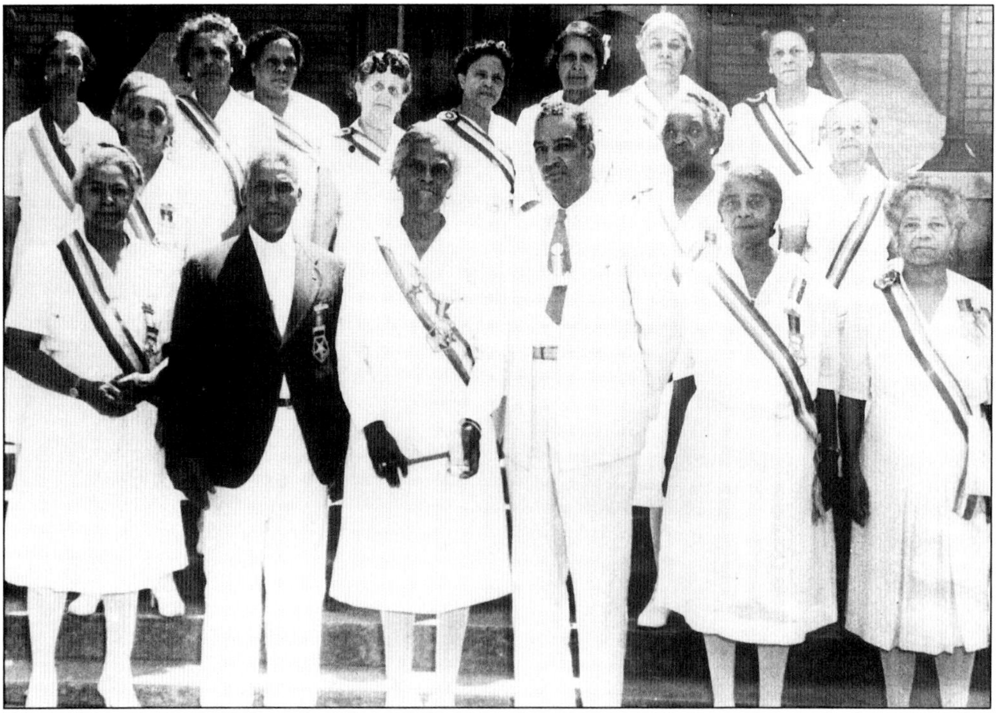

Pictured is E. Porter Hatcher Sr. (fourth from left). He was an officer of the Eastern Star Lodge. (*c.* 1945.)

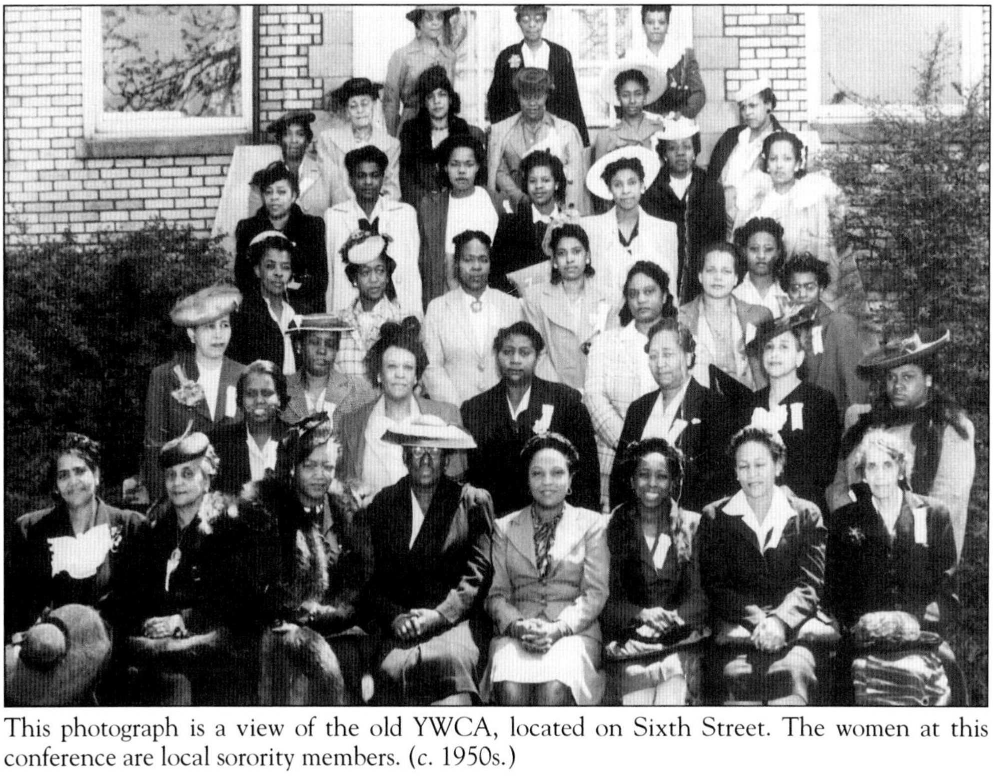

This photograph is a view of the old YWCA, located on Sixth Street. The women at this conference are local sorority members. (*c.* 1950s.)

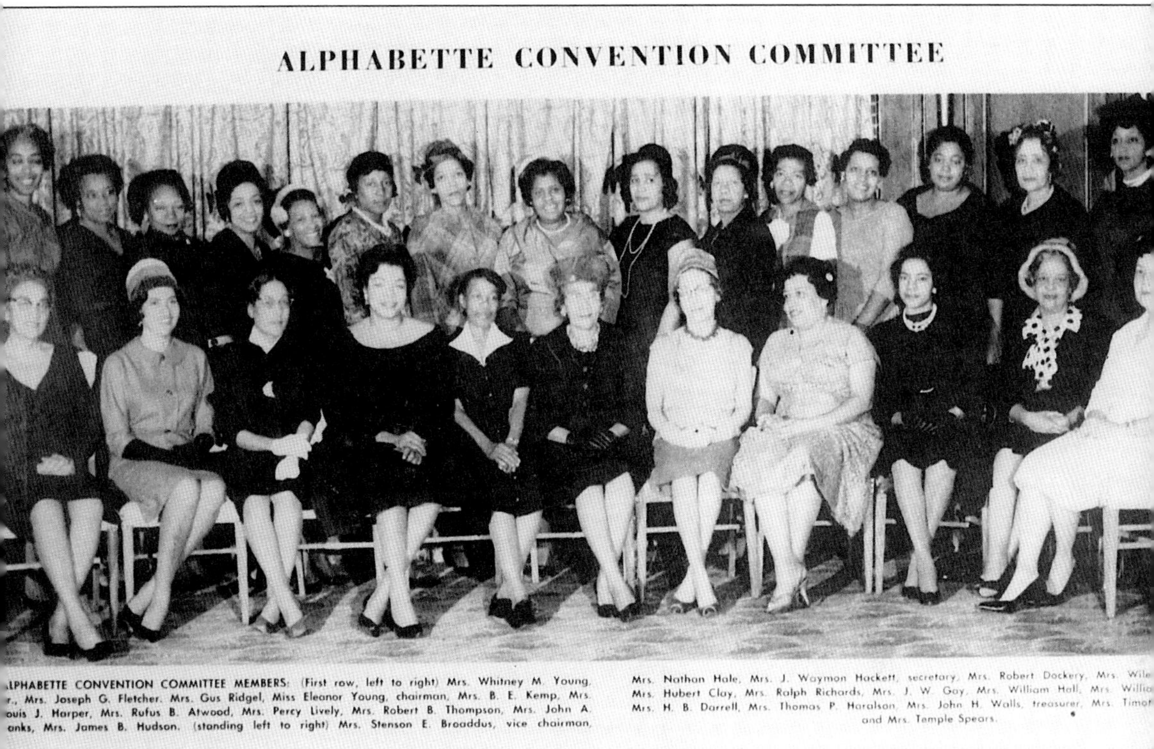

The Alphabette Convention women's committee is seen here hosting the December 1961 Alpha Phi Alpha convention in Louisville.

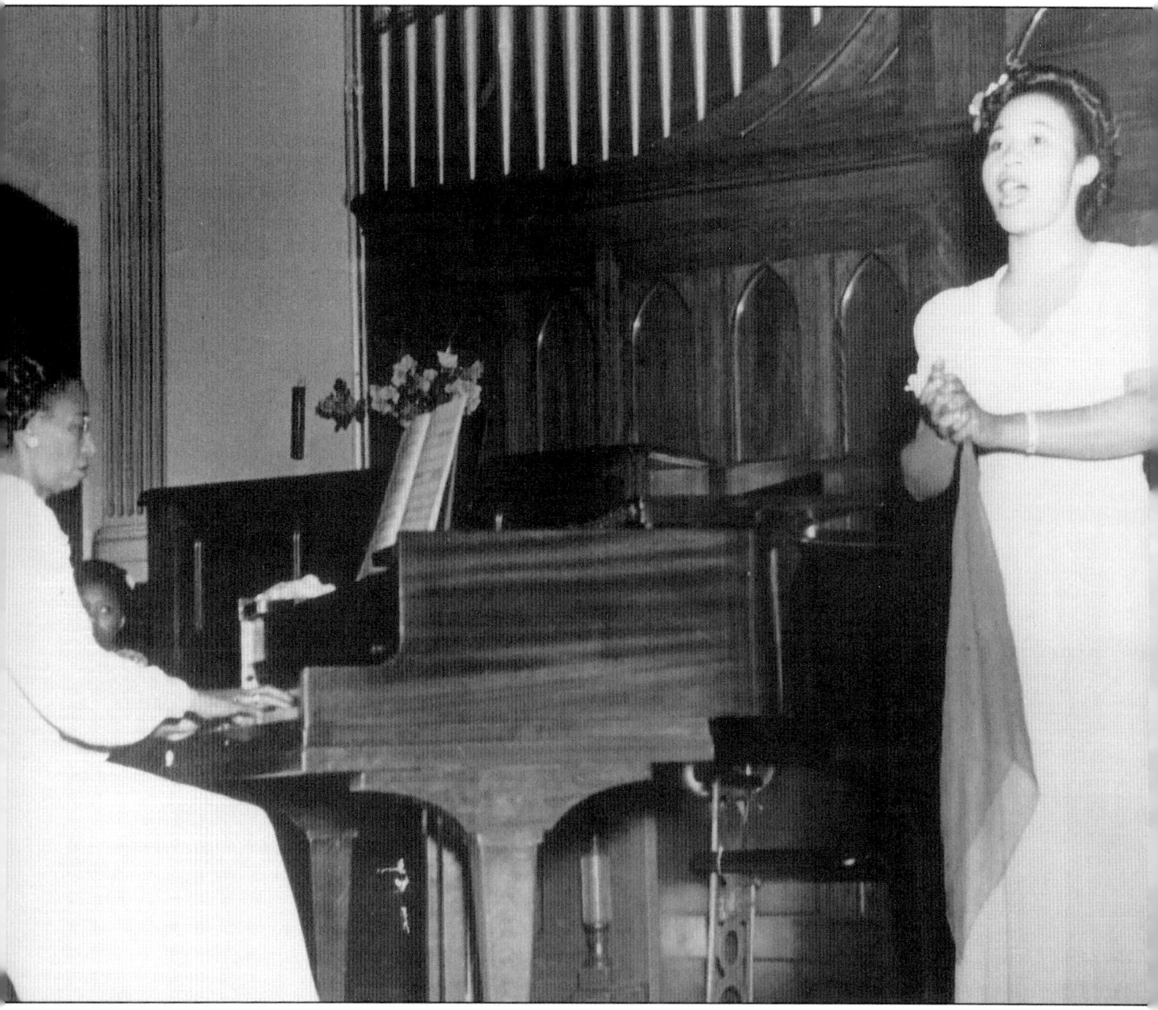

This concert for the Alphas was held at Quinn Chapel A.M.E. Church during the 1961 convention.

Eight

SWIMMING POOLS

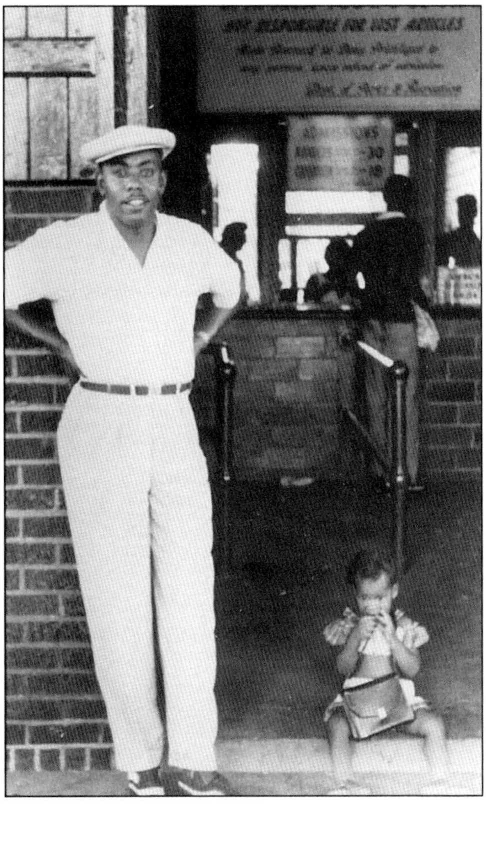

Charles Thomas stands in front of a pay entrance to Sheppard Park pool, which was located between Sixteenth and Seventeenth Streets on Magazine Street. This segregated pool was reserved for African Americans under Louisville's apartheid laws. (*c.* 1950.)

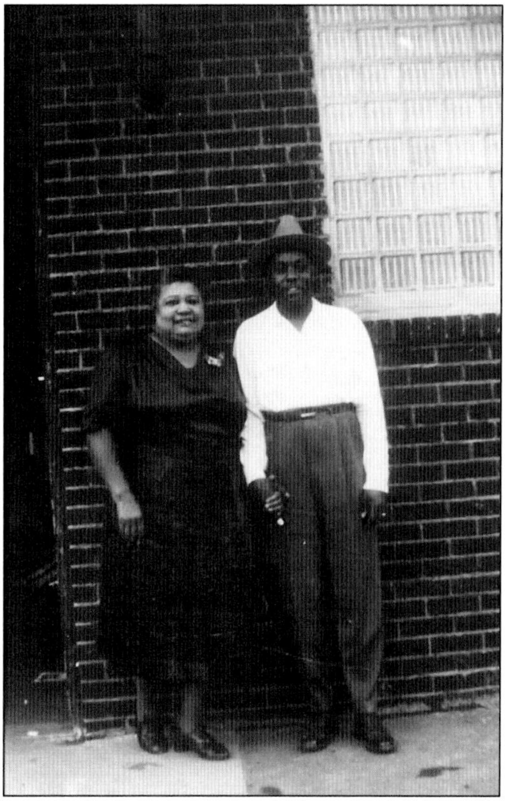

Charles Thomas is pictured with a Sheppard pool cashier named Sarah Martin. In earlier years, she was a blues singer for Fletcher Henderson's Orchestra.

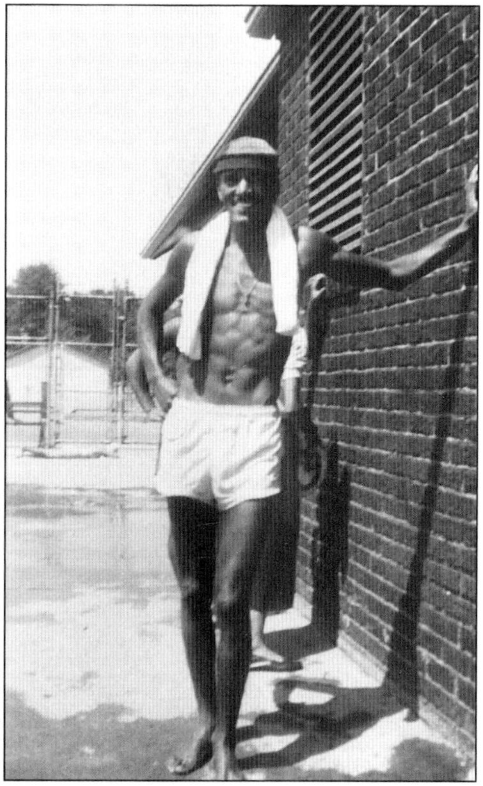

Pictured is Newt McCravey, a Sheppard pool lifeguard.

Pictured are two Sheppard pool swimmers.

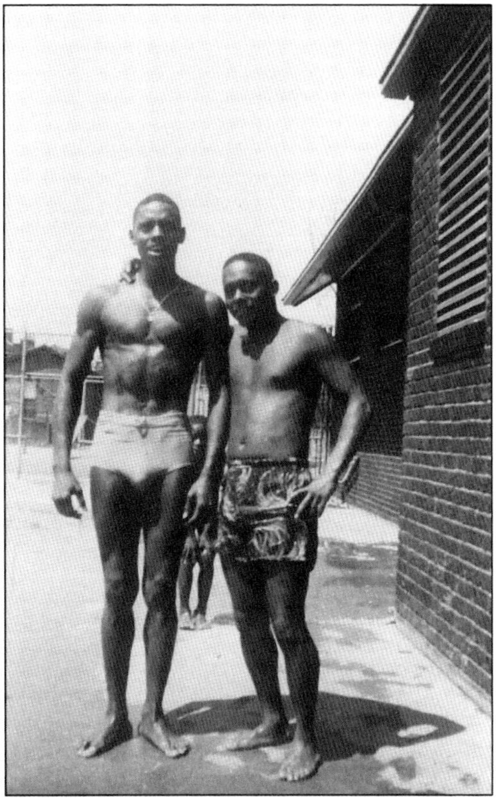

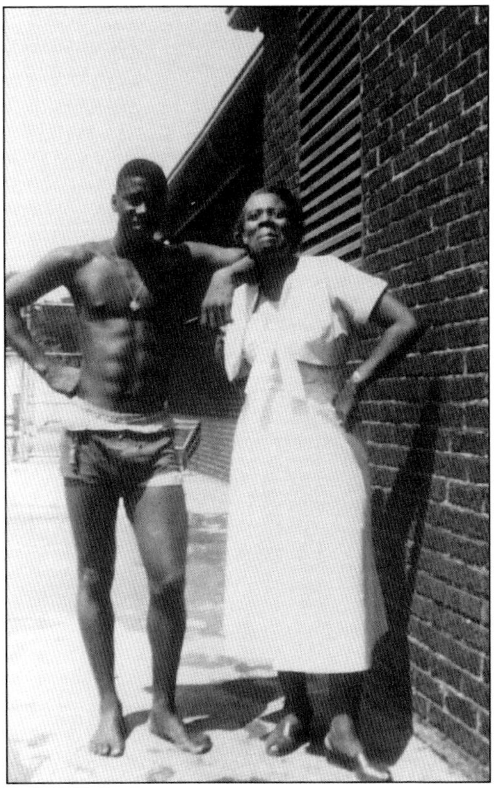

Eddie Lee Davis, a student and athlete, is pictured with Ruth Anderson, a Sheppard pool cashier. Sheppard Park pool closed around 1958.

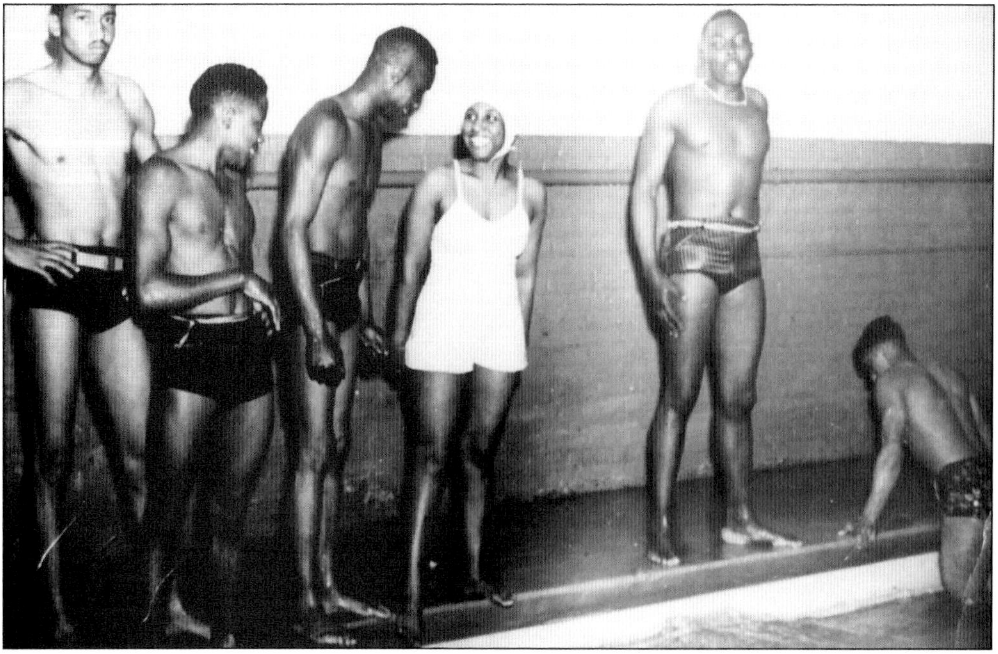

In this WW II era photograph, these Fort Knox soldiers are enjoying the old YMCA pool on Chestnut Street (between Tenth and Eleventh Streets). It was an indoor pool. In 1955, city pools were ordered to be desegregated by Mayor Andrew Broaddus. As a result, Algonquin, Shelby, and Wyandotte Park pools were democratized.

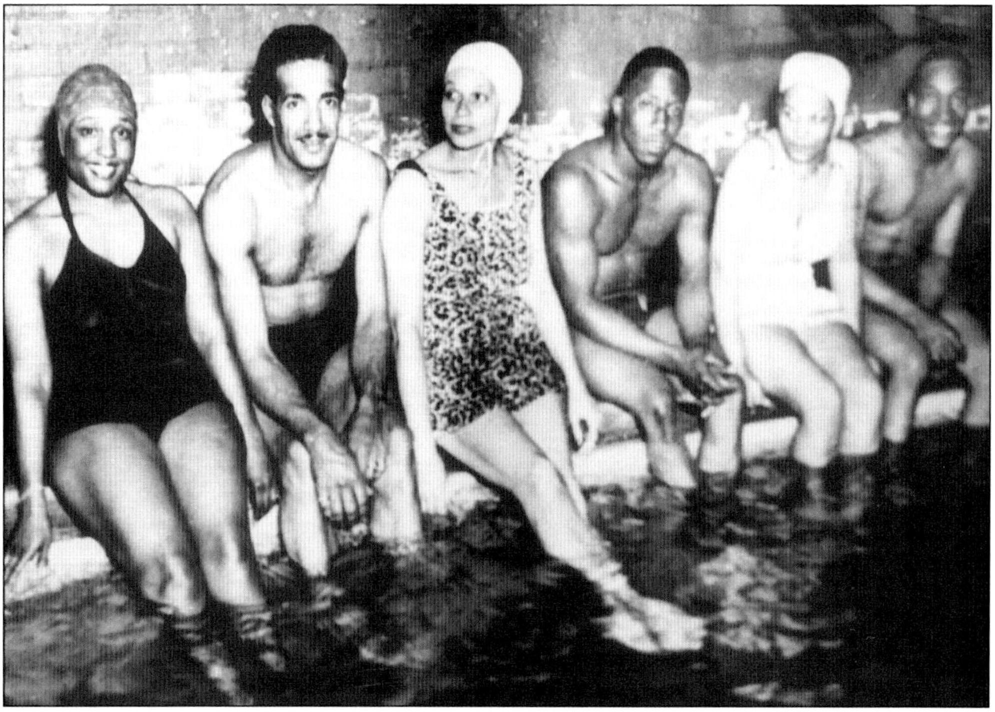

This c. 1943 photo is a view of a YMCA-USO club pool party held at the corner of Tenth and Chestnut Streets.

Nine

Community Businesses

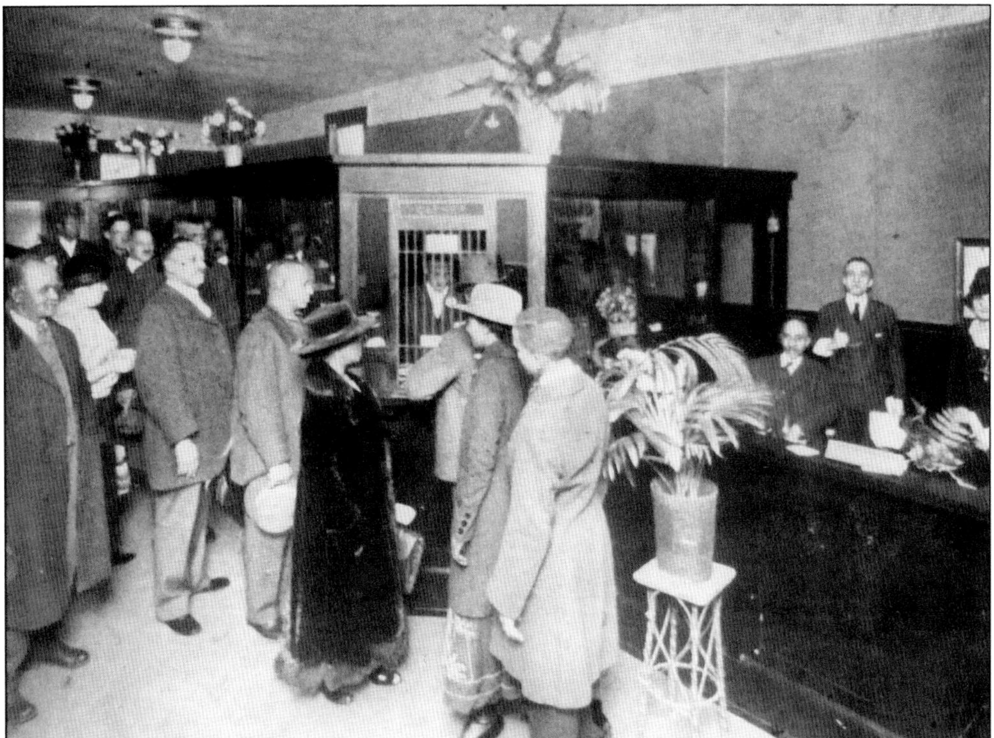

The First Standard Bank, located at Sixth and Walnut Streets, collapsed during the Great Depression under Roosevelt's Bank Holiday edict. (1922.)

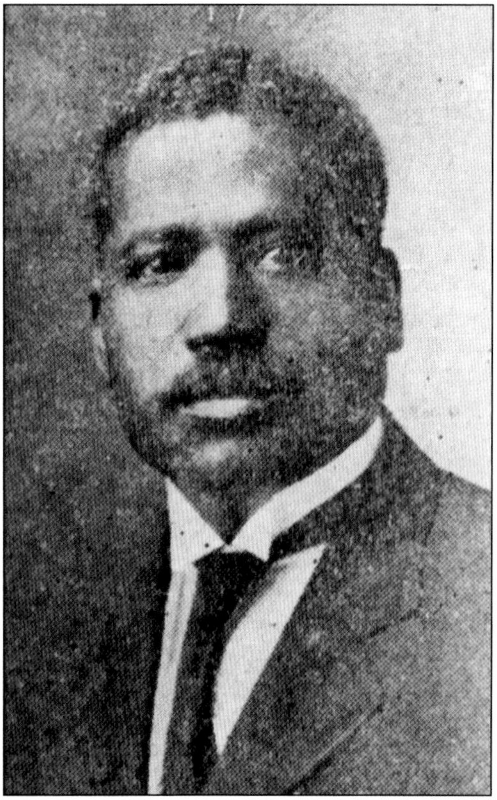

Doctor P.R. Peters, pictured here, was one of the first African-American doctors in the city of Louisville. (1922.)

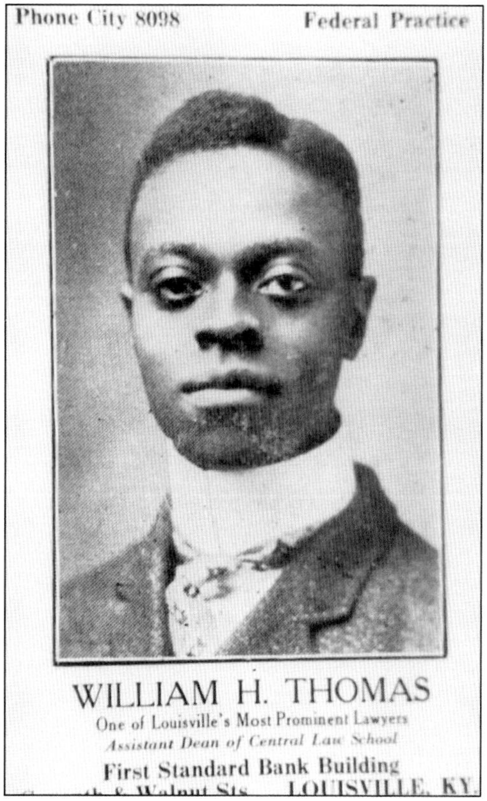

Attorney William H. Thomas was also the assistant dean of Central Law School, an African-American college. (1922.)

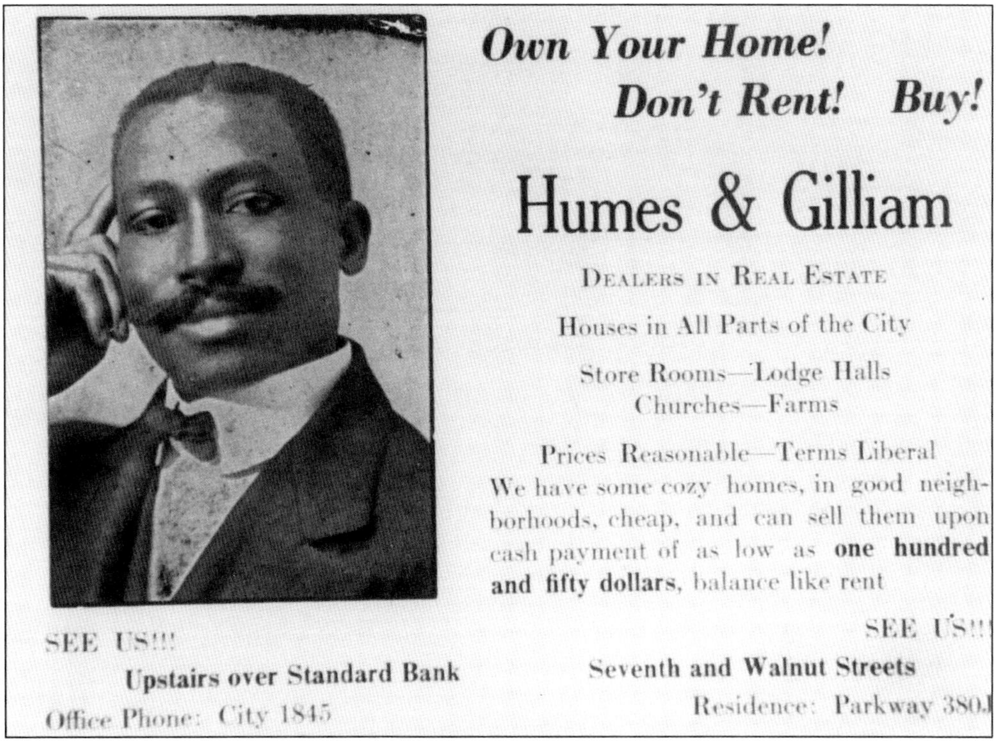

John Humes and Gilliam, real estate partners, had offices located at Seventh and West Walnut Streets. (1922.)

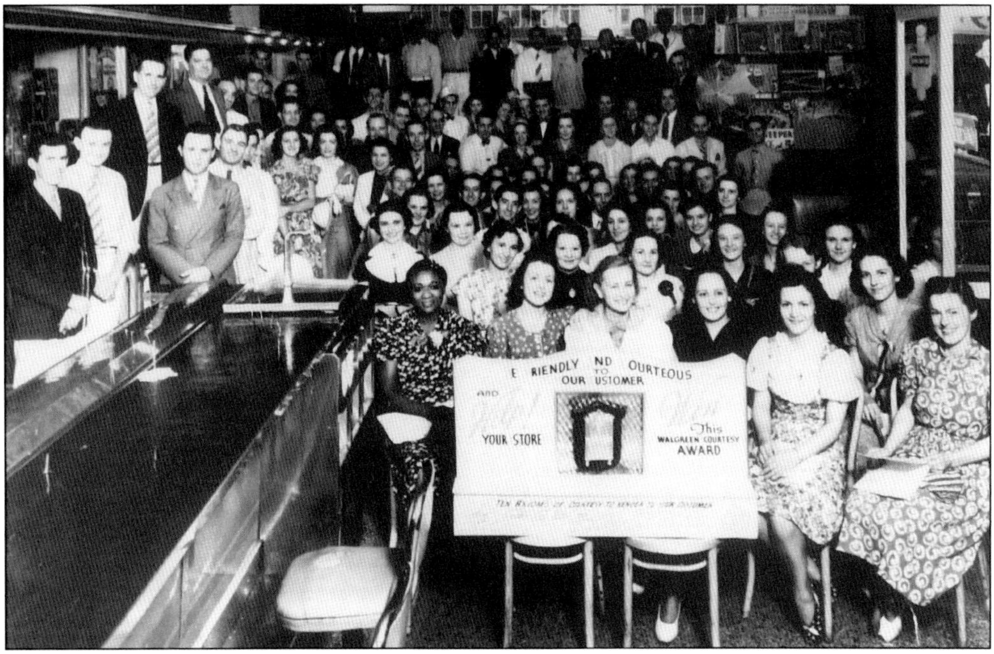

Walgreen's Drug Store and headquarters, located at Fourth Street and Broadway employed African Americans, even during the Depression in the 1930s. Des Moines Beard and other Blacks worked at this store. (1936.)

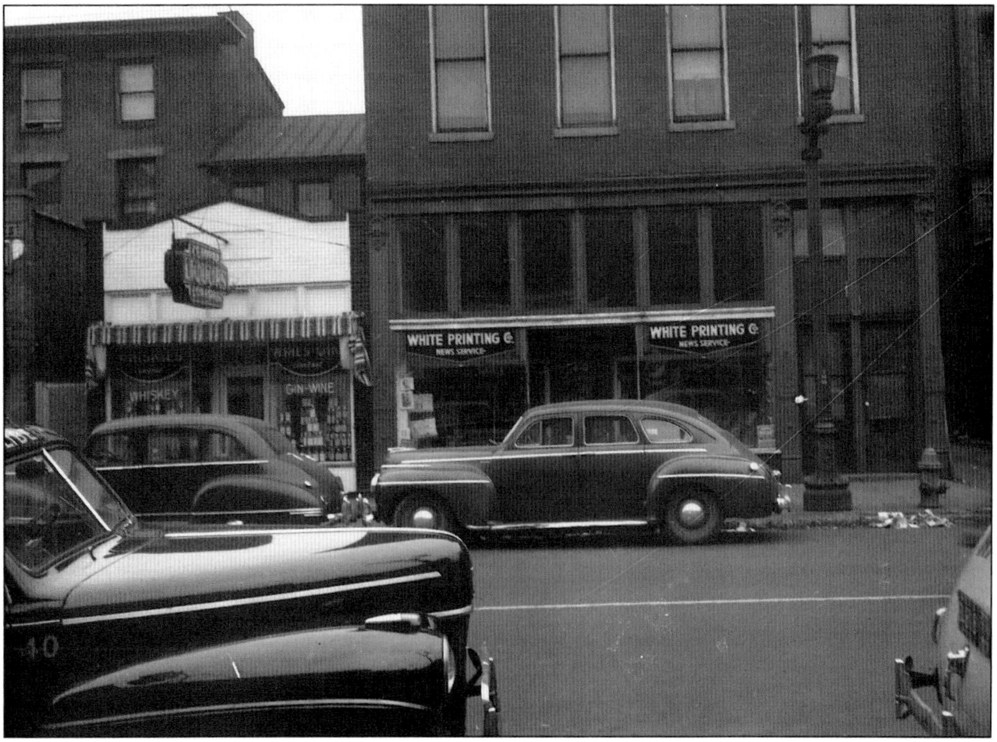

White Printing Company and News Service was located at 619 West Walnut Street. The taxicabs parked in front belong to the Liberty Cab Company, a Black-owned business. (c. 1939.)

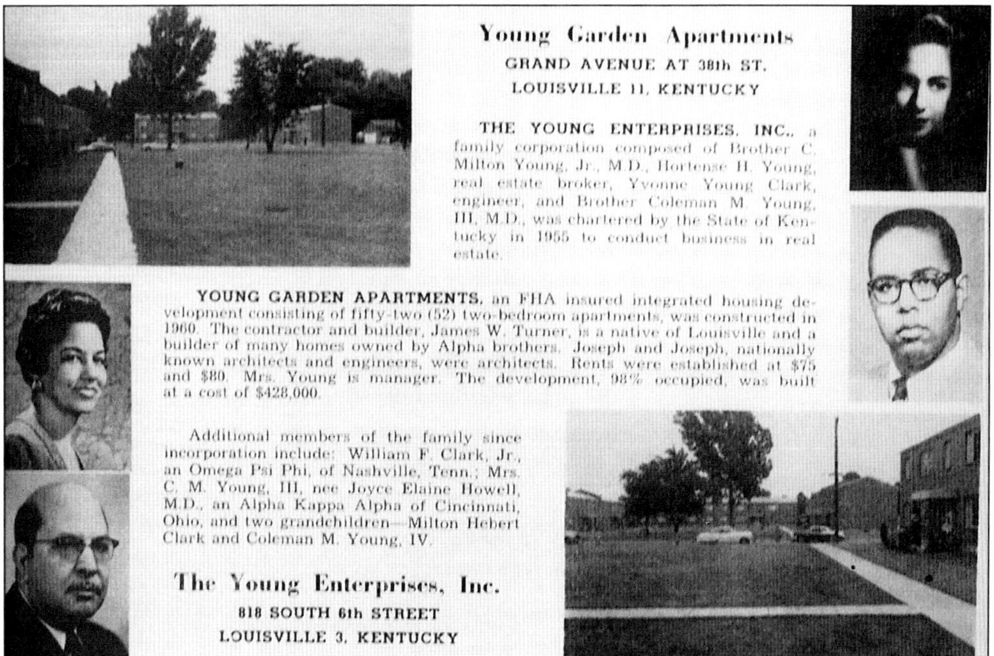

Young Garden Apartments
GRAND AVENUE AT 38th ST.
LOUISVILLE 11, KENTUCKY

THE YOUNG ENTERPRISES, INC., a family corporation composed of Brother C. Milton Young, Jr., M.D., Hortense H. Young, real estate broker, Yvonne Young Clark, engineer, and Brother Coleman M. Young, III, M.D., was chartered by the State of Kentucky in 1955 to conduct business in real estate.

YOUNG GARDEN APARTMENTS, an FHA insured integrated housing development consisting of fifty-two (52) two-bedroom apartments, was constructed in 1960. The contractor and builder, James W. Turner, is a native of Louisville and a builder of many homes owned by Alpha brothers. Joseph and Joseph, nationally known architects and engineers, were architects. Rents were established at $75 and $80. Mrs. Young is manager. The development, 98% occupied, was built at a cost of $428,000.

Additional members of the family since incorporation include: William F. Clark, Jr., an Omega Psi Phi, of Nashville, Tenn.; Mrs. C. M. Young, III, nee Joyce Elaine Howell, M.D., an Alpha Kappa Alpha of Cincinnati, Ohio, and two grandchildren—Milton Hebert Clark and Coleman M. Young, IV.

The Young Enterprises, Inc.
818 SOUTH 6th STREET
LOUISVILLE 3, KENTUCKY

This snapshot, taken in 1961, is a view of Young Garden Apartments on Grand Avenue at Thirty-eighth Street. Dr. C. Milton Young Sr. and his son were doctors.

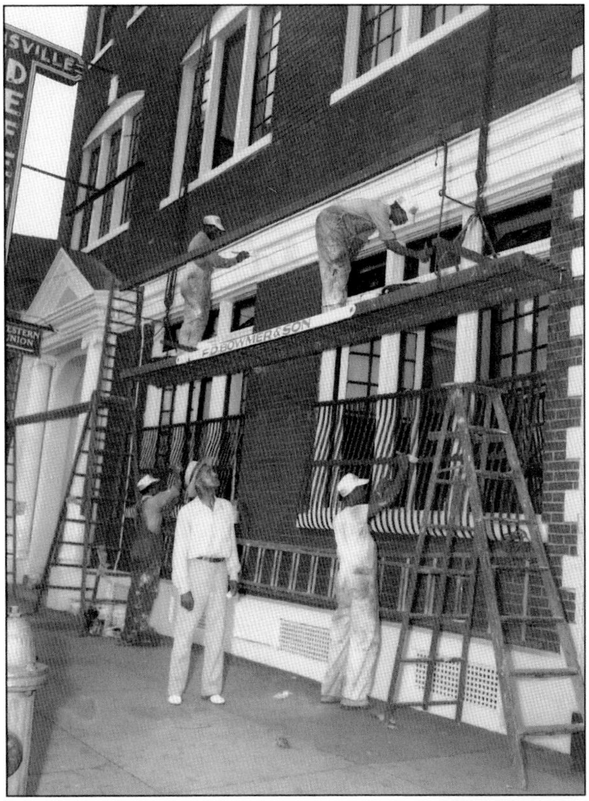

The Louisville Defender's office, located at 418 South Fifth Street, is pictured here undergoing renovation. Western Union and the Louisville Urban League had offices in the building. (*c.* 1943.)

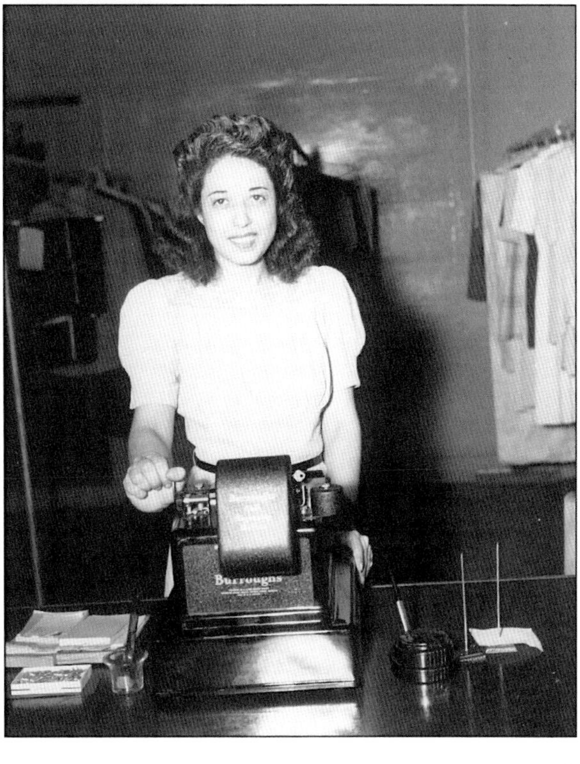

Pictured is a clerk in a black-owned cleaners. A number of African Americans owned and operated cleaners in Louisville. (*c.* 1939.)

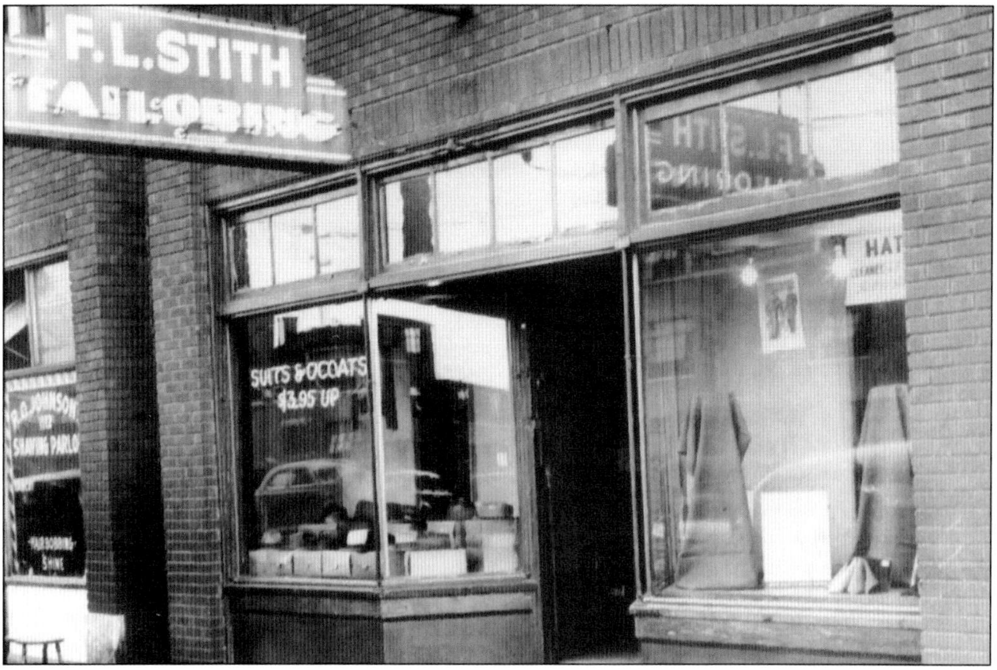

Pictured is Frederick Louis Stith's tailoring and clothing shop was located at 1114 West Walnut Street, beside the R.O. Johnson Shaving Parlor. The shaving parlor also included such services as hair-bobbing and shoe shines. (c. 1939.)

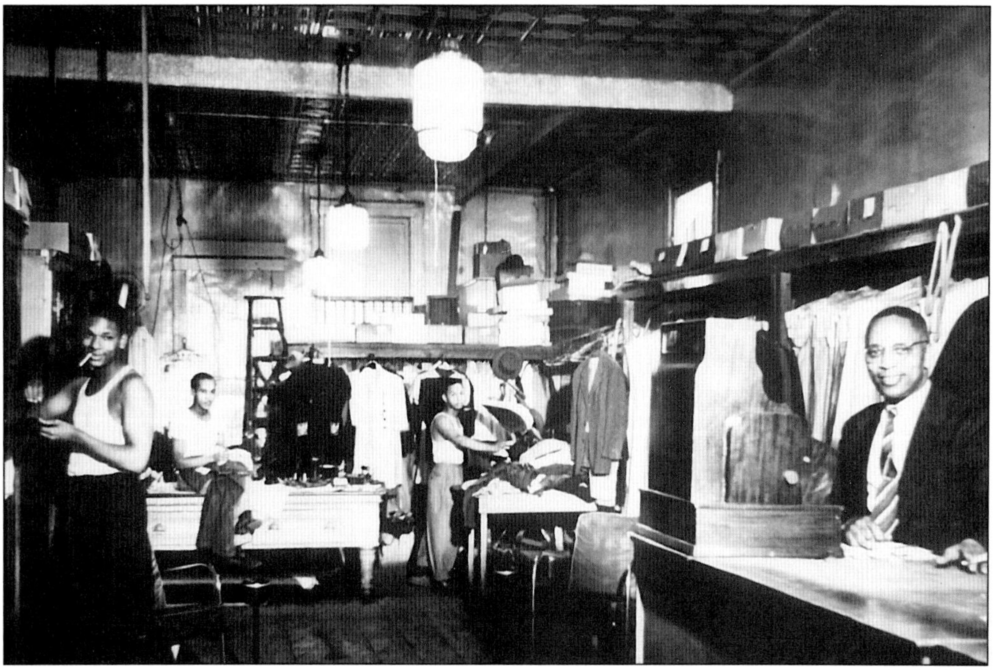

Frederick L. Stith in his cleaners at the cash register, his son John C. Stith on the right, James Dailey at the tailoring table and Elmer Cowden on the right at work. c. 1939.

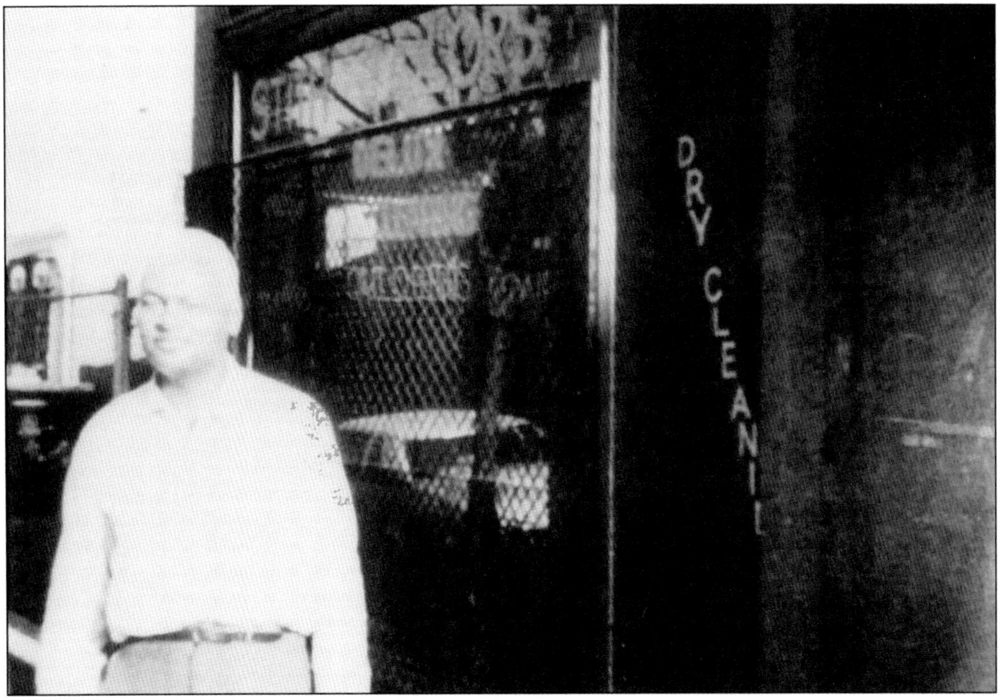

Frederick Lloyd Stith, the son of Frederick Louis Stith, stands in front of the cleaners store his father passed on to him. The cleaners was located at 2348 West Chestnut Street.

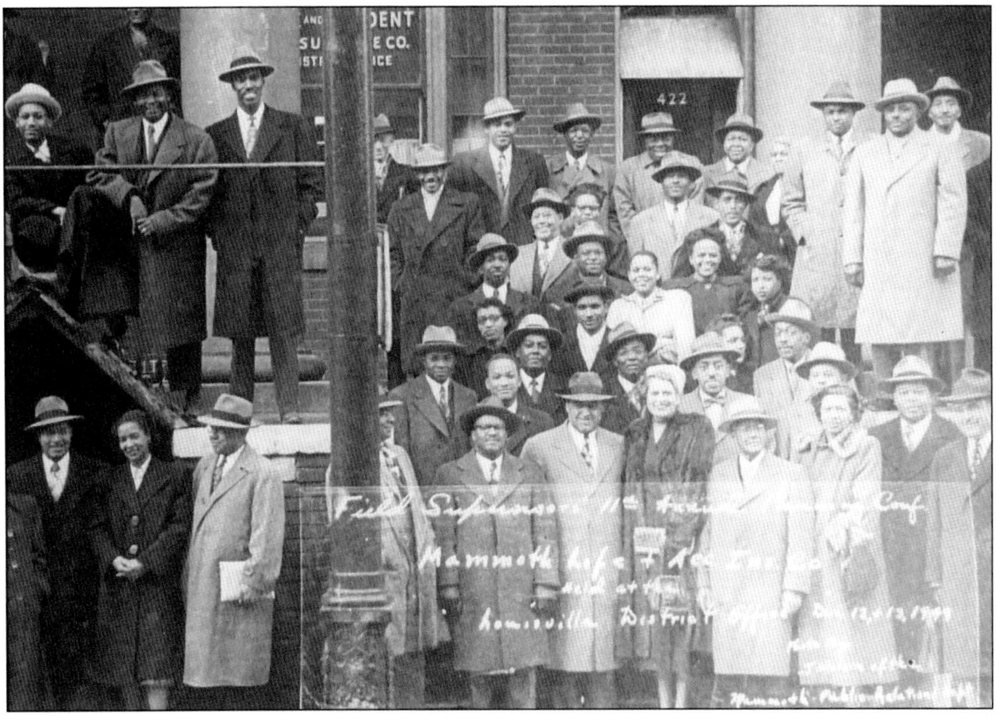

This photograph is a scene from Mammoth Life and Accident Insurance Company's Annual Planning Conference. The meeting was held at the Louisville district office in December 1949.

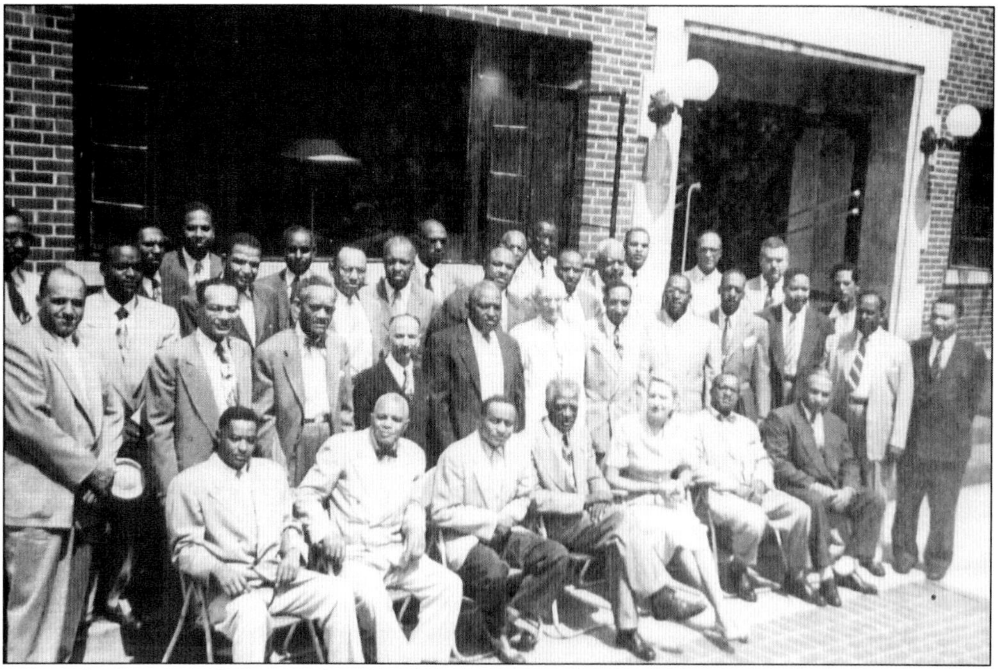

Pictured is a group of Mammoth Life Insurance employees and officers.

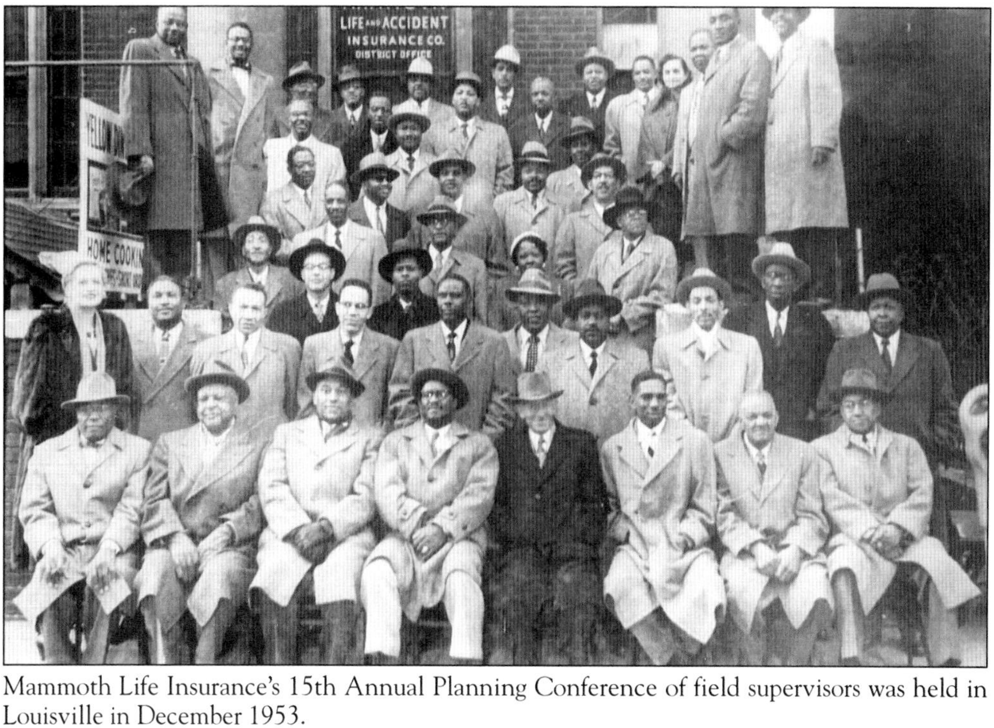

Mammoth Life Insurance's 15th Annual Planning Conference of field supervisors was held in Louisville in December 1953.

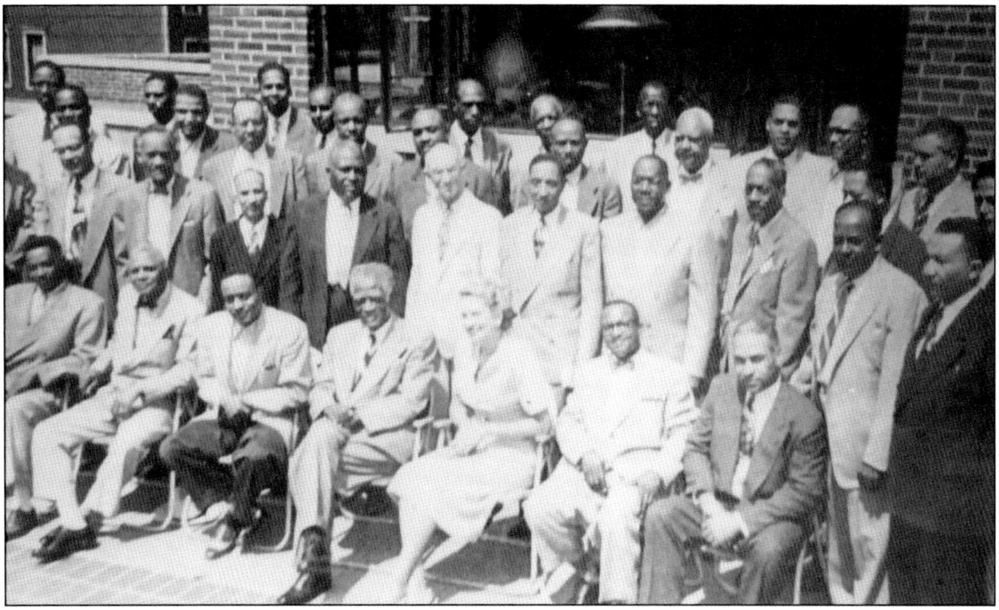

Pictured is the Mammoth Life Insurance managers convention in Cincinnati. Mae Street Kidd (center) became a Kentucky state legislator.

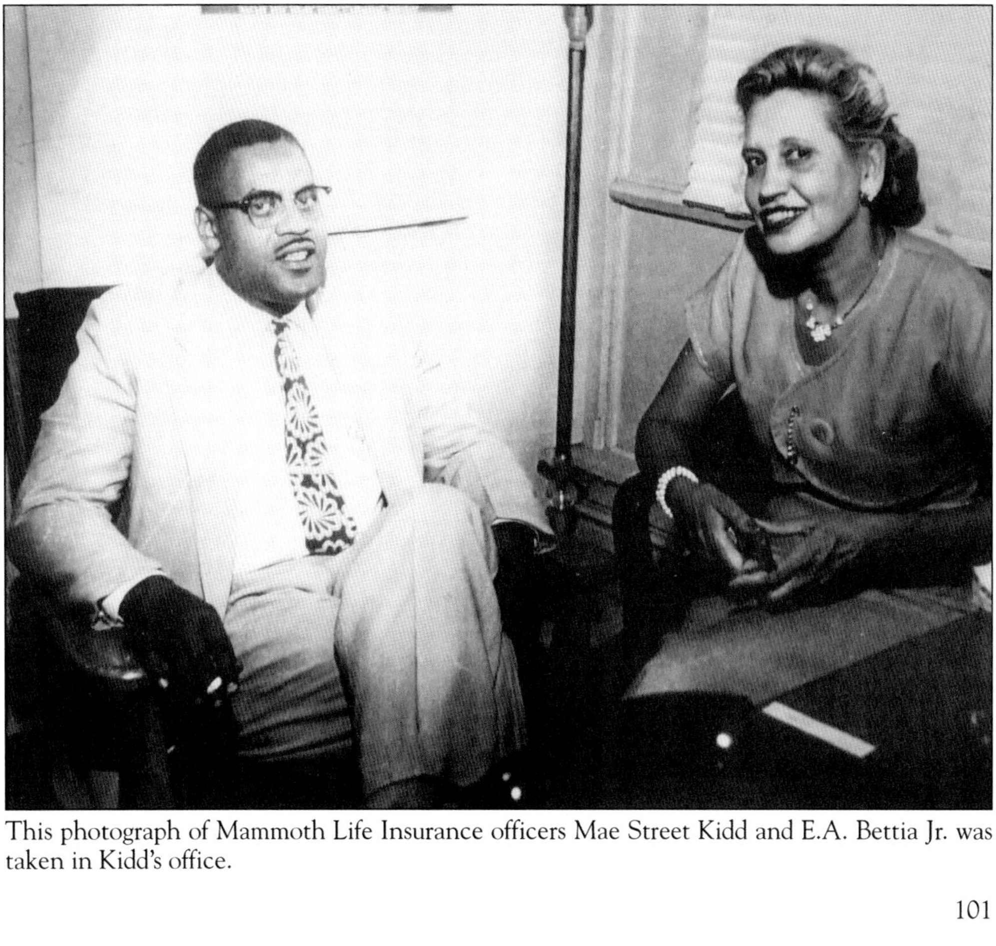

This photograph of Mammoth Life Insurance officers Mae Street Kidd and E.A. Bettia Jr. was taken in Kidd's office.

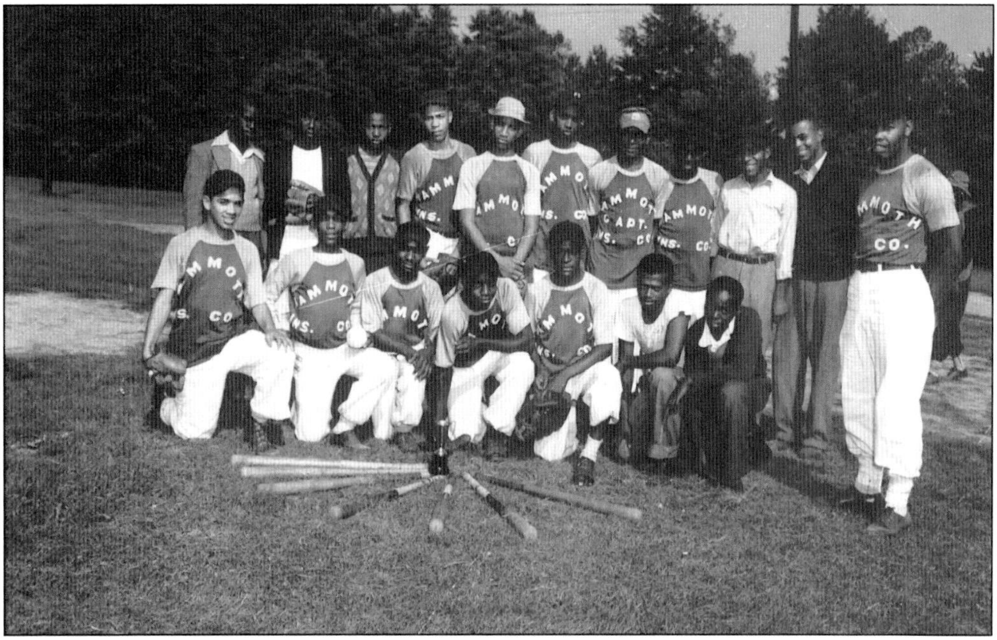

Mammoth Life and Accident Insurance Company sponsored this baseball team.

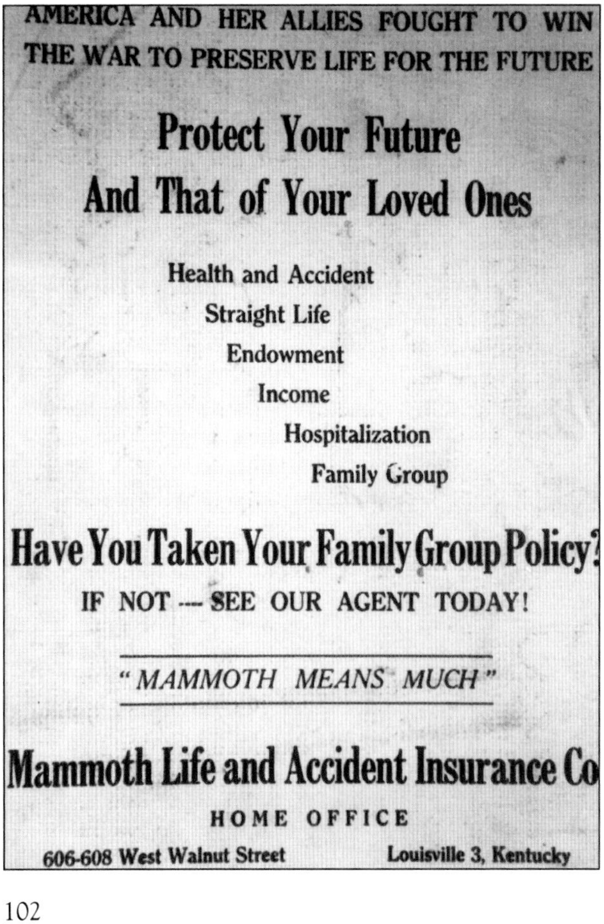

This 1945 advertisement for Mammoth Life and Accident Insurance Company was used during WW II.

Charles Thomas worked weekends at Harry's Pawn Shop and sold the popular "Mr. B's" shirts worn by singer Billy Eckstein. (c. 1949.)

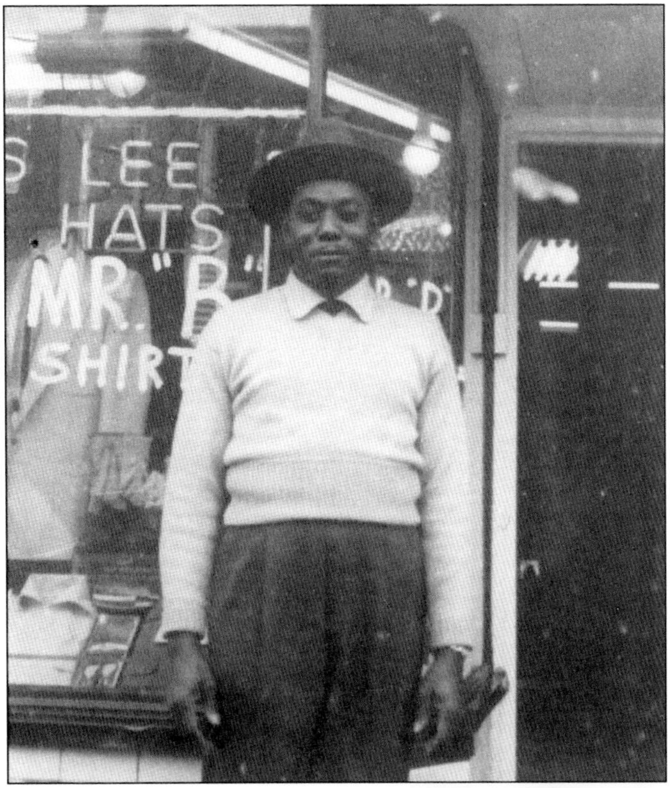

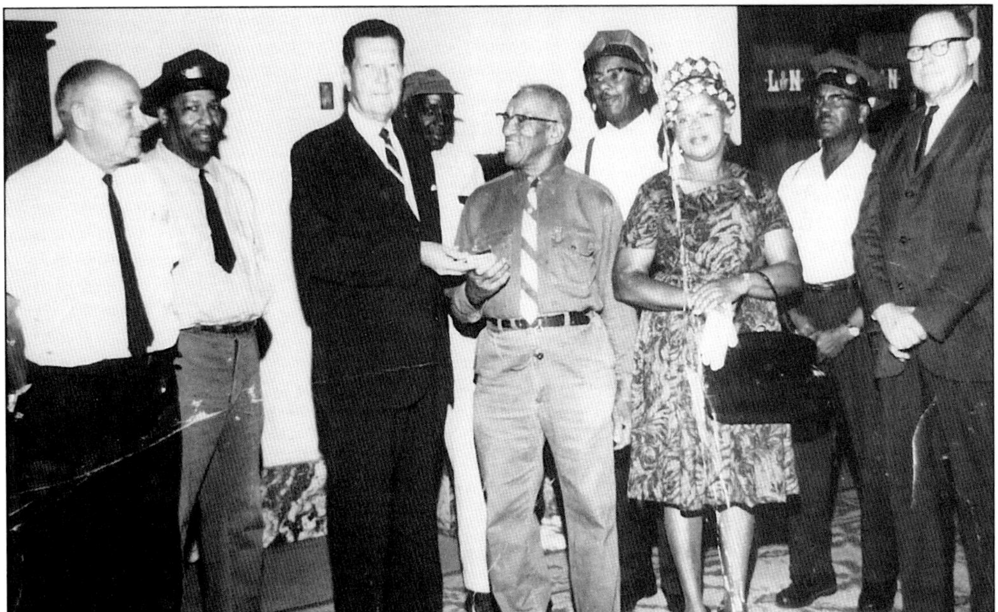

Louisville and Nashville Railroad officials are seen here celebrating the retirement of William "Panky" Thomas with his wife in 1960. Thomas was a chief cook for the vice president of the L&N Railroad, and he was a red cap. John Weathers, (pictured) was a station porter and later, a messenger.

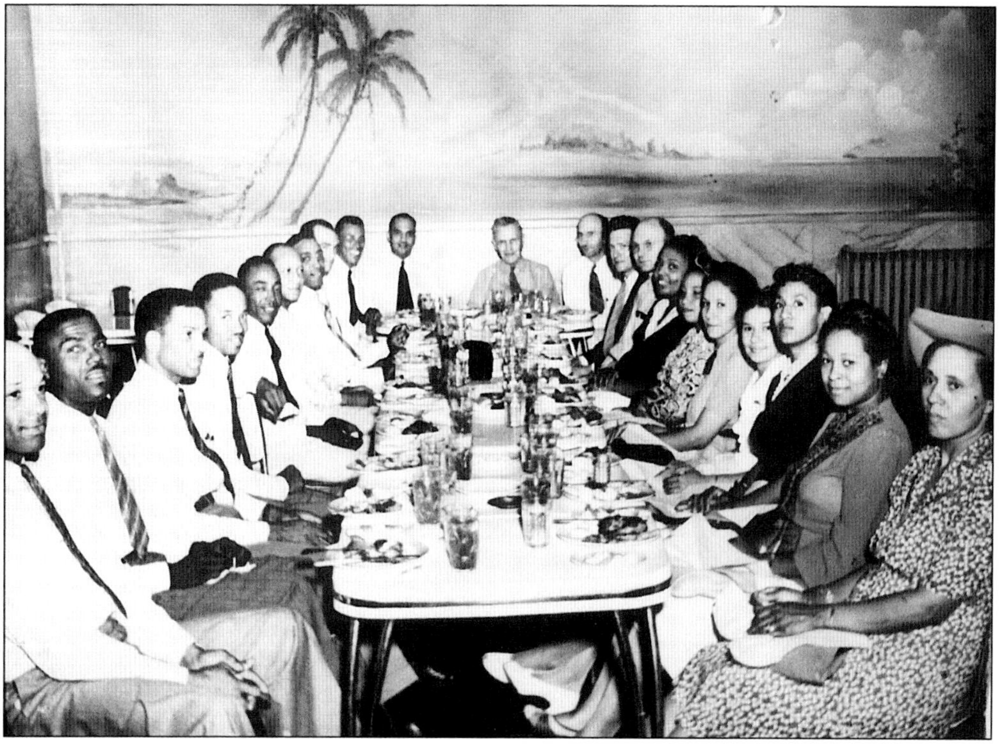

These African-American professionals are enjoying their dinner at the Brock Building, located at 639 South Ninth Street. (c. 1944.)

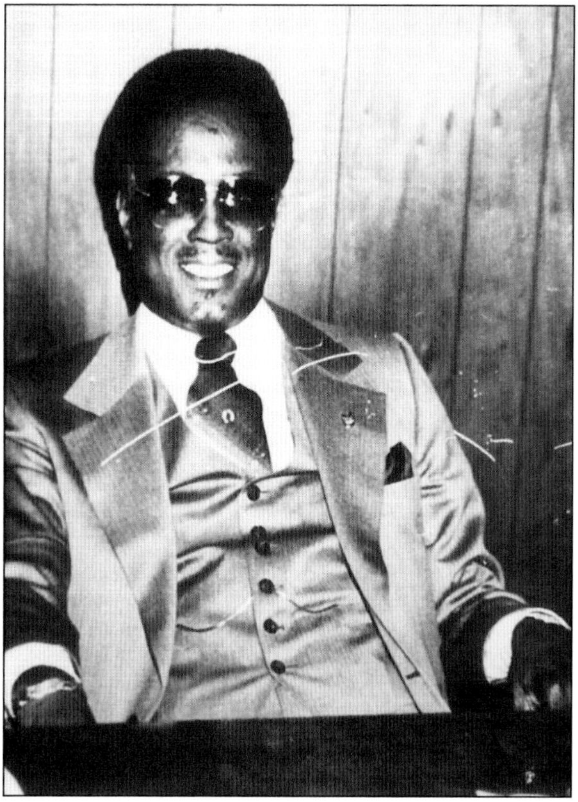

William E. Summers III, a businessman who owned the WLOU radio station, became a minister and community leader in Louisville. His son, William E. Summers IV, is presently the deputy mayor of the City of Louisville.

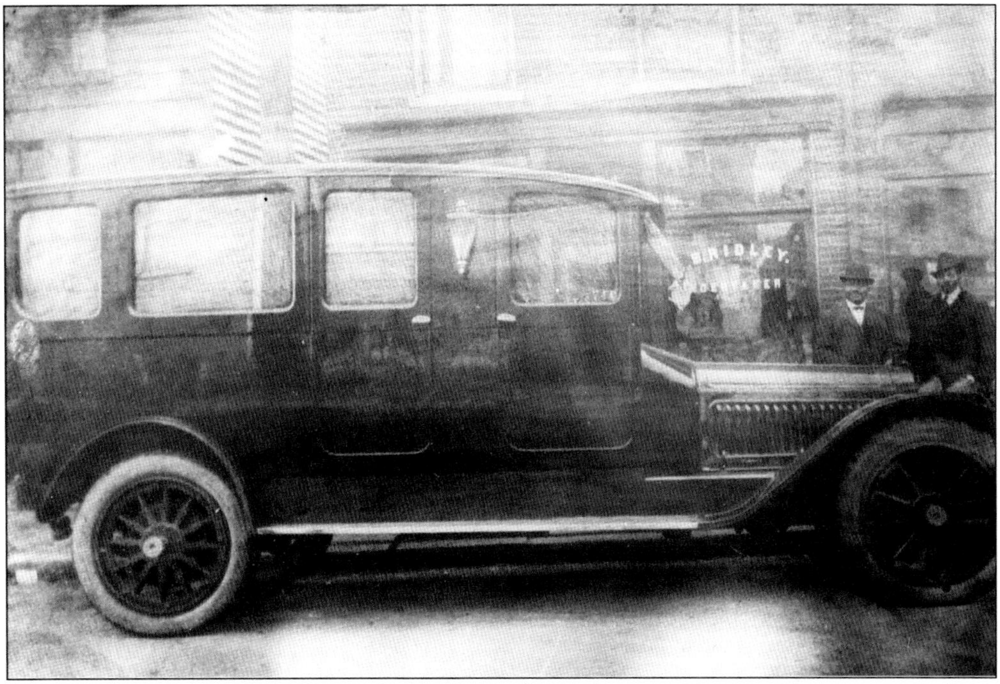

Undertaker A.B. Ridley's office and chapel were located at 1024 West Walnut Street. Ridley's and J.B. Cooper's were the major funeral homes for African Americans. (*c.* 1920s.)

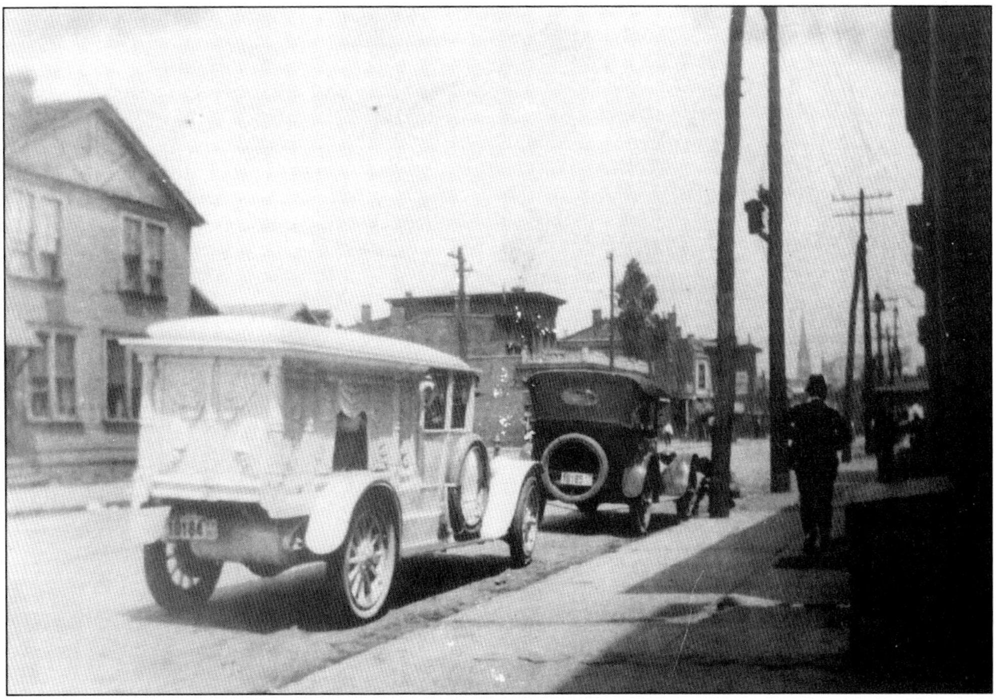

In this *c.* 1920s photograph, A.B. Ridley stands with a white hearse in front of his funeral home.

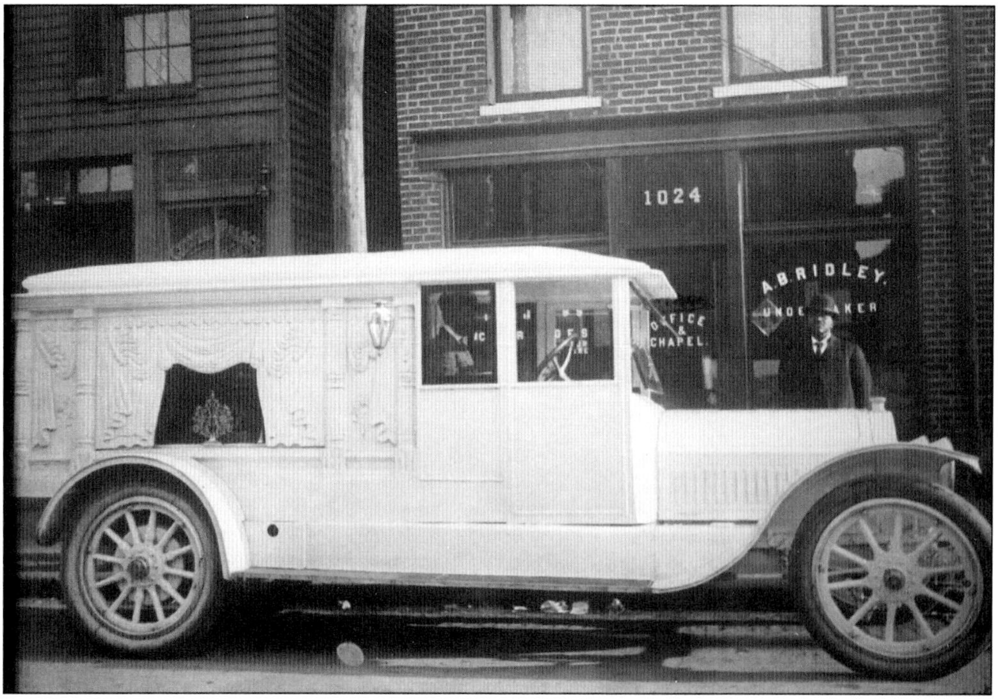

A.B. Ridley also used his hearses as makeshift ambulances. (*c.* 1920s.)

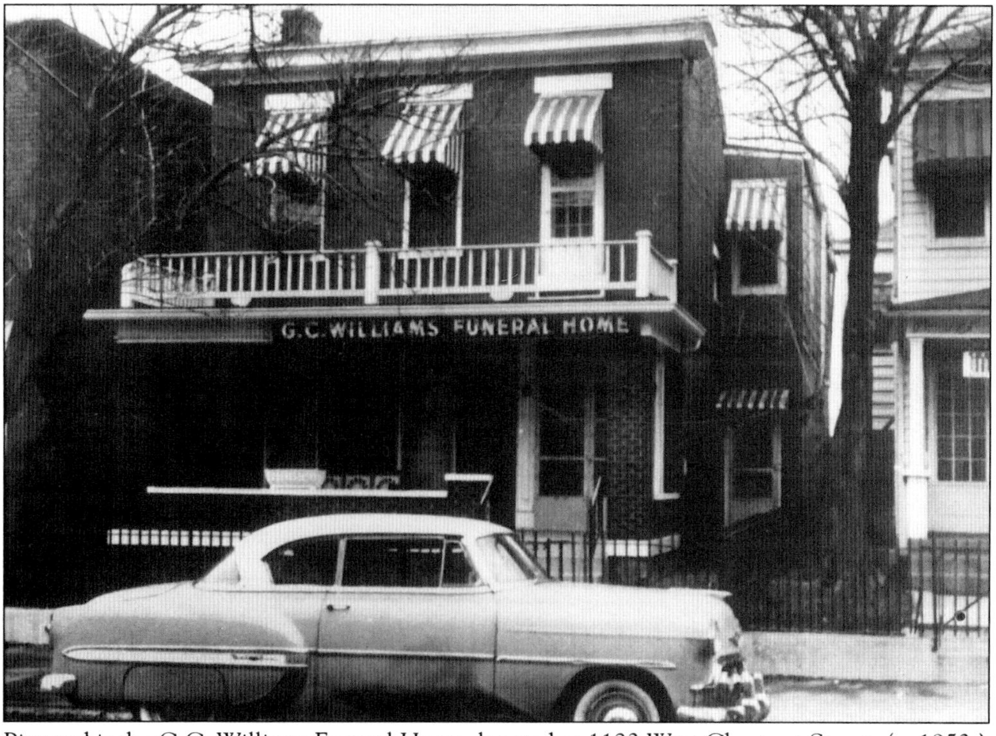

Pictured is the G.C. Williams Funeral Home, located at 1123 West Chestnut Street. (*c.* 1953.)

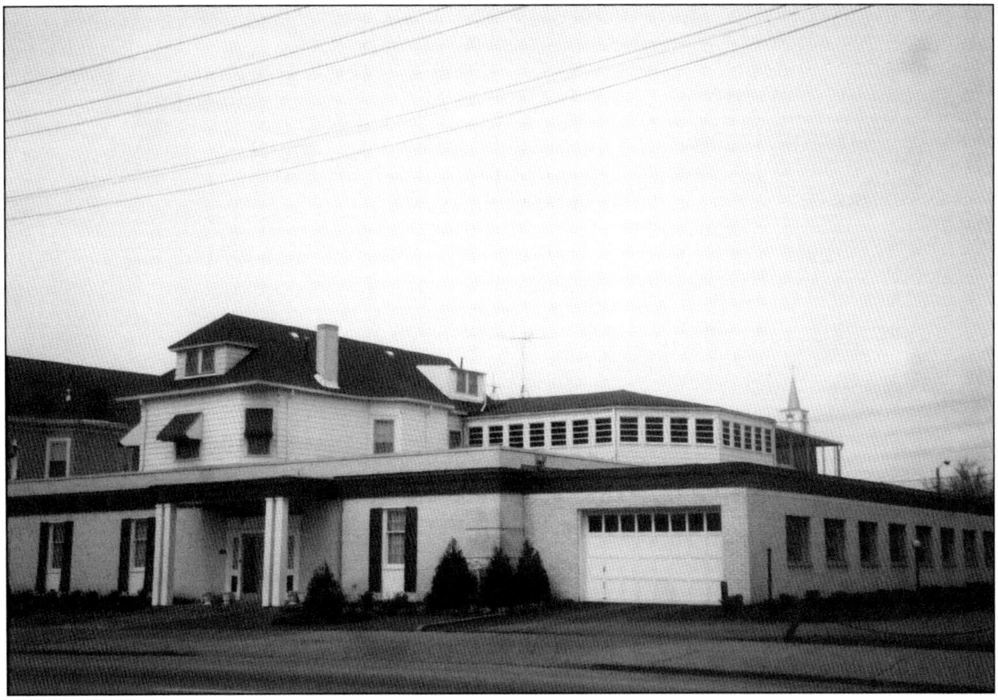

Calvin Winstead bought the W.W. Beckett Funeral Home in 1962. Pictured is the funeral home still used today.

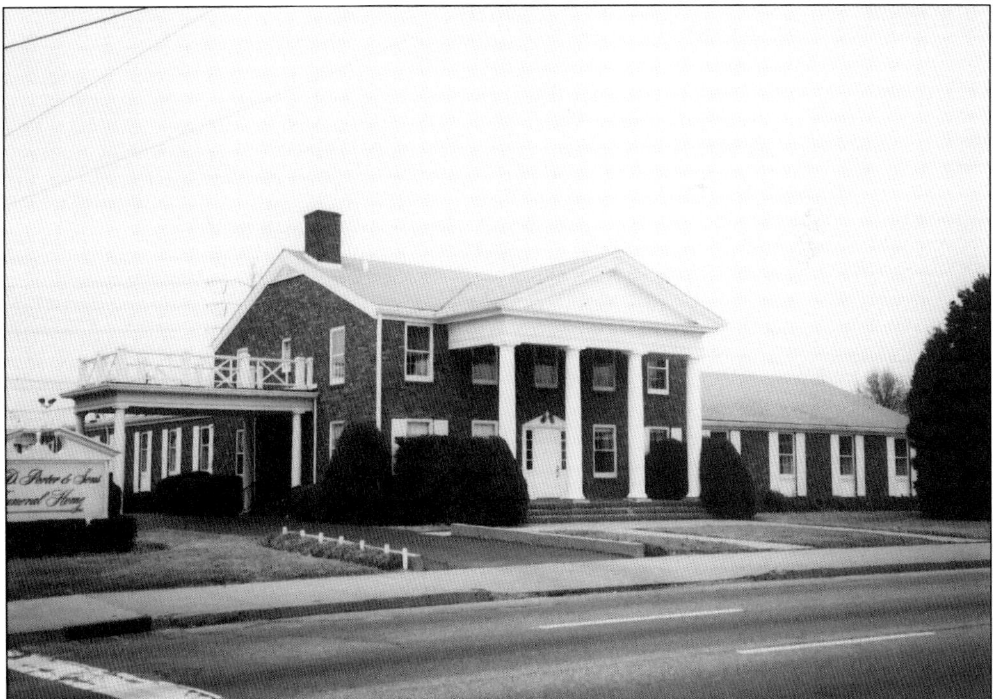

A.D. Porter and Sons Funeral Home, located at 1300 West Chestnut Street, began in 1907. A.D. Porter learned the trade from Ratterman Funeral Home and his family.

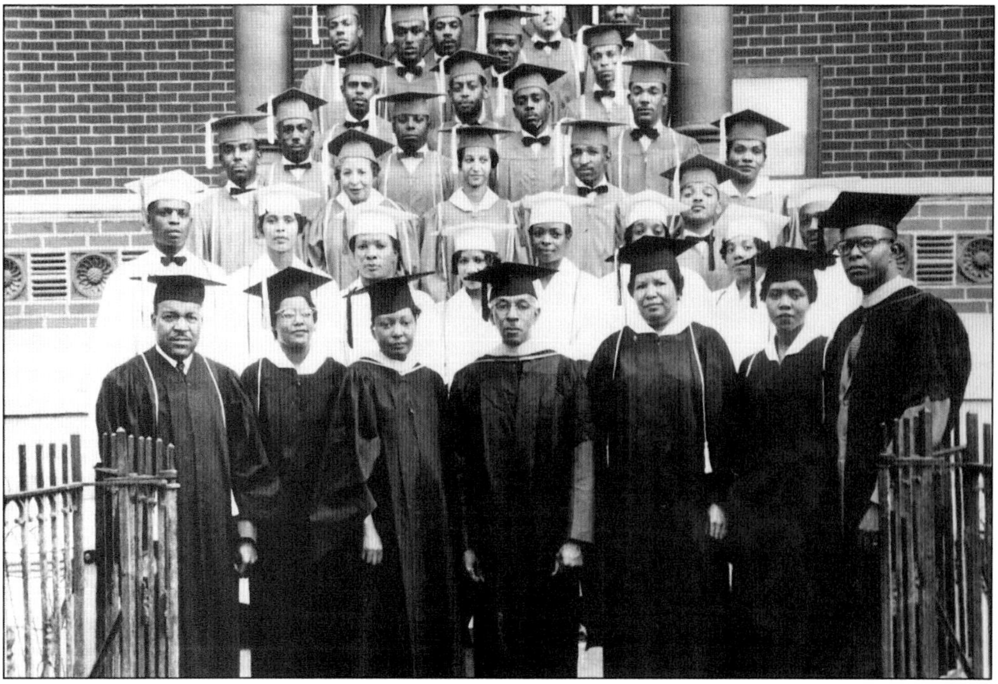

Pictured is a 1958 graduating class of barbers and beauticians. Kenneth Bradley can be seen on the third row (far right).

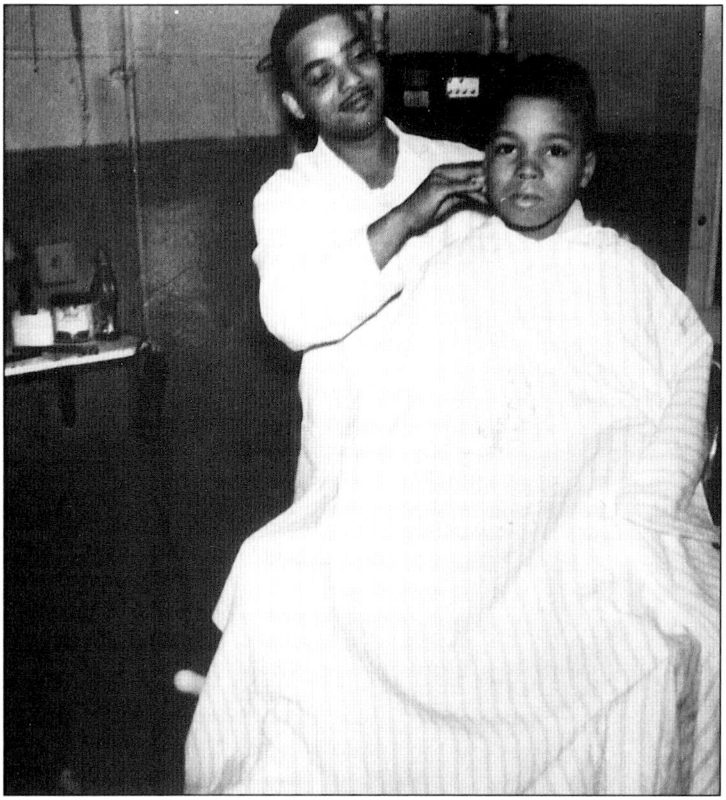

Kenneth Bradley, seen here cutting a young resident's hair, graduated from an African-American barber and beauty college in Louisville. (1958.)

Ten

PUBLIC HOUSING AND NEW SOCIETY

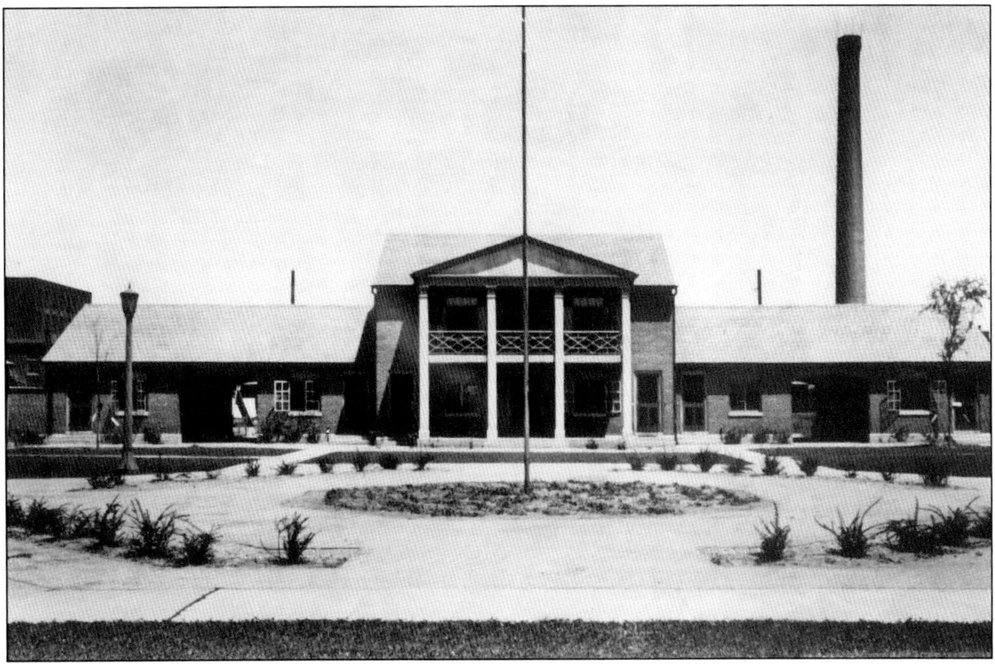

College Court Public Housing Project was dedicated by the Louisville Municipal Housing Commission on February 6, 1938 as a new low-cost public housing program. It was part of President Franklin D. Roosevelt's New Deal policy. This project targeted African Americans under the policy of racial separatism. College Court was named as a result of a naming raffle.

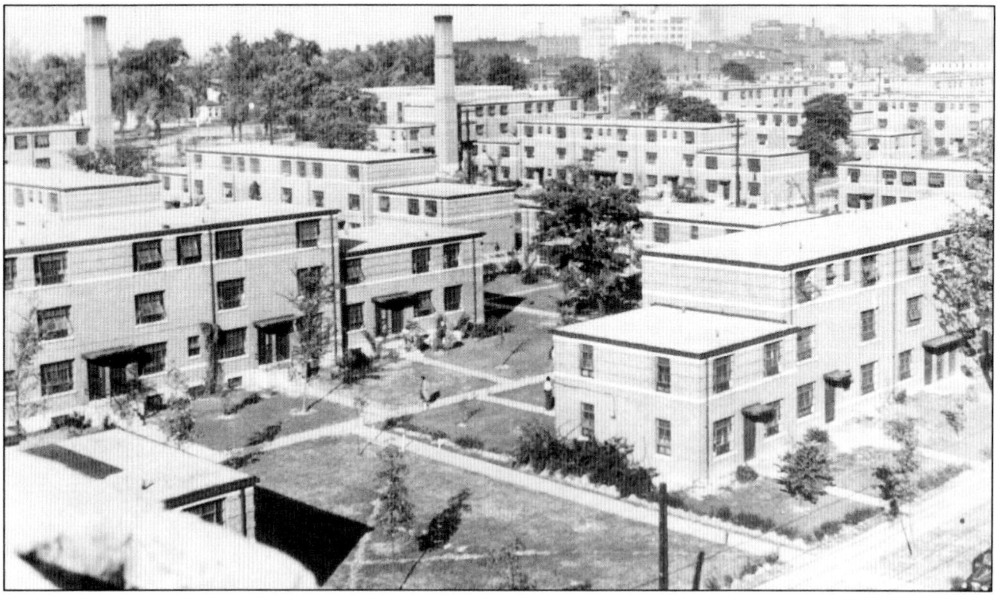

Beecher Terrace was opened in 1940 as another all-black housing project. Earle Pruitt was the manager. New public housing was a major advancement from the dilapidated housing which did not have running water. Outhouses were common in the poor sections of Louisville.

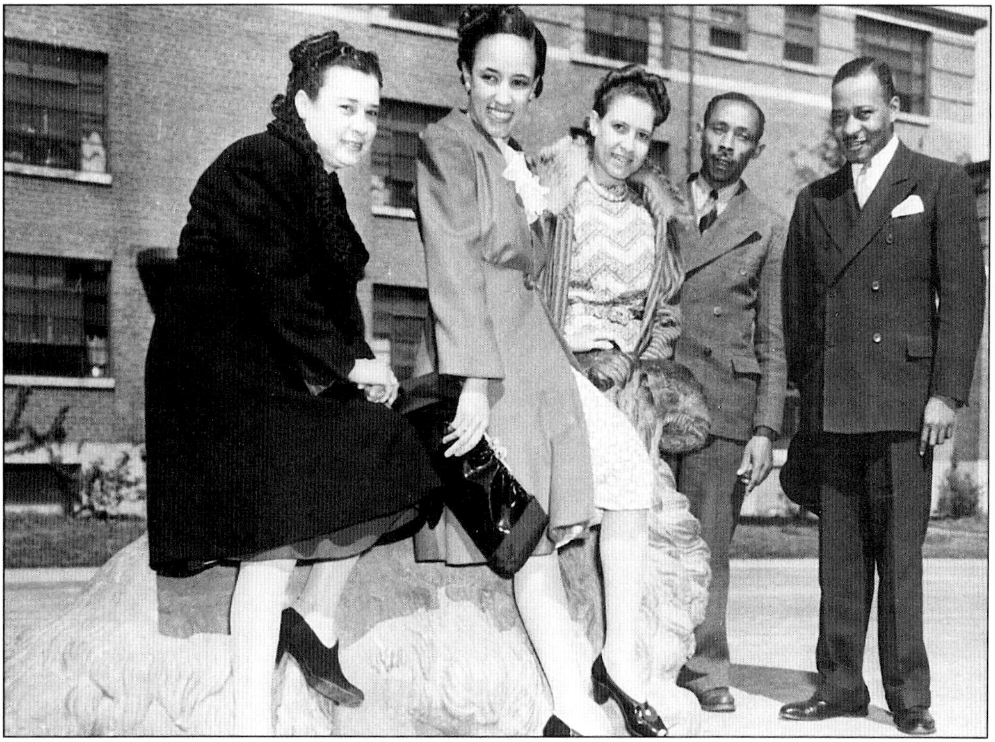

Beecher Terrace had concrete walruses and camels in its housing area. Pictured from left to right are as follows: Della Pruitt (wife of Earle Pruitt), Mrs. Perossier, Pauline Wade, Theodore Wade, and Earl Pruitt (manager). Beecher Terrace was named for Rev. Henry Ward Beecher, a New York minister and a member of the famous Beecher family. (*c.* 1948.)

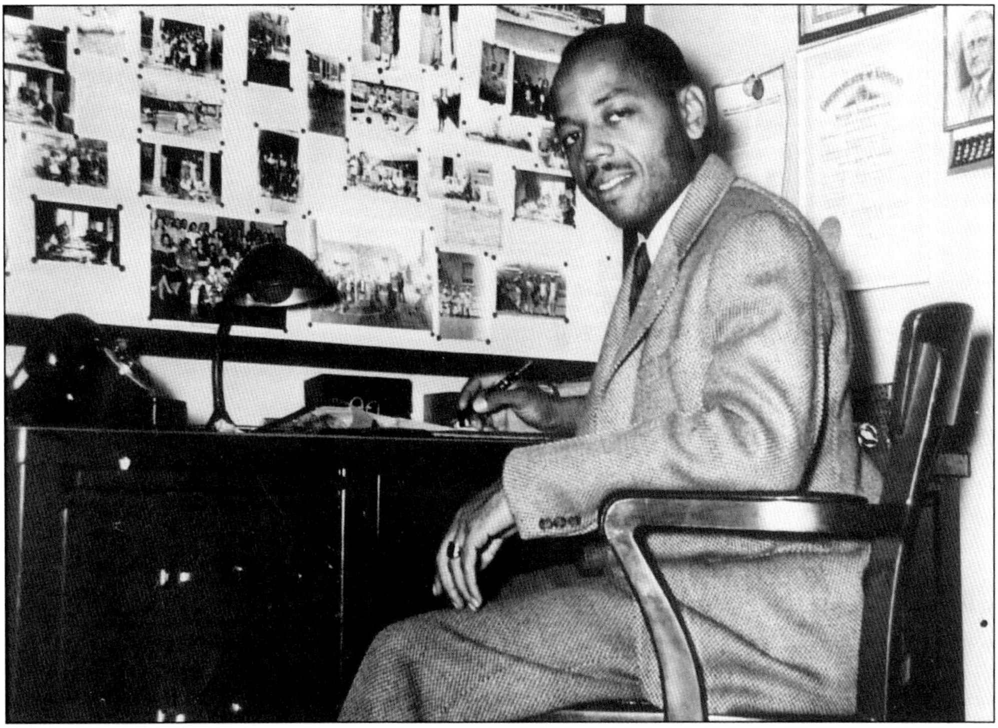

Manager Des Moines W. Beard is seated at his desk in his College Court office. Public housing allowed many working people to live like the middle class. (1940.)

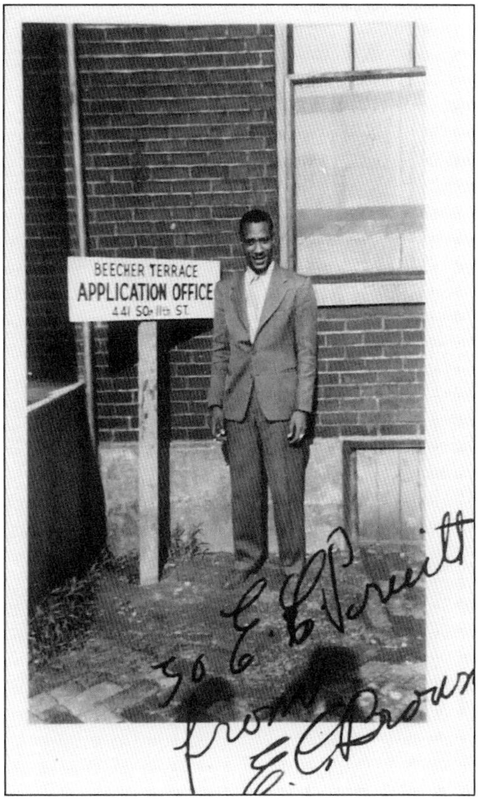

At the Beecher Terrace application office (441 South Eleventh Street), E.C. Brown processed applications and became a public housing manager. Beecher Terrace and Sheppard Square became public housing that gave priority to workers in war industry jobs. (1940.)

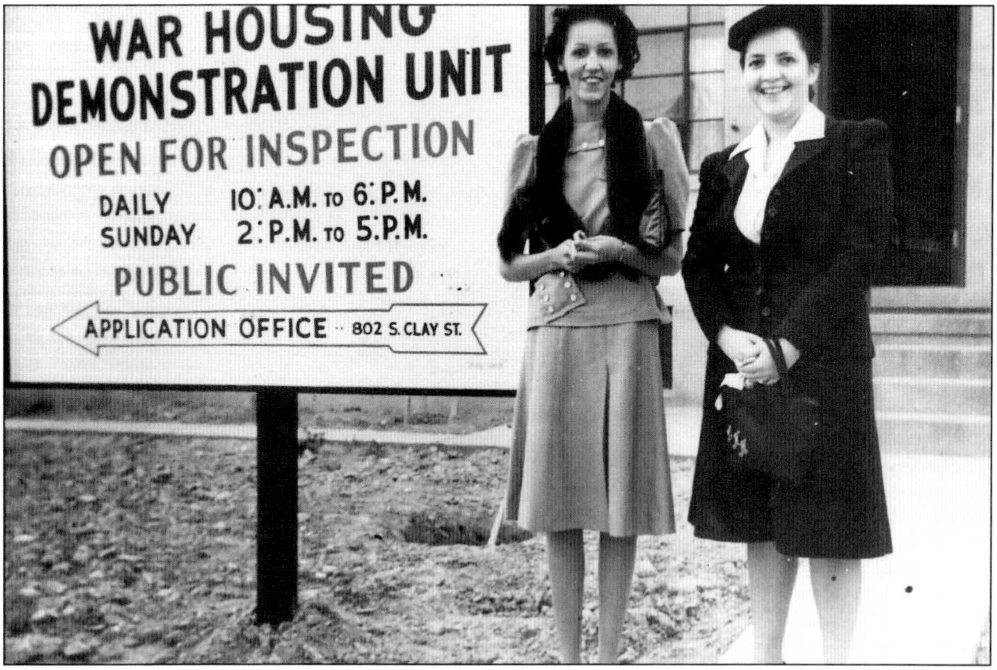

Miss Laura Cordery and Lillian Hudson are seen here conducting a war housing demonstration unit at the Sheppard Square Public Housing Project. The all-black project was named in honor of William Sheppard, an African-American missionary to Africa.

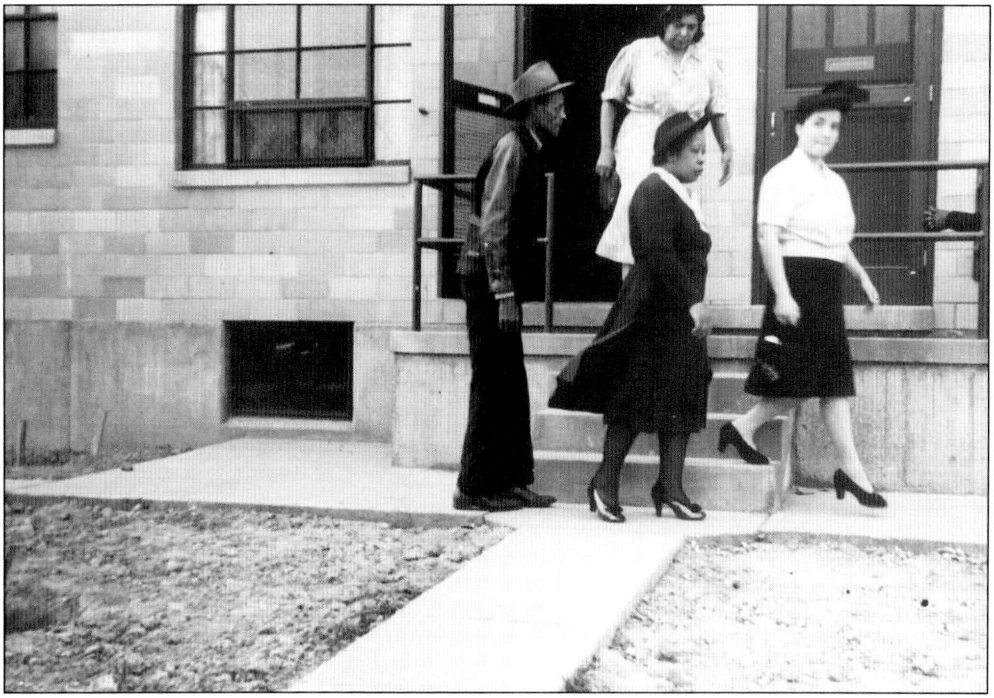

This is a view of the Sheppard Square Public Housing project. Mrs. Lillian Hudson leads the way from an apartment to the laundry room. (1940.)

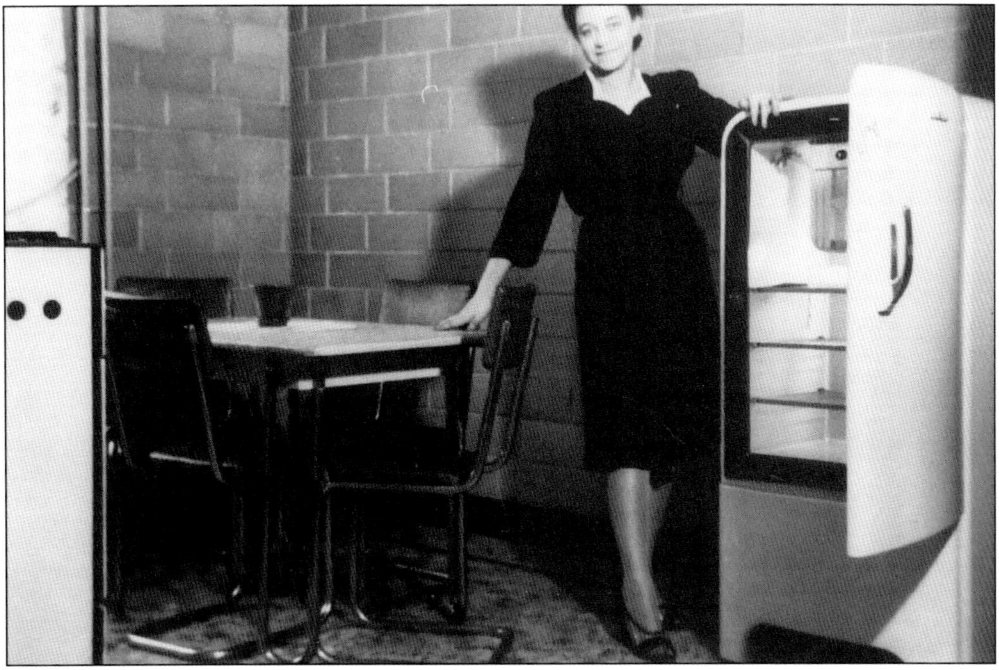

Miss Margerie Clark is seen here showing an apartment at Sheppard Square. (1940.)

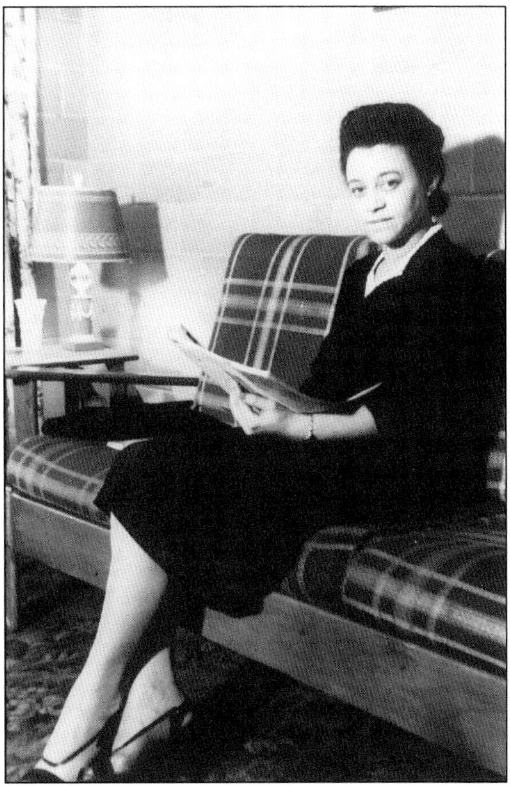

Miss Margerie Clark shows a newly decorated apartment at Sheppard Square to inspire new tenants to live gracefully, with inexpensive furniture. (1940.)

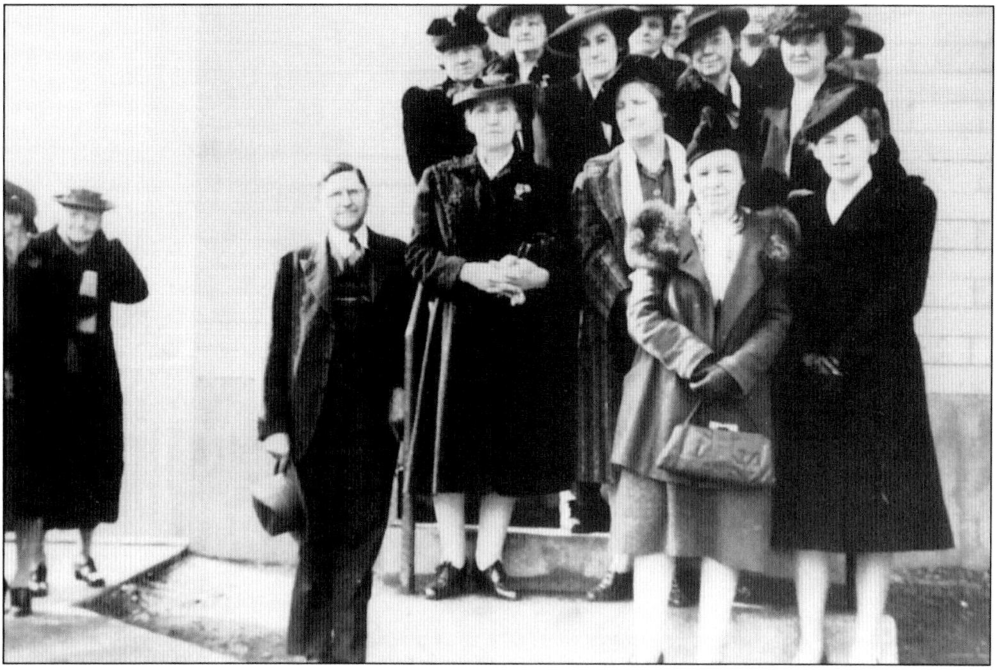

Pictured is a project tour given by the Women's Confederation of Louisville. Many people—white and black—adults, children, youths, and officials of every type, came to view the new public housing projects. The tour went on for some time.

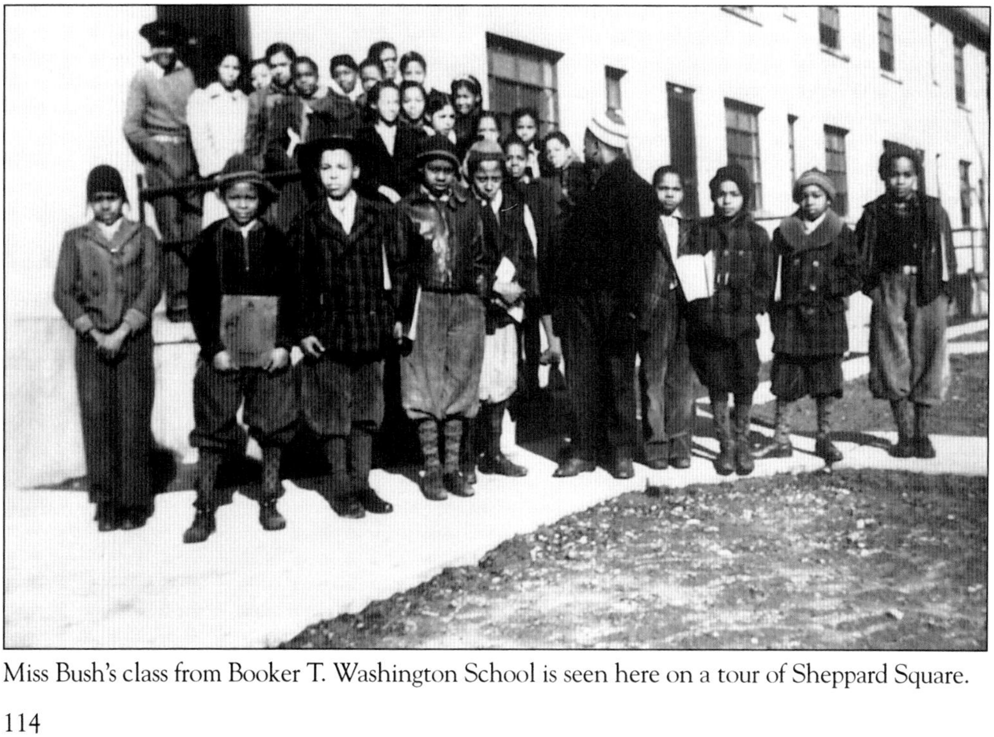

Miss Bush's class from Booker T. Washington School is seen here on a tour of Sheppard Square.

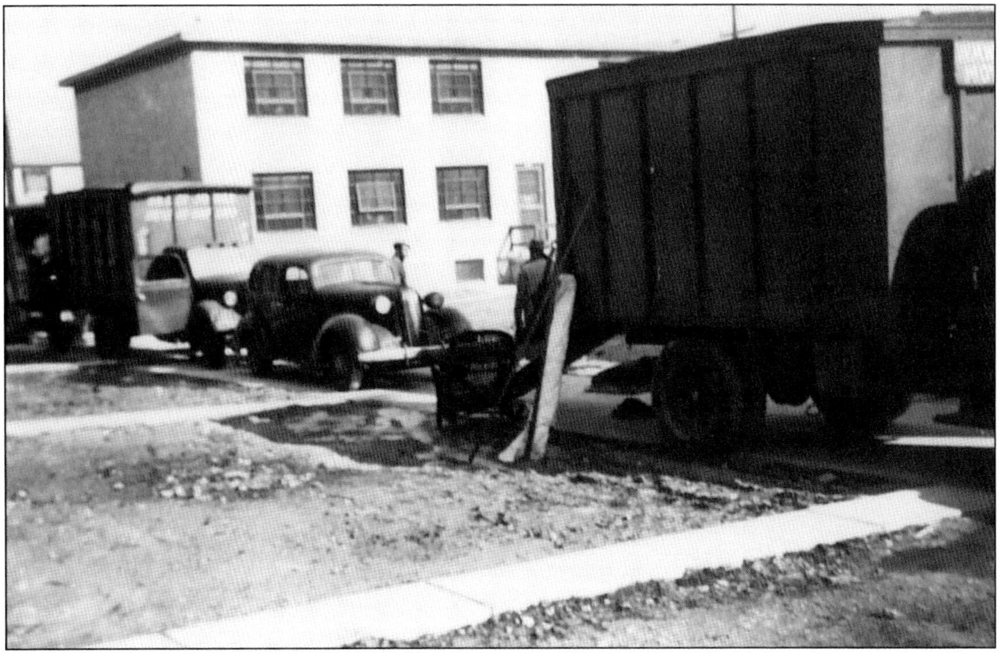

New tenants are pictured moving into their new home at the Sheppard Square housing project.

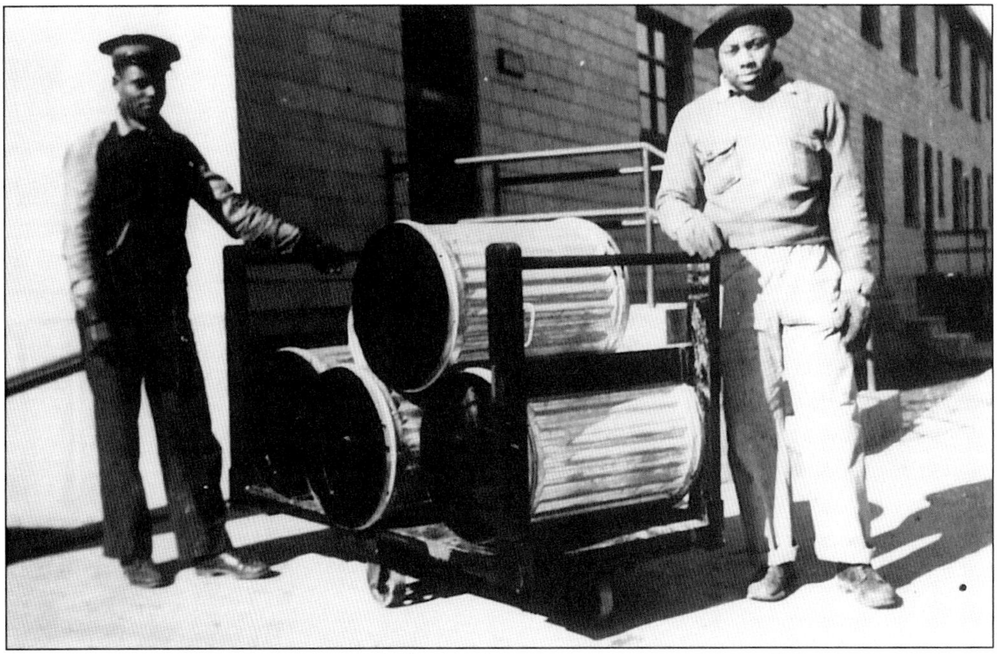

Pictured in this view are members of Sheppard Square's maintenance staff.

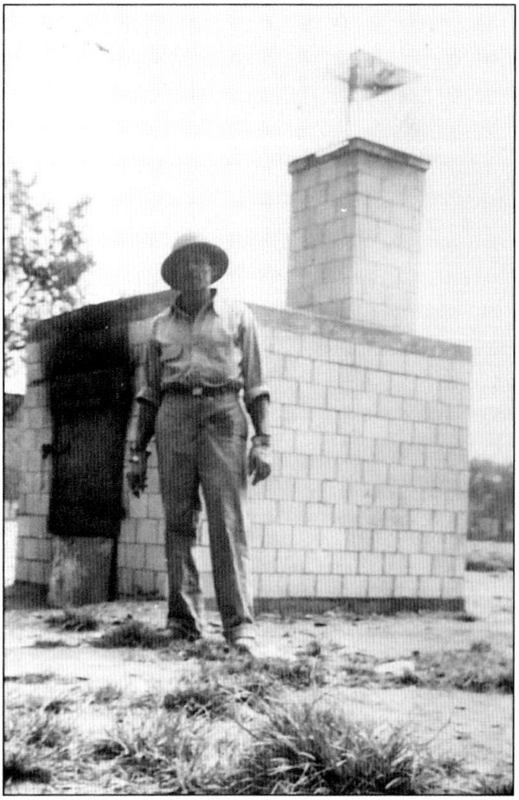

Pictured is a public housing maintenance worker. A trash incinerator can be seen in the background.

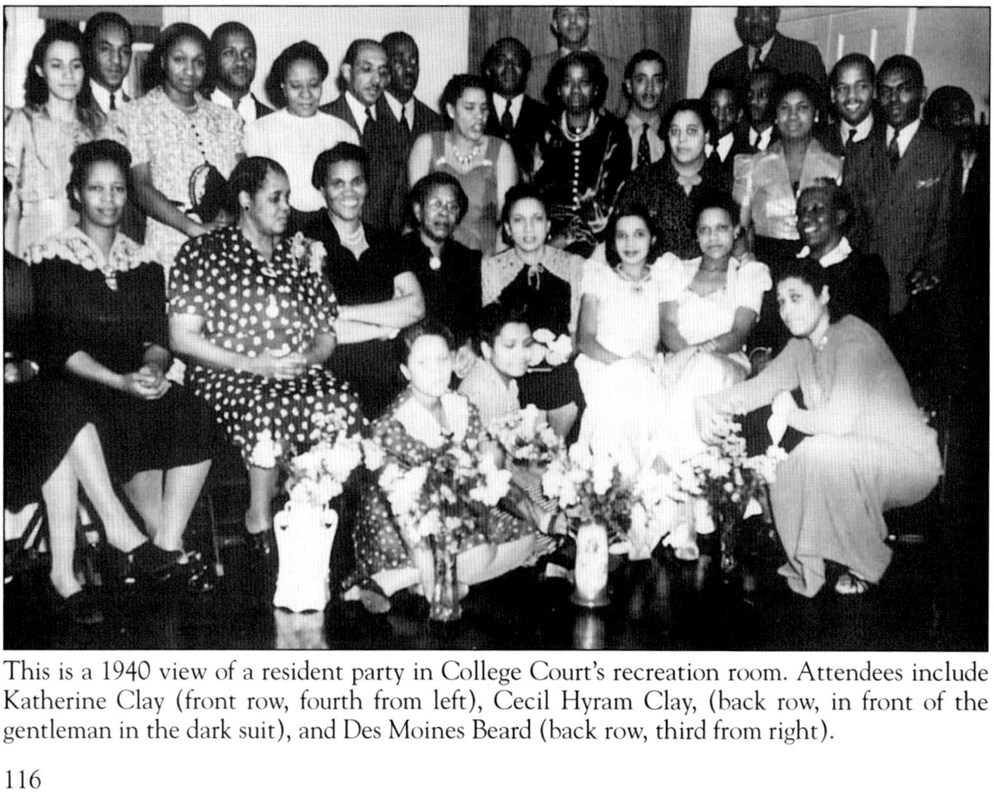

This is a 1940 view of a resident party in College Court's recreation room. Attendees include Katherine Clay (front row, fourth from left), Cecil Hyram Clay, (back row, in front of the gentleman in the dark suit), and Des Moines Beard (back row, third from right).

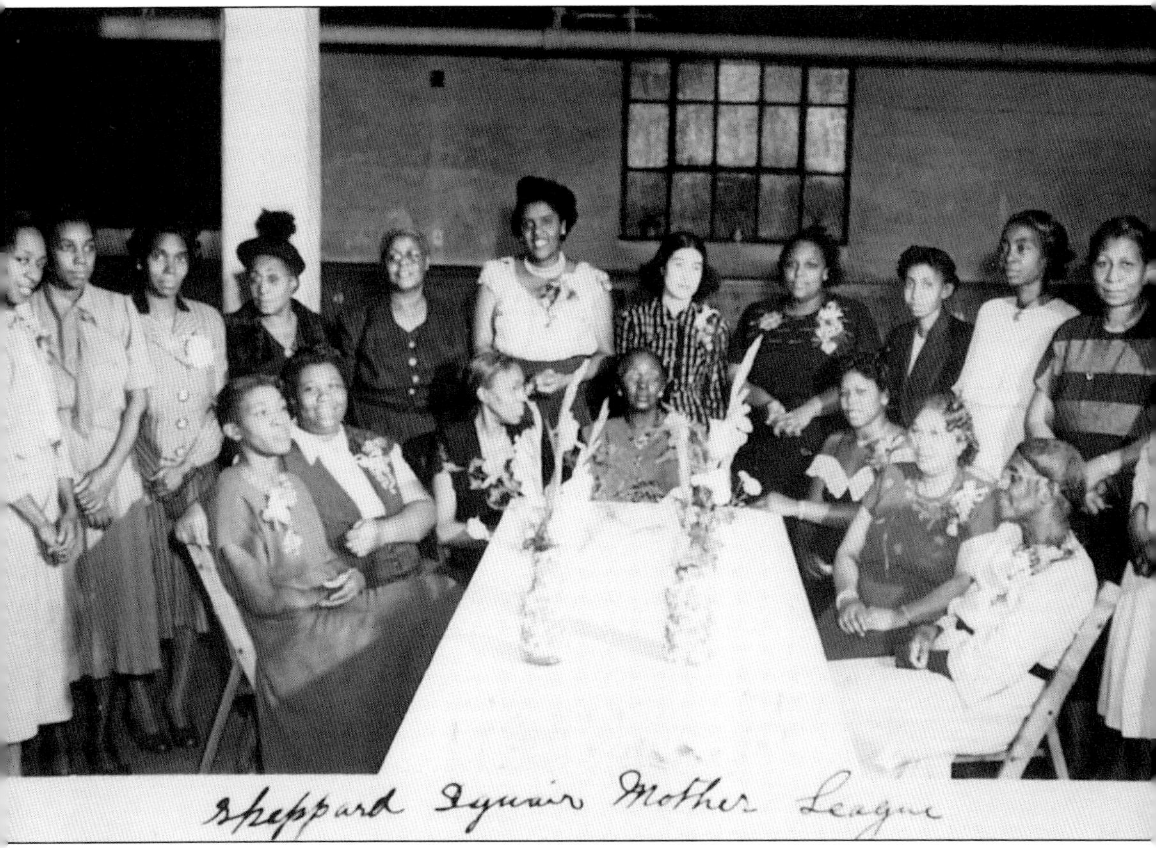

This is a view of the Sheppard Square Mothers' League meeting, which was held in the basement of the recreation center. These women planned and supervised events for their children. (1949.)

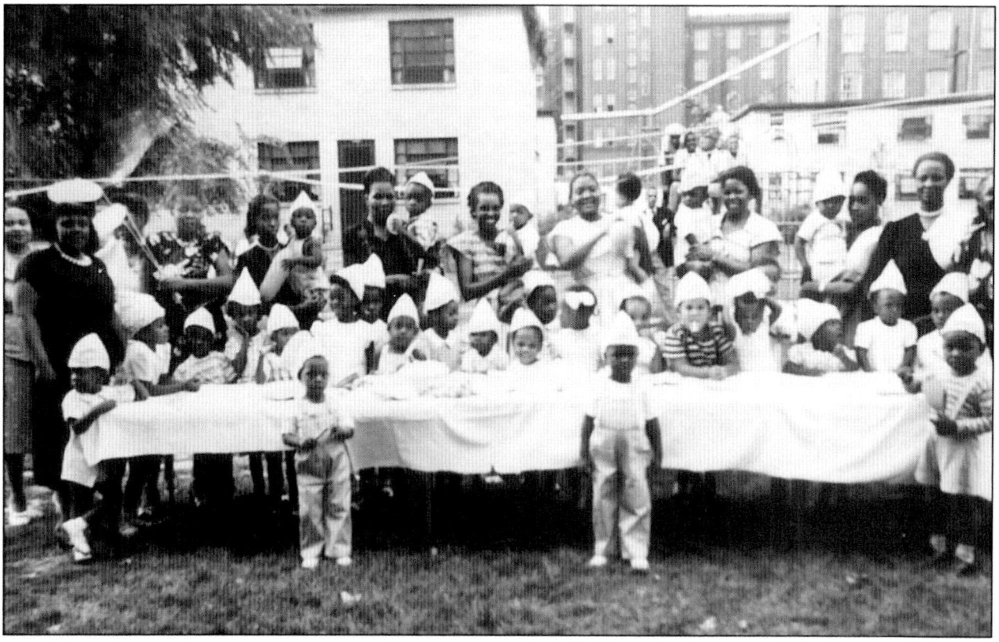
The Sheppard Square Mother's League celebrates a birthday with a party for the children.

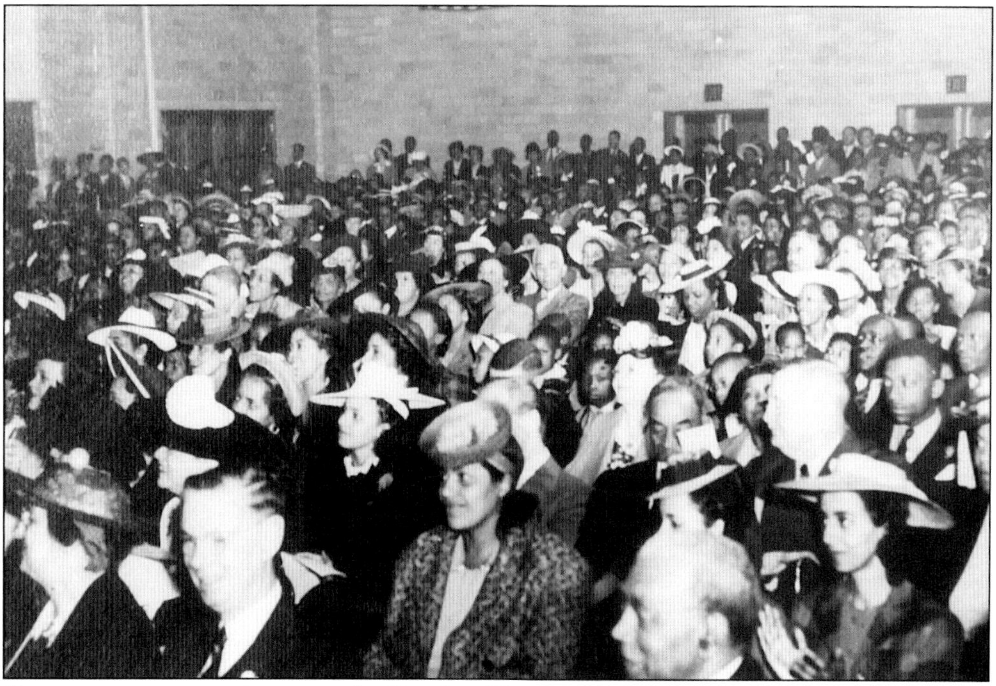
Huge turnouts were the norm for Beecher Terrace community meetings. Public housing elevated its tenants to immediate middle-class housing standards, and they were often envied, in a positive way, for their good fortune.

Eleven

The Brock Building
and Other Social Clubs

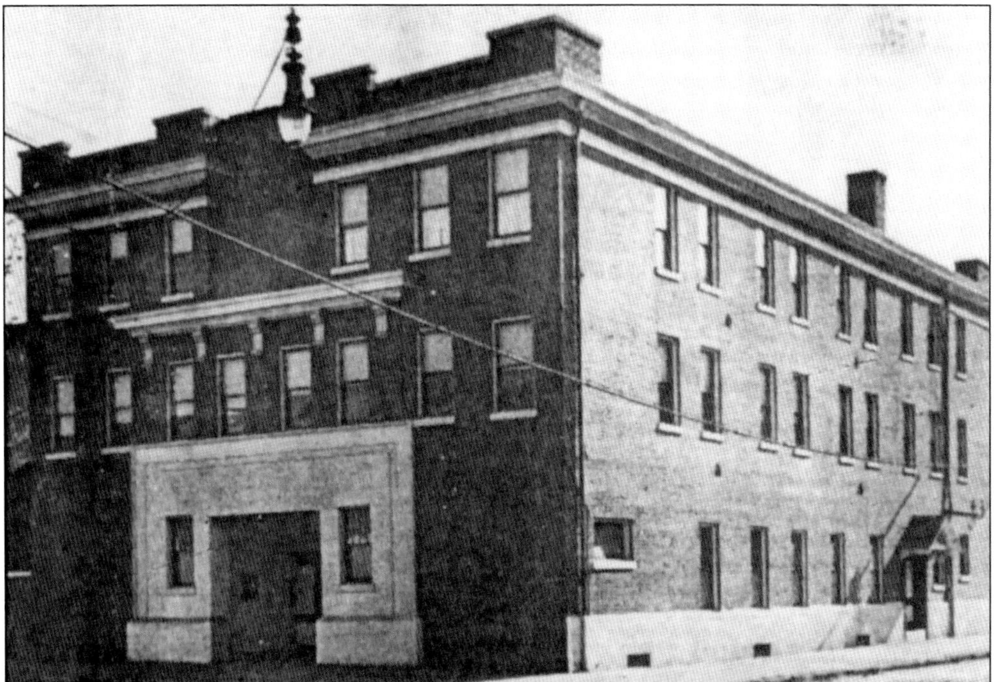

The Brock Building, located at 639 South Ninth Street (near Madison Street), was owned by Dr. Theophilus Clay Brock. Born in Louisville on December 7, 1887, Mr. Brock became a dentist and a WW I officer who served in the American Expeditionary Force. His wife was Mamie Brock. The Brock Building, pictured here, was originally called the Bessie Allen Music and Dance School. (1941.)

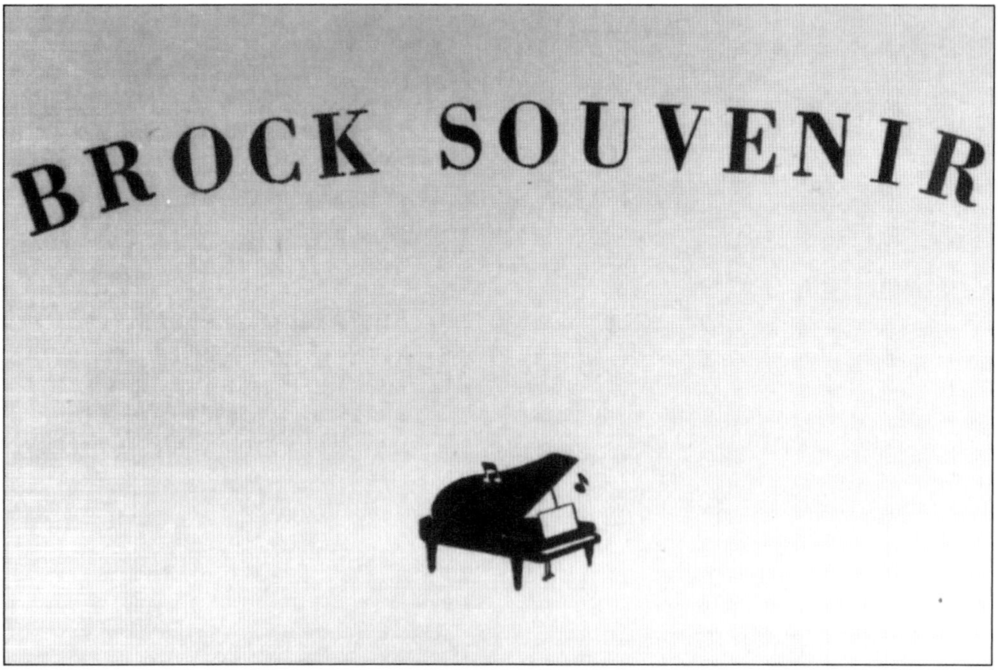

This is a photo album cover for pictures that were taken at the Brock Building.

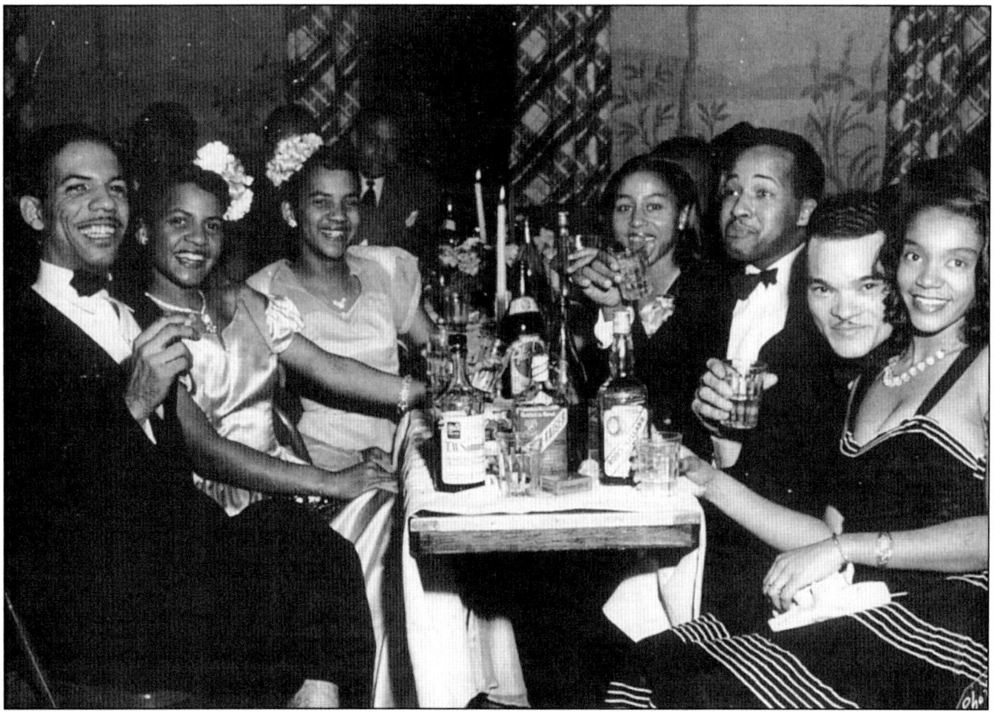
Pictured are Edward Sumpter and his wife, Francis (far right), in front of the Brock Building, a popular red-brick, three-story building with a ballroom. (c. 1948.)

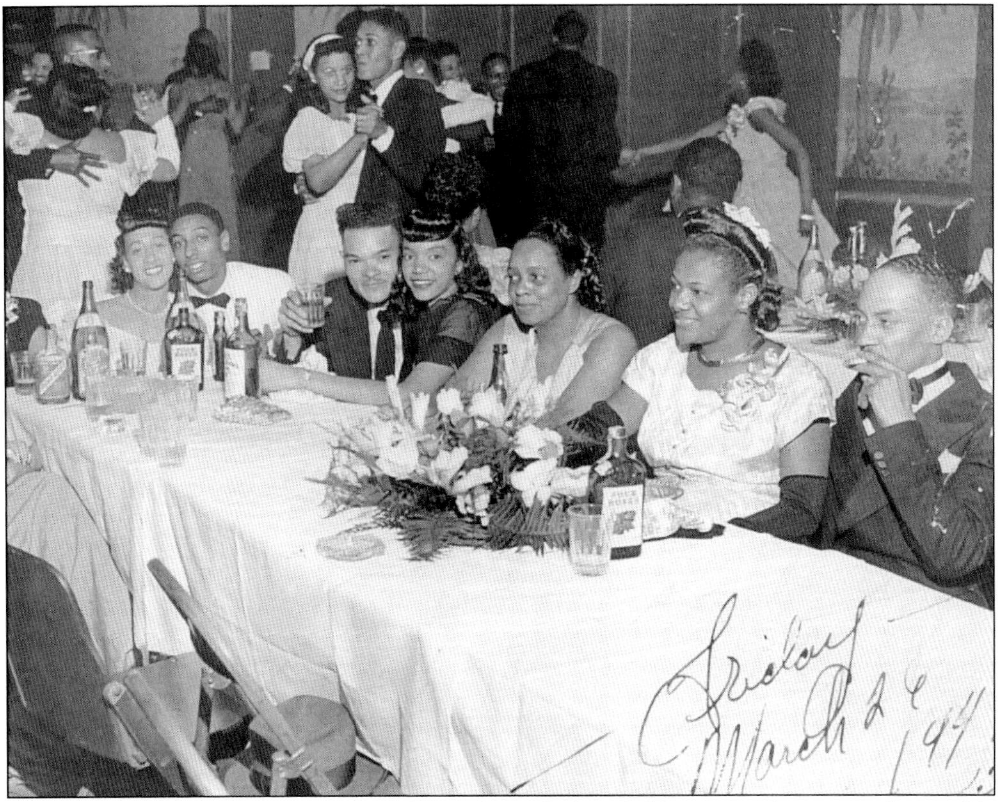

Edward Sumpter and his wife, Francis (second couple from left), are seen here, seated at a table with friends during a dance at the Brock Building.

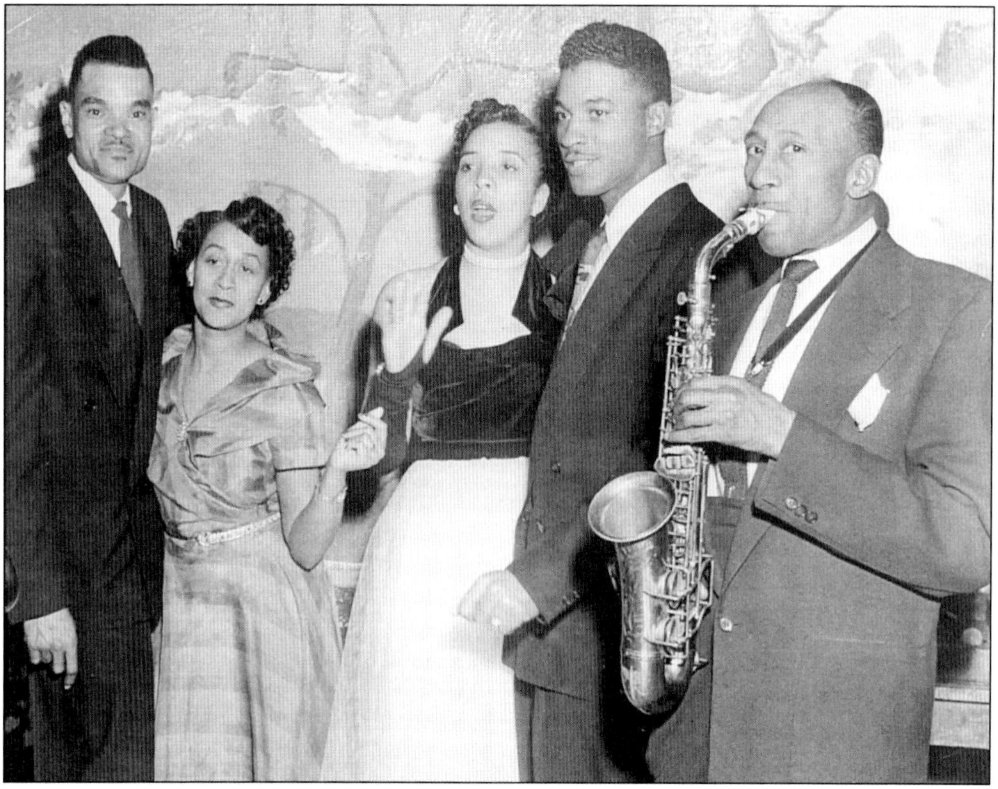

Pictured are Edward Sumpter and a social club friend (left) on the bandstand at the Brock Building's ballroom with live entertainment. (March 28, 1948.)

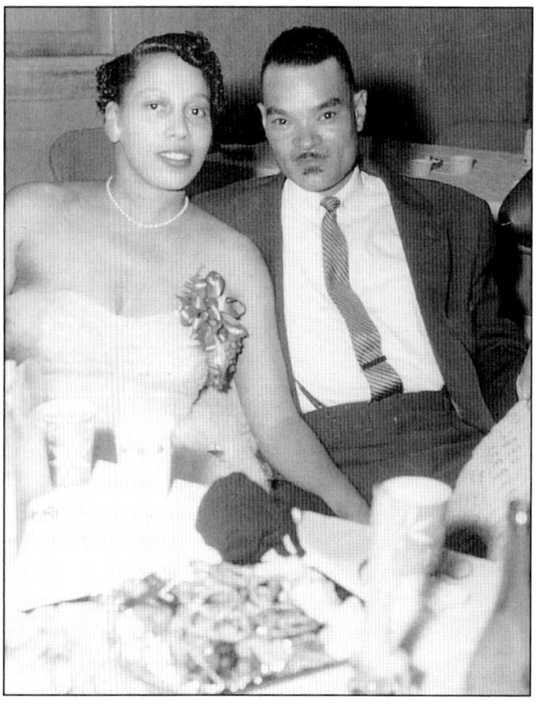

Edward Sumpter and a friend mingle at a party at the Brock Building. Sumpter was a WW II veteran who served in the navy. He was injured in an explosion aboard ship from enemy fire.

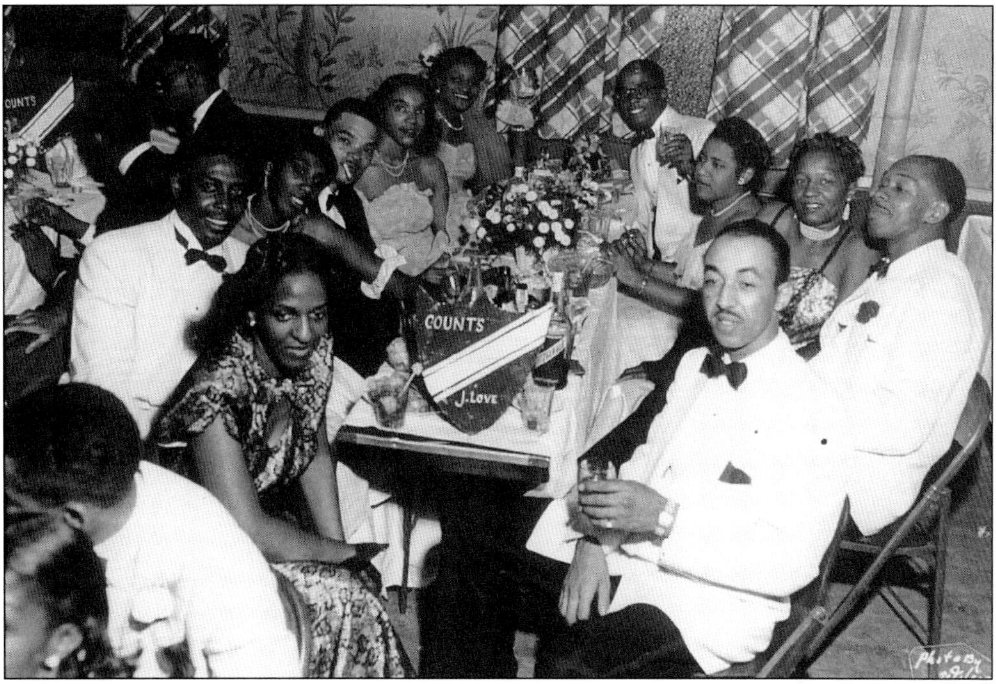

Seen in the background of this 1948 photograph are Edward Sumpter and a social club friend seated at a table. The social club "Counts, J-Love" gave a party once a year. Social clubs of men and women were popular from the 1940s to the 1960s, and they collected dues for their annual parties.

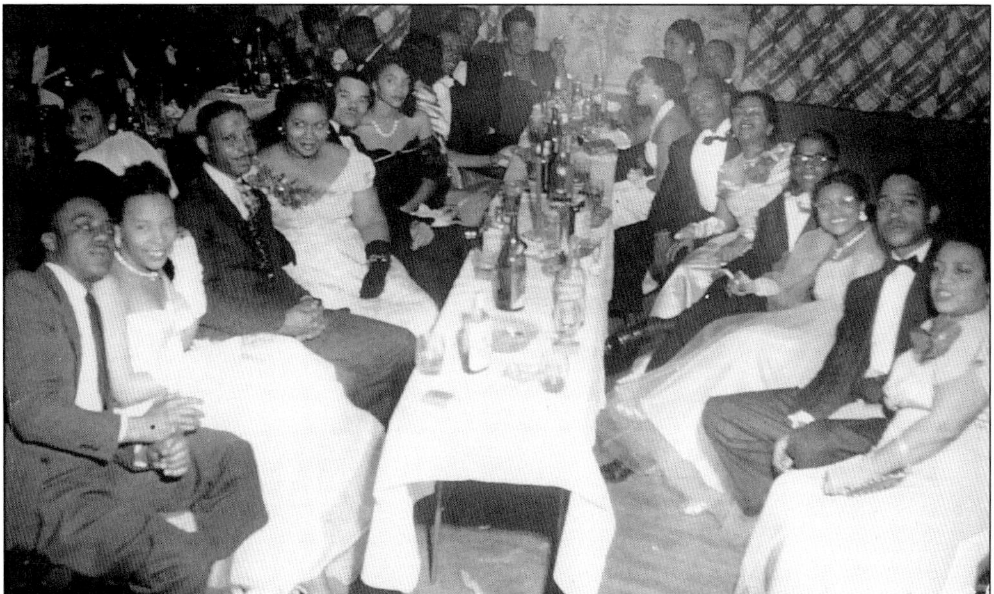

Francis and Edward Sumpter (seated left) are attending a Brock Building party. The couple enjoyed the night life in Louisville's African-American community. They turned racial segregation into positive ethnic congregation in a celebration of life and culture. (December 9, 1950.)

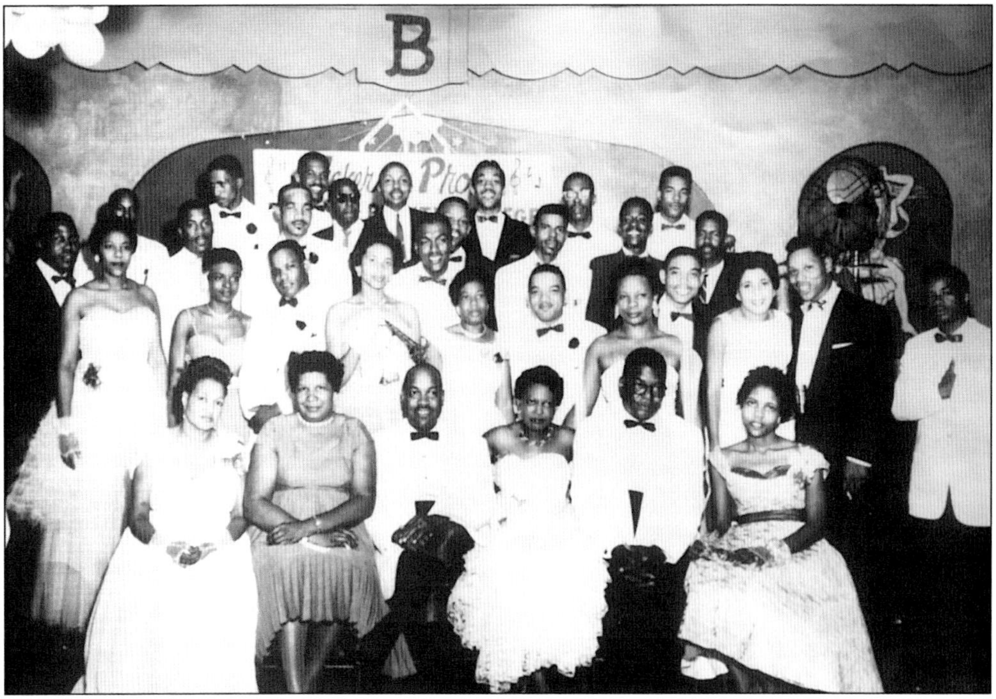

Pictured is a graduation party for recently graduated beauticians and barbers in the 1950s. Kenneth Bradley is the sixth gentleman on the second row.

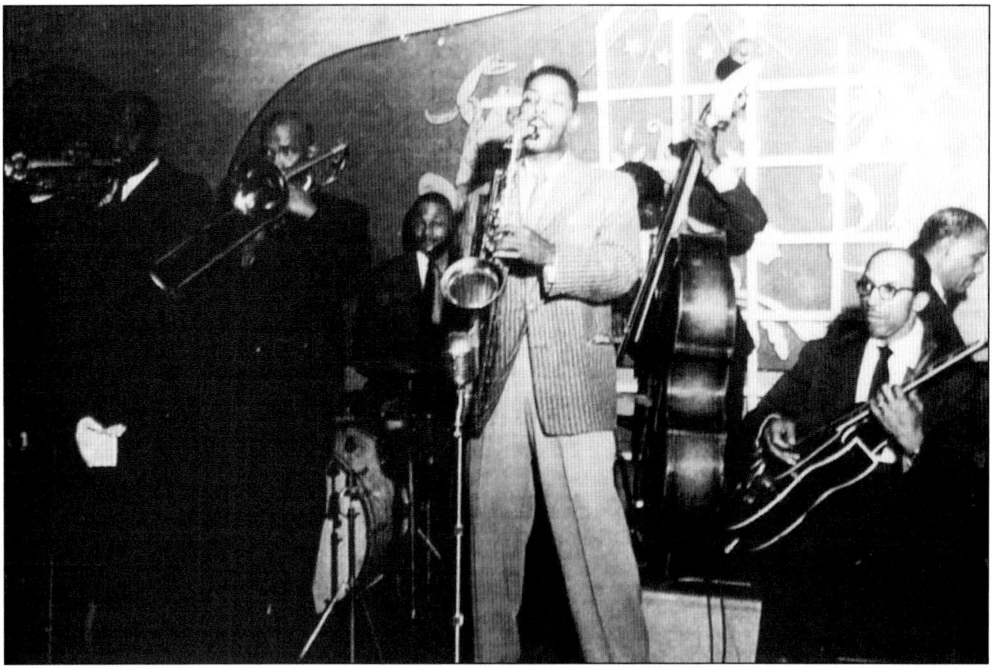

This jazz group is playing for a party at the Brock Building in the late 1940s. Band members, from left to right, are as follows: Lorenzo Goatley (trumpet), Milt Robinson (trombone), Frederick L. Stith (drums), Grovley Thompson (tenor sax), Saint Elmo Tucker (bass), John Wood (guitar), and Sylvester "King" Purdue (piano).

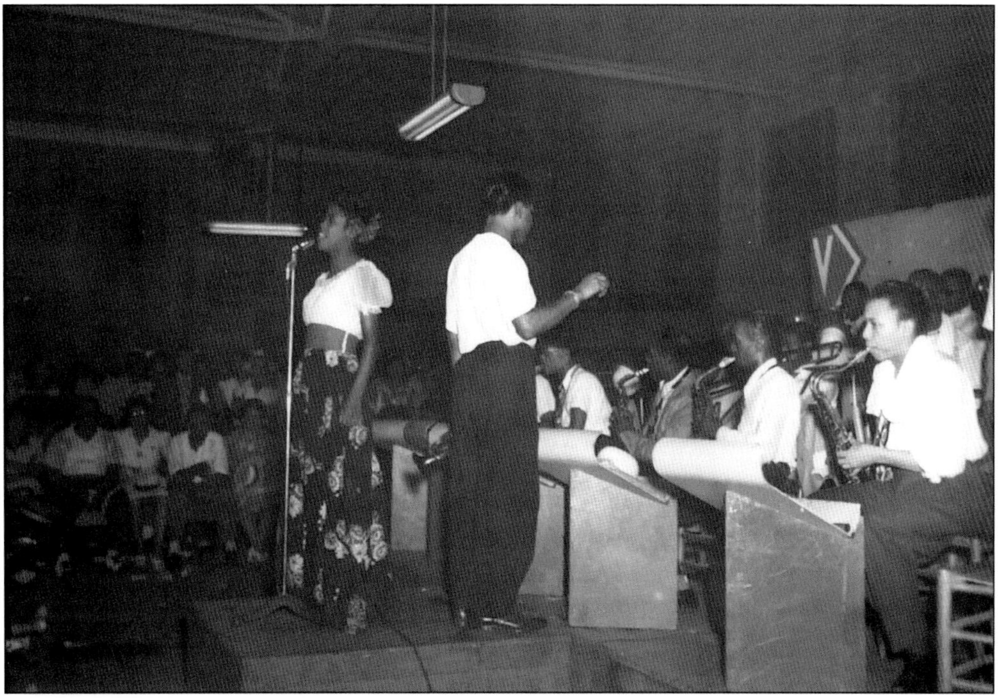

Pictured is a big band performing at the Madison Square (Skating) Rink , located at the corner of Ninth and Madison Streets. (c. 1940s.)

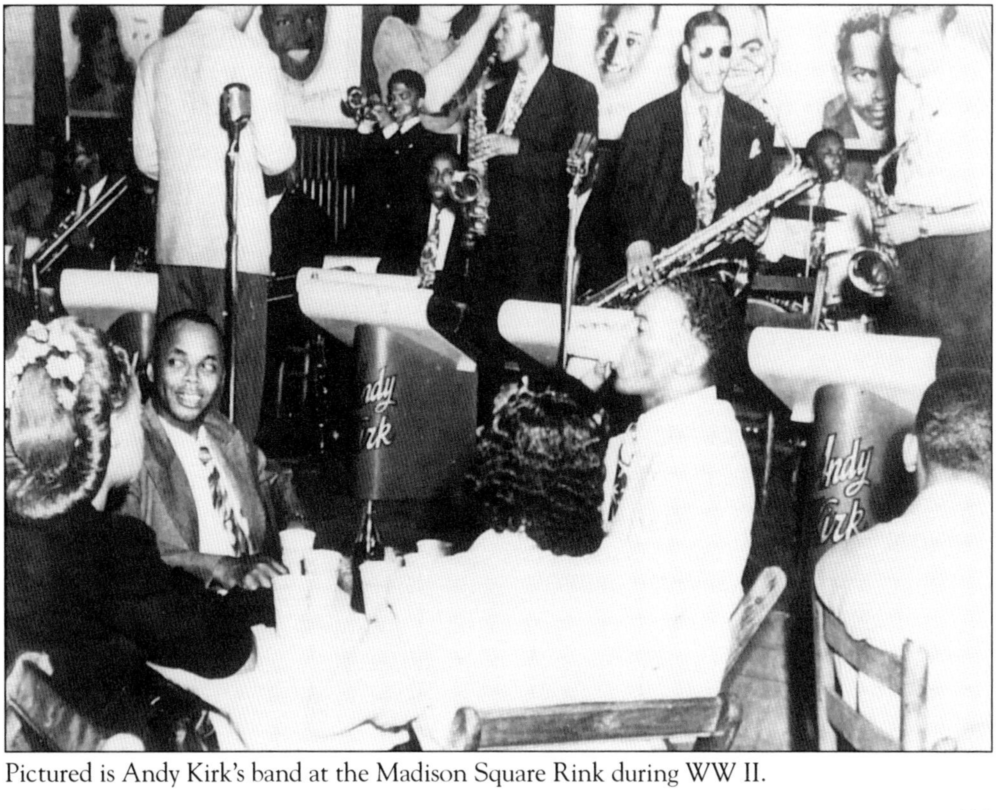

Pictured is Andy Kirk's band at the Madison Square Rink during WW II.

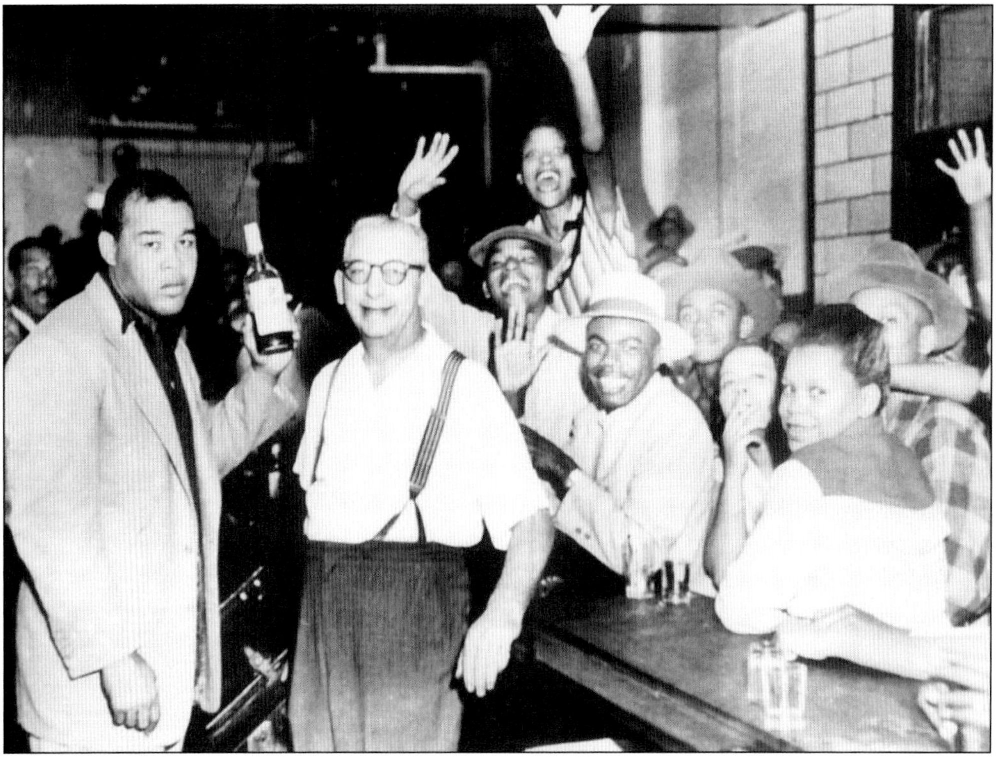

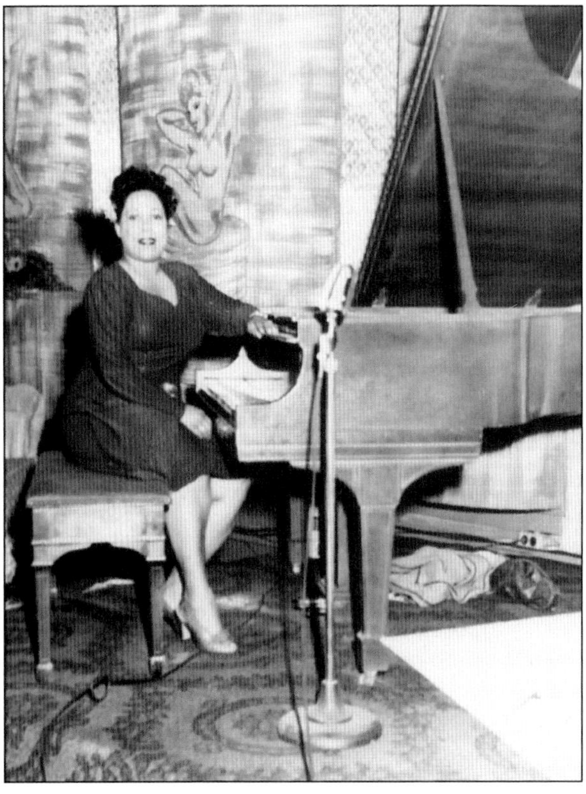

Boxer Joe Louis is pictured at the J and H Club, near Hancock and Clay Streets, in an area called Smoketown. Joseph Krenitz, the club owner, stands in the center with Louis. Behind Krenitz is Kenneth Bradley (wearing a cap), and Joe Hammond (left) can be seen in the background. Louis is promoting "Joe Louis" liquor, which was named after him. (c. 1950s.)

Pictured here is Helen Humes at the piano. She was an important jazz and blues singer and made a number of records.

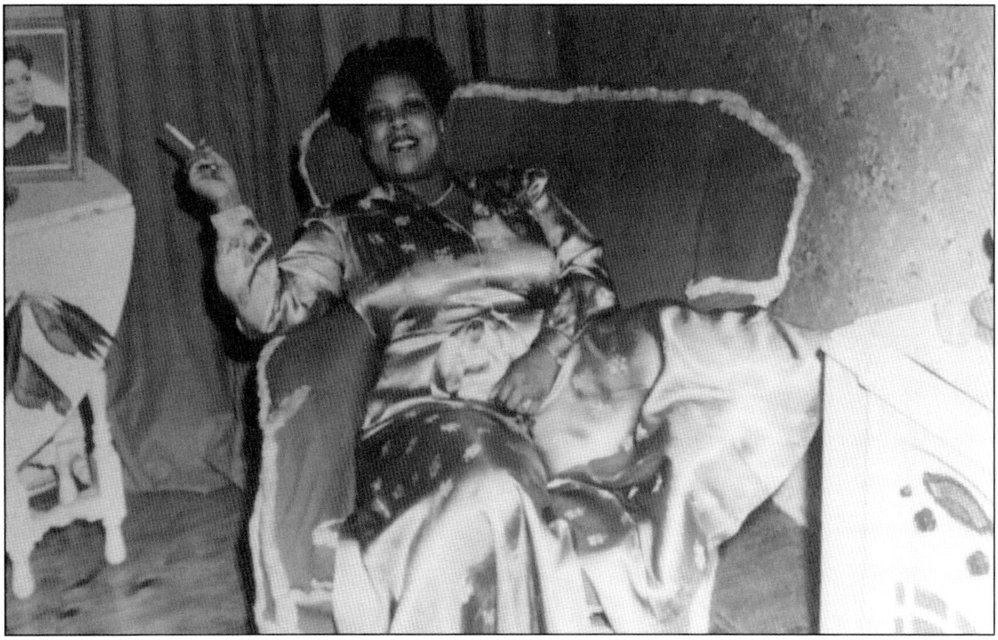

Helen Humes relaxes and enjoys her career as a blues and jazz singer.

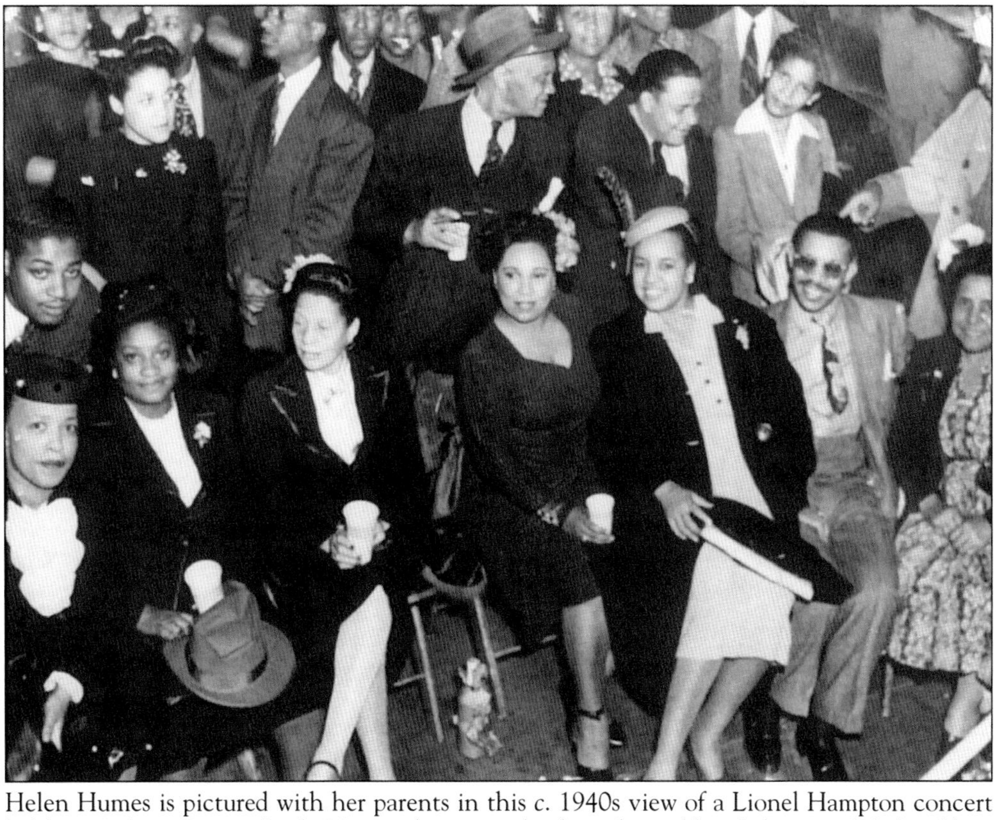

Helen Humes is pictured with her parents in this c. 1940s view of a Lionel Hampton concert held at Madison Square Rink. Her mother is on the far right and her father stands behind her, wearing a hat.

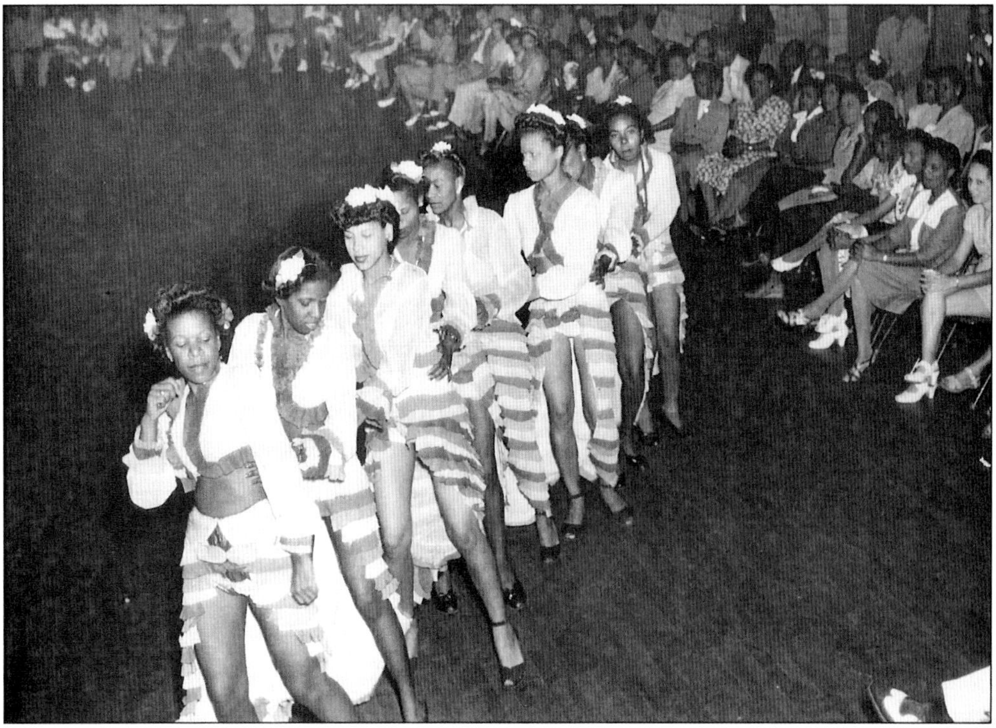

These dancers are performing an exotic dance at Club La Conga. The club was located at Baxter Center in the Beecher Terrace Public Housing Project.

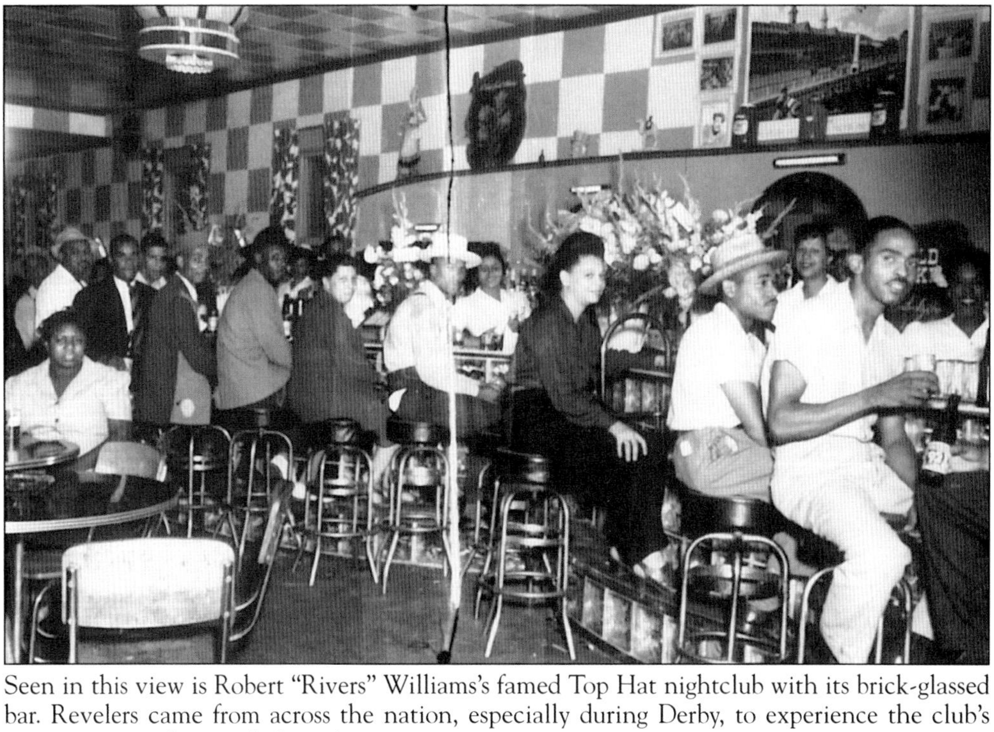

Seen in this view is Robert "Rivers" Williams's famed Top Hat nightclub with its brick-glassed bar. Revelers came from across the nation, especially during Derby, to experience the club's exciting atmosphere and clientele.